TESTIMONY ON TRIAL

BRIAN ARTESE

# Testimony on Trial

## Conrad, James, and the Contest for Modernism

UNIVERSITY OF TORONTO PRESS
Toronto   Buffalo   London

© University of Toronto Press 2012
Toronto Buffalo London
www.utppublishing.com
Printed in Canada

ISBN 978-1-4426-4368-0 (cloth)

Printed on acid-free, 100% post-consumer recycled paper with vegetable-based inks.

**Library and Archives Canada Cataloguing in Publication**

Artese, Brian, 1969–
Testimony on trial : Conrad, James, and the contest of modernism / Brian Artese.

Includes bibliographical references and index.
ISBN 978-1-4426-4368-0

1. Conrad, Joseph, 1857–1924 – Criticism and interpretation.   2. Conrad, Joseph, 1857–1924 – Technique.   3. James, Henry, 1843–1916 – Criticism and interpretation.   4. James, Henry, 1843–1916 – Technique.   5. Narration (Rhetoric) – History – 20th century.   6. Narration (Rhetoric) – History – 19th century.   7. Truthfulness and falsehood in literature.   I. Title.

PR6005.O4Z5475 2012      823'.912      C2011-907699-3

University of Toronto Press acknowledges the financial assistance to its publishing program of the Canada Council for the Arts and the Ontario Arts Council.

 Canada Council   Conseil des Arts
for the Arts   du Canada

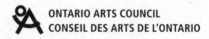 ONTARIO ARTS COUNCIL
CONSEIL DES ARTS DE L'ONTARIO

University of Toronto Press acknowledges the financial support of the Government of Canada through the Canada Book Fund for its publishing activities.

# Contents

# Acknowledgments

My sincere thanks go to Charlotte Artese and Christine Froula, who thought with me about every paragraph, and to Christopher Herbert for his generous insight. I am grateful, too, for the patience of Barbara Porter and Miriam Skey, and for the unwavering support of Richard Ratzlaff at UTP. Without knowing it, perhaps, Nancy Armstrong, Susan Griffin, and Brian Richardson were indispensible to the project. For their intellectual and moral encouragement, I also thank my family, Nick Beauchamp, Paul Breslin, Michael Bryson, Christine Cozzens, Steve Guthrie, Christopher Hager, Tony Jackson, John Martin, Michael Paul, Libbey Paul, Kathryn Pratt, Josh Russell, Peggy Thompson, Rob Thompson, and Rachel Trousdale.

# TESTIMONY ON TRIAL

# Introduction

If there is any idea in narrative theory that has achieved permanent recognition even among general readers of fiction, it is surely that of the 'unreliable narrator.' When I teach a novel that makes use of first-person narration, the phrase will crop up even among first-year undergraduates. Our suspicion of a narrator who is also a character within the story is not limited to fictions that send specific signals or clues that he is not to be trusted, or that he is ignorant of crucial facts, as in the well-known case of Ford Madox Ford's *The Good Soldier*. Even when reading Joseph Conrad's *Heart of Darkness*, for instance, students will remind me that the facts of the story are necessarily suspect because its central actor is telling the tale. As with any mortal, Charlie Marlow's vision of his world is naturally clouded and distorted by the limits of his single perspective. His story, in other words, is mere testimony.

Like the literary modernism it helped to inaugurate, Conrad's fiction frequently presents itself as the testimony of locatable human agents, as opposed to an omniscience whose narrative purportedly is not subject to the disputability that testimony implies. Whether chiding or championing it for doing so, literary criticism takes it as a given that modernism is interested in testimony because it raises questions about our access to truth and reality. As it examines the epistemological assumptions behind such criticism, this book will demonstrate that they belong to a much broader intellectual orientation, maintained in cultural institutions beyond the literary, that degrades the authority of testimony in general. It will become clear, for instance, that Conrad's famous break from prevailing narratological norms is inextricable from his explicit loathing of the progressively more powerful institution of the press. With its increasingly non-localized and omniscient posture in the latter half of the nineteenth century, the newspaper situated both the politics and the metaphysics of what might be called anonymous versus testimonial authority. Conrad's novelistic theatre, in which all social and even juridical narratives are carefully *located,* and where no interrogator escapes visibility or responsibility, is deliberately opposed to an increasingly influential power of anonymous authority at the turn of the century. In the 'irresponsible paragraphs' of the daily press, anonymity had become a tool for, not against, 'commercial and industrial interests.' The British Board of Trade, for instance, was 'free in this world and the next from all effective sanctions of conscientious conduct.' Its corporate anonymity allowed it to operate as a 'ghost,' according to Conrad, 'a mere void' without 'a shadow of responsibility' ('Some Reflexions' 305–7, 309).

Suspicion of testimony in the novel – and to some extent in public discourse in general – is the product of an ongoing cultural reaction against literary modernism, one that emerged long before that term was coined. The epistemological problems that testimonial narration purportedly brings in its wake are usually said to be part and parcel of modernism's penchant for obscurantism. Over the course of the nineteenth century, as anonymous omniscience came to represent a reader's unfettered access to the truth of the diegetic world, testimonial narration could be perceived as an obstacle to truth. Although part of the purpose of this book is to investigate how and why literary modernism came to be peculiarly associated with a blinkered and truth-denying subjectivity – a charge that has been passed onto postmodernism as well – one could argue that it is difficult to conceive in any other way a body of work whose peculiar name is identified with contemporaneity in general. It is not wholly facetious to suggest that our conception of literary modernism is partly governed by the fact that, wherever and whenever critical consciousness exists, 'the new generation' is always accused of an awkward self-awareness, stylistic obscurity, and corrosive irony, in contrast to the old days when sincerity and transparency prevailed. As Borges suggests in his famous 'Pierre Menard, Author of the *Quixote,*' the contorted self-consciousness that critics perennially attribute to their contemporaries is more likely to be a projection of the sophisticated readers themselves. Menard, we may recall, is a writer who manages to recreate, miraculously, huge portions of *Don Quixote* by synthesizing within himself Cervantes's personal and historical consciousness. Borges's academic narrator compares the authors' works. On the subject of 'truth,' Cervantes writes that its 'mother is history,' which the critic sees as 'mere rhetorical praise of history.' But when that same line emerges from the modern Menard, the narrator is staggered by its implications. 'Historical truth, for Menard, is not "what happened"; it is what we *believe* happened' (94). Borges's satire is but a small exaggeration of an intellectual habit that persists long after his *Ficciones*. Fredric Jameson, for instance, insists that when Conrad's *Lord Jim* is presented as the testimony of the fictional Charlie Marlow, who in turn communicates Jim's narrative, this 'elaborate narrative hermeneutic' demonstrates an 'ideology of the relativity of individual monads' (222). Yet no critic would ever perceive such knotty 'ideological' demonstrations in, say, Samuel Richardson's 1740 novel *Pamela*, despite the fact that the narratological structure created by Pamela's reiteration of Mrs Jewkes's narrative is identical to that in *Lord Jim*.

The post-poststructuralism that Jameson represents, however, has been superseded by a reconsideration of modernism that, as a necessary response to long-standing critical blind spots, has become almost exclusively the purview of postcolonial criticism. Conrad has remained the central embodiment of modernism in postcolonial studies, however, not simply because his subject is Western imperialism – and he its subject – but because his definitively modernist narrative technique is readily conceived as saturating the deep weave of a given work with any and all colonialist ideologies that modernism has been said to instantiate. Narrative structure is said to 'speak' a colonialist ideology, however conceived, independent of any particular discourse in the work. The poststructuralist critique I bring to bear on such narratological assumptions clears the way to a coherent vision of modernist testimony in its colonial milieu. The final chapter of this book takes advantage of this new perspective by anatomizing an overlooked historical lynchpin in Conrad's work: a prolonged reference in *Heart of Darkness* to the New York *Herald* and its production of an African drama that enraptured the globe.

Most contemporary critical approaches, it is true, have moved away from defining modernism primarily in terms of its formal innovations. Yet they continue to ascribe to Conrad far-reaching epistemological and philosophical assertions because they suppose them to be necessary, structural consequences of his testimonial narrative techniques. If the critical survey in this study seems at times weighted toward 'narratology' – a term that necessarily encompasses not just its 'classical' instantiations, but its multiform contemporary hybrids as well – it is not because narratological readings have been especially influential in crafting our understanding of Conrad, testimony, and modernism. I examine the formulas of narratology solely because that is where the enabling terms and concepts of these erroneous structural premises have been fostered. From Marxism to cosmopolitanism, new historicism to 'new modernism,' literary criticism persists in rendering questions of testimony with narratological tropes of 'embedded' narration, 'filtering consciousness,' and the various guises of 'external focalization.' Such are the figures by which we have come to understand, with Jameson, that Conradian narrative and the modernism it heralds are primarily concerned with an ahistorical psychic interiority, the limits of subjectivity, and an 'ideology of the relativity of individual monads' (222).

When Conrad was hoping for a wider distribution of his own works in the United States, he seemed to anticipate that critics would project difficulties, which the general reader had not yet been taught to perceive, onto a narrative technique that takes a 'purely human' point of view. In a 1913 letter to Alfred Knopf, hoping to sustain the publisher's interest in the nearly finished novel *Chance*, Conrad writes:

> I stand much nearer the public mind than Stevenson, who was super-literary, a conscious virtuoso of style; whereas the average mind does not care much for virtuosity. My point of view, which is purely human, my subjects, which are not too specialized as to the class of people or kind of events, my style, which may be clumsy here and there, but is perfectly straightforward and tending towards the colloquial, cannot possibly stand in the way of a large public. (*Collected Letters* 5:257–8)

To a modernist of this period, as Patrick Collier reminds us, the 'public mind' did not denote 'a narrow, bourgeois audience,' but 'something much closer to universality . . . unified only by the common denominator of literacy' (20). Conrad's diagnosis of his narrative technique in relation to the 'average mind' was apparently correct. *Chance* exploded the author's previous sales record, and the obscure artist's writing finally achieved popularity. Yet literary criticism has insisted for decades that he was, in fact, wrong – that *Chance* represents an apotheosis of convolution and self-involvement in Conrad's narrative art, and is all but intolerable to anyone other than literary critics and narrative theorists. As Norman Page writes:

[T]he popular success of *Chance* is surprising, since the novel is far from being an easy read on account of a mode of narration that has been variously described as cumbersome and absurd. Marlow, who tells the story to the narrator, himself reports much of it at second or third hand. The general verdict has been that the gain in subtlety or dramatic effectiveness is so slight as hardly to justify such lengths of elaboration. (112)

Just as it would probably have bewildered the 12,000 people who bought *Chance* less than two months after its release, this 'general verdict' among literary authorities has long mystified me as reader. Like most people, I suspect, who read *Chance* or *Lord Jim* for the first time – another novel whose narrative 'entanglement,' according to Gérard Genette, threatens 'the bounds of general intelligibility' (*Narrative Discourse* 232) – the stories somehow unfolded for me in a perfectly 'straightforward' way, as Conrad had anticipated. Of course one can make a strong case that the high modernism of Woolf, Eliot, and Joyce 'constituted itself through a conscious strategy of exclusion' directed particularly against 'an increasingly consuming and engulfing mass culture'; but despite Andreas Huyssen's formulation, that phenomenon can hardly be attributed to 'modernism' *tout court* (vii). As Mark Morrisson demonstrates throughout *The Public Face of Modernism*, avant-garde writers before the First World War were eager 'to bring modernist literary experiments into broader public discourse' (16). It is not simply the case, however, that the early experimentalists have been inappropriately lumped in with the later ones under the too-broad heading of modernism. The literary-historical narrative that had once enabled this broad brushstroke, now supposedly discredited, is that modernism displaced a realist narrative technique that was not formally complex, self-referential, or experimental, but rather a transparent window onto truth and reality. What will become clear in the following pages, however, is that this story has in fact been maintained in the deep weave of literary criticism by broadly accepted narratological premises, acknowledged or unconscious, about testimony.

One such classic assumption is that the testimonial intervention of a Charlie Marlow, the primary narrator of *Chance*, creates clutter among the normal or proper 'material' of a novel. This would probably come as a surprise to the general reader, who, as we shall see, has been perfectly comfortable with the notion that Marlow is an important subject of Conrad's tales, not just a narrative apparatus. Conrad's fabula, with its 'purely human' point of view, easily jibes with the historical fact that the daily 'colloquial' practice of storytelling almost always takes the form of first-person testimony. This conflict of perception between lay and professional readers is part of a larger and perhaps more familiar theoretical argument about how people use and perceive ordinary language in general. In a typical exchange, for instance, between Paul de Man and Meyer Abrams in 1983, de Man argues that the 'popular uses of language' are 'infinitely theoretical, constantly metalinguistic,' and that they are eager to 'theorize' and 'turn back' on themselves (De Man, *Resistance* 102). Abrams, on the other hand, takes the position that theories of language are conceived and pondered only by professionals. The corresponding premise in literary criticism – still prevalent, especially among narratologists – is that any novel that draws attention to its narrative condition thwarts the average reader's expectations and threatens to undermine her understanding and reception of the work.

In his 1988 book *Le Différend*, Jean-François Lyotard maps out one of the powerful logical paradigms that, historically, has removed epistemological authority from testimony. Even when it is taken for granted that all historiography ultimately hangs on testimony – individual or collective – this logic emphasizes the possibility that any one such statement is, if not a lie, corrupt because it is biased, or 'interested,' or sees only 'one side' of the event in question. If the witness to an event 'claims to see everything,' Lyotard writes, 'he or she is not credible. If he or she is credible, it is insofar as he or she has not seen everything, but has only seen a certain aspect' (45). The contemporary inquiry that draws Lyotard and others to this problem reveals the potential stakes of the debate. The never-adequate testifier is the witness to mass executions in Nazi concentration camps who has now been called back to the witness stand by scholars contesting the historicity of the Holocaust. This inquiry is often made possible by an apparent movement of 'zooming out,' to borrow the photographer's term: a reframing of the testimony from the purportedly wider scope that is the scene of inquiry itself – a scene of deposition that seems to encompass or comprehend the testimony. Before the reframing, the object of inquiry had been the 'content' or scenario depicted by the statement; now the object of inquiry is the statement as such, its content bracketed. Before, there was no other authority, no authoritativeness outside the testimony; but now the testifier is inescapably suspect, and final authority can reside only in an imaginary comprehension effected by the new scene of deposition. This comprehension purportedly escapes the limitations of testimony and takes on the capacity to 'see everything.'

The reframing that puts testimony under suspicion is a movement that takes place within the histories of both literary criticism and journalism. Late in the nineteenth century, the public histories-of-the-now moved into the 'new journalism.' The series of long testimonials that had once constituted the newspaper were now sifted, readily paraphrased, and framed with commentary, as Harold Herd writes, to 'help [the reader] in absorbing the news' (223). 'The journal' was thus elevated more distinctly above its constituent elements and attained an effectively extradiegetic purchase from which it could claim 'comprehensive coverage of . . . modern life' in general (223). As we will see, the promise of complete comprehension that came to be demanded of the newspaper would also be demanded of the novel.

Lyotard's writing on the witness has come under the consideration of Shoshana Felman, who offers a compelling argument that the Holocaust brought about a 'historical crisis of witnessing' and inaugurated our 'contemporary Age of Testimony.' Faced with the Holocaust as 'an event eliminating its own witness,' Felman claims that 'the cryptic forms of modern narrative . . . bear[] testimony, through their very cryptic form, to the *radical historical crisis in witnessing* the Holocaust has opened up' (*Testimony* 200–1, Felman's emphasis). It is precisely this picture, however, of modern narrative embracing the condition of the witness because of its inadequate comprehension that I would like to revise. Felman's portrayal of modernist narrative as a cryptogram, which presupposes a hidden but determined comprehension that such narration deliberately withholds or evades, contradicts without comment the modernist challenge to the very notion of comprehension beyond testimony. This ubiquitous and uncriticized metaphor of cryptography, I hope to show, has severely distorted our understanding of narrative in general. The criticism that compulsively attaches this metaphor to modernism in particular usually begins by pointing to the pre-war work of Conrad. For Conrad, the 'problem' of the witness is not that she cannot survive to tell the tale, or that she cannot perceive the facts, but rather that her report, as Lyotard suggests, is said to fall short of an imaginary narrative that would depict the event in its comprehensive entirety, beyond her mere 'perspective.' If there is an 'age of testimony' contemporaneous with literary modernism, as Felman suggests, it is one that grows out of a mounting tension at the fin de siècle between testimony and an anonymous authority to which the masters of public discourse increasingly appeal. My opening chapter takes a look at a few of these late nineteenth-century gatekeepers of public discourse, such as William Archer, L.F. Austin, and even Bernard Shaw, as they engage in a contentious debate about anonymous authority in the press. The larger part of that discussion, however, surveys and critiques the twentieth-century's reception of Conrad's narrative method, as articulated by critics from Henry James to Genette to Jameson. Dispelling the epistemological clouds these figures have gathered around Conrad's testimonial project, I go on to look at the crucial scene of public inquiry in *Lord Jim* in the clearer vision that emerges.

Another major objective of this book is to demonstrate that the very intelligibility of the novel as a cultural artefact is dependent on the question of testimony. In England, especially, and instantiated in fictions as diverse as *Robinson Crusoe* and *Clarissa*, the phenomenon of the novel is of a writing that emerges as the true testimony of a potential neighbour – the personal account of a historical contemporary, not distant in time or space, no matter if the narrative itself is exotic. Even when the dust settled on the question of whether these eyewitness accounts described historical realities, the constraints and the freedoms created by their rigorous testimonial structures are what made the novel what it was, distinguishing it from ballads and every other 'romance' that had circulated hitherto. That the modernist novel has, in literary studies, borne the brunt of its turn against testimony is evident in the fact, suggested above, that critics have never looked at the early novel's epistolary narrator with the epistemological suspicion that they have directed at a storyteller like Marlow. It is a critical inconsistency that fails to discern within modernism the vital legacy of epistolary and sentimental fiction, whose strategies of testimonial narration were so crucial to the novel's development. The second and third chapters of this book read the birth of the modernist novel, as embodied in both Conrad and Henry James, in the context of this sentimental ancestry. It will become clear that testimonial narration is indispensable to the major political task of the sentimental novel, which is to create and disseminate a conception of privacy acceptable for public consumption. The scrupulous use of testimonial arrangements in the early novel, with their complex machinery of letters, 'found' diaries, and exposing editors, is a reflection of a mimetic project that required the novel to depict the real-world conditions of personal narrative. But this reality puts an obstacle before another of the sentimental novel's primary goals: to confirm the inner sincerity of its letter-writing heroes and heroines, which may be hidden beneath the self-interest that could motivate any personal testimony. The early novel attempts to skirt this obstacle in at least two ways: rhetorically, by valorizing 'confession' as if it were not testimony, as if its claims of transparency and sincerity preclude the possibility of conscious self-representation and negotiation with the other, and structurally, by developing complicated scenarios wherein the protagonist's private testimony has been unexpectedly 'diverted' into the public sphere, or 'overheard' by third parties, thus mitigating the spectre of self-interested exhibitionism that inevitably haunts the very concept of testimony. One of the primary reasons omniscient narration comes to displace epistolarity over the nineteenth century is that it has the power to reveal a character's sentimentally appropriate interiority without requiring her to perform the self-interested act of articulating it herself.

When Conrad revives testimonial fiction at the dawn of the twentieth century, he therefore receives a dual inheritance: a well-developed strategy of sympathetic portraiture, on the one hand, but also a demanding ideal of sentimental accountability that, over the course of the preceding century, had merged with a moral injunction in Anglo-American society against any interiority or privacy that refuses to be accessible to public view. This particular moralism, however, suffers a distinct backlash in many nineteenth-century novels. Writers from Melville to Trollope to James react strongly against the perpetual personal transparency that sentimentalism seems to advocate, and they transform the formerly heroic agent of sympathy into one of the novel's primary antagonists. Sentimentalism becomes increasingly associated with mushy-headed social reform, a moon-eyed philanthropism, and feminism. Despite the generally condescending tone of the Victorian critique, it ultimately infuses sentimentalism with a dangerous political and social power, just as the concept of 'petticoat rule' would come both to ignite and assuage social-revolutionary fears. The nineteenth-century novel frequently portrays sentimentalism at the heart of a disciplinary nannyism that seeks to penetrate and bring order to both house and mind.

The rhetorical and narrative strategies by which Conrad and James render the disciplinary injunctions of sentimentalism will lead me to an extended reconsideration of influential literary criticism inspired by Michel Foucault. In its attempt to diagram what Mark Seltzer calls 'a continuity between . . . the social technologies of power' and 'the techniques of the novel' – specifically, the self-authorizing techniques of an external narrator 'seeing, knowing, and exercising power' over its diegetic world – this criticism posits precisely the operations of ideological representation and identification that Foucault attempted to think beyond (57). The novel's uncharted disciplinary function, I argue, will have to be found not in the mere 'political dream' of Bentham's panopticon (Foucault, *Discipline* 205), but where the document, literary or otherwise, exerts itself: at the multiform apparatus of registry that render the subject intelligible as such and affix the body to that subject with the lynchpin of the proper name.

At the apex of the novel's backlash against sentimentalism, Henry James joins Conrad in insisting on the prerogative of the individual to speak as a testifier as opposed to a confessor: to speak as a representative or 'ambassador' *for* the self in a culture with ever-increasing 'incitements to discourse' and an ethos of confessional transparency; to speak as one who maintains the 'space' or possibility of a personal reserve. Like his nineteenth-century models, however, James continues to let omniscient narration carry out the intrusions he claims to eschew, penetrating his subjects' psyches and policing their sentimental sincerity. Conrad's artistic method is thus unique within the general reaction against sentimentalism in its rigorous devotion to the real-world testimonial realities that sentimentalism tried to keep in view. It is a key element of the peculiar naturalism that carries his modernism away from that of James, distinguishing it even from the American master's new 'centre of consciousness' technique. The literary struggles Conrad and James undertake – sometimes together, sometimes in contest – will emerge in readings of *The Nigger of the 'Narcissus,' Lord Jim, Notes on Life and Letters, The Portrait of a Lady, The Reverberator,* and *The Ambassadors,* among several other stories and essays. Although the argument implicit within James's fiction vehemently insists on the prerogative of the individual to represent oneself as a testifier, the author firmly rejects personal testimony as a vehicle for artistic, philosophical, or historiographic knowledge. In the realm of literary criticism, in fact, I argue that it was James who first crafted the vocabulary that would forever put Conradian narrative under an epistemological cloud. As James, in an essay of 1914, ultimately dismisses Conrad's work precisely because it does not pretend to speak from a comprehension that would transcend testimony, the American creates a treatise praising the authority of the unlocated voice that belongs to no privacy and no testimony. This voice had already achieved cultural ascendancy in the anonymous yet colossal stance of the nineteenth-century newspaper.

In his fiction, Conrad scrutinizes the masterful comprehension of the press most explicitly in *Heart of Darkness.* Surprisingly, the mountains of criticism evoked by this tale have overlooked one of the primary targets of its satire: the 'newspaper stunt,' as Conrad once called it, perpetrated by the New York *Herald* in the 1870s, when the paper sent its travelling journalist Henry Morton Stanley on a sensational hunt into central Africa to find Dr David Livingstone. Revealing how *Heart of Darkness* conflates the seeker and the sought of this episode into the figure of the journalist Kurtz, the final chapter of this book returns to the broader context of nineteenth-century journalism. As we will see, the '*Herald* expedition,' as Stanley's venture was called, helped to grease the political wheels of the Belgian machine that would soon devour central Africa. The profit of Stanley's expedition was not only increased sales for the *Herald*, but the inflation, in print, of an 'African darkness' that the comprehensive light of the press would theatrically penetrate. *Heart of Darkness* recalls the powerful transformation, accomplished largely through the Anglo-American newspaper, by which the 'hidden' Livingstone became the hidden truth of Africa itself. The novella demonstrates, moreover, how such a theatre of exploration, incursion, and discovery effectively occludes its own stage management. If a drawn veil always exposes a once-hidden truth, even a purely staged motion of unveiling – a journalistic performance of 'eyewitness penetration' into the heart of darkness – will seem to guarantee the advent of truth. Through the comprehensive posture of the *Herald*, Stanley's apologias for colonial violence were suffused with a historiographic authority that transcends the 'mere testimony' of the adventuring witness.

# 1 'Speech Was of No Use': Conrad and the Critical Abjection of Testimony

Although the English novel began to strike out on its own in the eighteenth century, diverging from its travel-writing and printed 'newes' parentage, it maintained a protocol shared by all of these genres that required an open portrayal – or at least some account – of the narrator or witness who made the narration possible. Even the most fantastic tales in the novel's ancestry could not universally take for granted the premises of what we now call omniscient narration. The printed ballads of the sixteenth and seventeenth centuries habitually took the form of a first-person testimonial. An important part of their drama, in fact, would often include the spying activities that had been required of the narrating witness to get the story. Even where we seem to see omniscient narrators in the seventeenth century, they were usually born within the *conte* as an actor within the fiction itself.[1] The narrator was one who had won his story by successfully penetrating a private or otherwise circumscribed space. The attainment of this unobserved omniscience, whether by supernatural or covert means, was an element of the plot. The appearance of the narrator within the narrative is historically no more of an innovation to fiction than is the 'third-person' narration that does not account for itself as either testifier or witness.

Over the course of the nineteenth century, however, the testimonial protocol fell away, for news as well as for its cousins in fiction. Even more, the acknowledgment within a narrative of its testimonial nature became an admission of a fundamental unreliability, a renunciation of epistemological and historical authority. This new conception became fairly explicit in the British and American press. By the end of the nineteenth century, the personal accounts that had formerly constituted textual 'news' – whether or not they were later designated as fiction – were now testimonials within 'the journal.' The newspaper had become, in William Archer's words, an 'impersonal force' that seemed to transcend and comprehend its constituent reporters, witnesses, correspondents, and even editors. The press can now exert itself, Archer writes,

> from behind a mask of superhuman, ineffable wisdom which imposes so ludicrously on the multitude . . . Men tell each other with bated breath, 'The *Tribune* says this, the *Oracle* says that; the *Reverberator* is of such an opinion,' forgetting that *Tribune, Oracle*, and *Reverberator* are only Hobson, Dobson, and Jobson speaking grandiloquently through a resonant mouthpiece. (Hopkins, 'Anonymity? I' 530)

In the novel, too, the 'superhuman' extradiegetic literary voice reached its normative apex at this period.[2] When Joseph Conrad's 'Marlow' narratives hit the literary scene at the beginning of the twentieth century, therefore, they arrive with a force of contrast, spinning their tales almost entirely through the testimony of one or more characters within the fiction. Conrad was seen by at least one of his contemporaries as speaking to the more general question of how a reading society ought to acknowledge – or efface – the ultimately testimonial nature of all its narratives. In an essay that asks in its title 'Why Marlow?' and investigates 'the spell of that "veiled glance" of his, akin to the glittering eyes of another Ancient Mariner,' Francis Wentworth Cutler seems to see in Conrad's narrative strategy a call for democratic polyvocality in public discourse (28):

> We have seen [Marlow] ignoring the rules of narration: that a story should have but one teller, to whom nothing in his tale is unknown; that the psychological story in particular demands the omniscient author-narrator . . . In so doing he has, we have seen, obeyed a higher law than that of textbooks – the law of his vision of reality created of human contact . . . The older novel, the simplification of life, gave us the creative process achieved, the decision handed down. From the verdict on Becky Sharp or on Rosamond Lydgate there is no appeal. But with Conrad we actually enter into the creative process . . . For the art of Conrad is literally a *social* art – the collaboration of many tellers and of many listeners . . . For the verdict on Jim and Flora [in *Chance*] rests with us at last. (37–8)

Sharing Cutler's determination to frame this issue in juridical and social terms, Conrad's *Lord Jim* goes so far as to use a scene of public inquest to model the condition of testimony in general. Twelve years after the novel was published, as will be explored below, Conrad reiterates the terms of this drama and its internal polemic in his heated participation in the public inquiry surrounding the crew of the USS *Titanic*.

The touchstone of this chapter will be these scenes of deposition in Conrad and their diagnosis of the effectively extradiegetic voice that had come to hold sway both in the literary world and among the apparatus of mass communication in 'this age of knowledge.'[3] I will also investigate the critical legacy that has effectively obscured Conrad's critique by subsuming it into a 'modernism' reportedly trapped in psychic introspection and aesthetic withdrawal. The epistemological and cultural criticism inherent in the author's fiction, as well as his positive assessment of the conditions of public discourse, have been buried under a conception of Conradian modernism as a writing entirely 'made for itself and submerged by itself' (Bradbury and McFarlane 29).

In an 1889 edition of London's the *New Review*, Tighe Hopkins initiated a colloquium on anonymity in the newspaper. Unsigned articles had long been the norm in the English press, and another debate about how well they protect voices of social and political reform from persecution would have been unremarkable, especially in a reform-minded publication like the *New Review*.[4] But here at the twilight of the century, Hopkins and several journalistic and literary allies argue at length against anonymity. The progressive voices that had once feared the blunt power of crown and title now saw a new enemy: anonymous authority itself, a power said to be conjured by the very organs of mass communication that had been weapons against the old order. 'The power of the press,' writes L.F. Austin, who would ultimately oppose Hopkins in the debate, 'is a purely impersonal force . . . The *Times* is the power, not the men who write in it.'[5] The *New Review* debate was not about whether the use of an anonymous voice really does effect a distinct and instrumental authority. All of its participants, including Bernard Shaw, agreed that anonymity creates an identifiable, autonomous authority with an operative power. At issue, rather, was whether the press ought to wield the 'mysterious power,' as James Runciman put it, 'which the anonymous article gives' (Hopkins, I 528).

Whereas Hopkins and his allies lament a reading public 'willing to impose on itself . . . a belief that the use of the "We" in place of the "I" endows [a] writer with a semi-miraculous wisdom' (I 524), Austin and a handful of others warn that 'the power of the press in England' would be devastated without its anonymous voice (I 517). Austin contrasts English practice with that of Paris, where 'the authority of this or that journal is of no account' precisely because articles are attributed to particular writers. The Parisian news reader 'enjoys the performances of his favourite literary swordsmen, the clash of whose weapons amuses the Boulevards and sometimes startles the birds in early morning in the Bois de Boulogne' (I 517). Open acknowledgment that articles are ultimately constituted by the personal testimony of particular writers and witnesses turns the serious business of journalism into a contemptible game. Austin's argument is a glimpse into a crucial nineteenth-century use of the term 'literary' to signal the distance of a given text from reliable reportage. French journalism is said to deserve demotion into the literary not because it is tainted by fictitiousness, but because it does not affirm a transcendental relation to the personal testimony of which it is composed. A report bound to a signature or name will, for that reason alone, contribute more to the memoir than to the history, more to the literary than to the real. Few of the *New Review* contributors fail to compare, favourably or not, the English habit of anonymity with France's systematic attribution. The portrait of a French public discourse rendered impotent by its rejection of anonymous authority is made intelligible by a cultural logic well known to Austin's readers. The greater insistence across the Channel on the testimonial nature of journalism is readily understood as an expression of the debilitating relativism and subjectivism for which Paris is the Western world's bastion. The *New Review* debate reveals the extent to which an industry whose product is public discourse had come to depend on cultural codes and philosophical imperatives that establish the moral value – and even necessity – of anonymous authority in itself.

Marc DaRosa argues that the participants of Hopkins's colloquium conceive the newspaper as 'a text that invalidates the notion of an originating consciousness' (829). The *New Review* observers thus display a prescient anxiety, DaRosa concludes, about the uncontrollable autonomy of text once it leaves the author's control, an autonomy that, in the end, is simply the predicament of any iteration, and which will later be signalled – alarmingly, to some – as 'the death of the author.' DaRosa's conclusion is tempting, but it ultimately requires a blindness to the authority these writers consistently recondense into a surrogate point of origin: the journal itself, an entity discrete but unlocalized. For Hopkins and his colleagues on both sides of the debate, neither anonymity nor any appeal to an authority that would transcend personal testimony threatens their sense of a journal's seminal univocality. As Edward Russell writes, a newspaper had 'an individuality . . . a continuity, a policy and even a manner independent of its personnel' (I 517). The *New Review* writers consistently and automatically project behind the article an 'originating consciousness'; they reify an 'author effect' even in the absence of a determinate author, even where there is no possibility of signature. The conceptual effect of corporate or anonymous histories-of-the-now – written in a voice that would be extradiegetic in relation to the world it reports – has not been the dissolution of the author. Rather, the projection of comprehensive consciousness behind the extradiegetic pose has been fully normalized – precisely, I suggest, by the massive proliferation of this writing leading to the 'new journalism.'[6] As we shall see below, the consequence of this normalization in relation to other printed scenes of narration and deposition is the negative marking of personal testimony within the non-local univocality of the article.

One of modernity's most explicit treatments of the institutional and juridical power of anonymous authority, and of the press's role as the medium of that power, can be found in two essays Conrad published in 1912 issues of *The English Review*. 'Some Reflexions . . . on the Loss of the *Titanic*' is certainly the most passionate public statement the author ever penned, and its sequel, 'Certain Aspects of the Admirable Inquiry into the Loss of the *Titanic*,' is only slightly more restrained. 'It is with a certain bitterness,' the first essay begins, 'that one must admit to oneself that the late S. S. *Titanic* had a "good press."' Despite having 'no great practice of daily newspapers' and 'scant respect for the "organs of public opinion,"' Conrad ultimately attributes to their 'irresponsible paragraphs' the manufacture of 'an absurd and vulgar demand for [the] banal luxury' of 'floating hotels' (*Notes* 213, 229, 214, 223). The real objects of Conrad's ire, however, are the public inquiries, in both England and the United States, whose purpose in the wake of the tragedy is to deflect responsibility from the profit-motivated decisions of technocrats and 'commercial men' to the ship's crew and captain (214). All the 'established authorities' at work in this deflection – the Board of Trade, the 'passage-selling Combines,' the 'high priests' of technology (who would 'fain forbid the profane from inquiring into its mysteries') and even a U.S. Senate board of inquiry – are implicated together in the 'calumnious, baseless . . . lie charging poor Captain Smith with desertion of his post by means of suicide' (216, 241, 230, 228). This charge, Conrad writes in conclusion to the first essay, is 'the vilest and most ugly thing of all in this outburst of journalistic enterprise' (228). This crescendo infuses into 'journalistic enterprise' all the 'commercial and industrial interests' under scrutiny throughout the essay (219). Exerting themselves through both the tribunal and the newspaper, all these authorities, Conrad suggests, contribute to the single 'admirable inquiry' of the later essay's title.

As in these essays, the ubiquitous and pivotal term in the *New Review* colloquium on anonymity is 'responsibility.' Echoing the arguments of Hopkins and his allies, Shaw reports that he writes 'more carefully, and with a keener sense of direct personal responsibility for the soundness of my utterances, when what I write appears over my signature' ('Anonymity? II' 271). Of greater concern on the other side of the debate is 'the journal' as a distinct corporate entity. 'The editorial "We,"' writes Lynn Linton, 'is the sign of a unified multitude, and its force is both great and legitimate . . . By the adoption of the signature the journal repudiates responsibility' (I 516). Conrad's 'Reflexions,' by contrast, finds something spectral in such unified multitudes. Among the forces scapegoating the ship's captain, Conrad singles out the British Board of Trade, citing 'some exasperated wit' who described such entities as having

> no souls to be saved and no bodies to be kicked, and thus [are] free in this world and the next from all effective sanctions of conscientious conduct [. . .] The Board of Trade is composed of bloodless departments. It has no limbs and no physiognomy, or else at the forthcoming inquiry it might have paid to the victims of the *Titanic* disaster the small tribute of a blush. (307)

The Board is composed of 'irresponsible gentlemen . . . with no care in the world; for there can be no care without personal responsibility – such, for instance, as the seamen have . . .' Among the principal initiators of the *Titanic* public inquiry Conrad can find no responsibility, no named accuser to which the crew can respond: 'A Board of Trade – what is it? . . . A ghost . . . Less than nothing; a mere void without as much as a shadow of responsibility' (216–17).[7]

Conrad's own testimony in this proceeding is made possible by the authority he claims as a former marine officer. Yet the essays are surprisingly hesitant to appeal to personal experience – that is, to stress its testimonial mode – in order to further their argument. The shift in the 'Reflexions' away from its caustic editorial stance is distinct and clearly announced, but it also comes reluctantly, even apologetically. It is 2,500 words into the essay before Conrad offers for instruction an 'incident I witnessed' during his tenure at sea, one that had not been 'boastfully paragraphed all round the Press, because that was not the fashion of the time' (313). He tells his story 'not for the vain pleasure of talking about my own poor experiences, but only to illustrate my point' (310), assuring his *English Review* audience that 'what I am going to relate' is a 'fact.' He interrupts his account with a repeated assurance that 'I am sticking all the time to my subject to illustrate my point' (313). The defensiveness of the storyteller finding himself amid this journalistic proceeding, now just one of many voices in a public debate – this, combined with the diction and especially the circumstance of the remarks, calls to mind one of the climactic moments of *Lord Jim*, when that sailor attempts to give his testimony in a public inquiry. Like that of the *Titanic*'s crew, the testimony that Jim gives at his tribunal must compete with a history of the *Patna* affair already articulated, already refined and elaborated by a network of conversation that begins with a 'cable message' and is kept in circulation by the likes of the *Home News* edition that a stranger later hands Marlow in a café. Marlow's acceptance of the French lieutenant's paper ('which I didn't want') leads the pair to their common interest in 'the irrepressible *Patna* case' (*Lord Jim* 85, 93). By that authorless tale, the product of a communication network he tries but fails to outrun, the relevance of Jim's testimony is measured and he is evaluated. The mariner's formerly spontaneous, self-generated, and gratuitous rime becomes, under Conrad's pen, coerced testimony in a courtroom.[8] As elsewhere in modern fiction, the courtroom proves to be *the* crucial trope in exhibiting the degraded status of the witness or testifier in a culture of anonymous authority.

In the novel, the inquiry is no more closed an affair than that of the *Titanic*: the entire Malay Archipelago, the whole of the seafaring world attends. The magistrates 'wanted facts. Facts! They demanded facts from him' (22). The young seaman has hope, at first, in 'a meticulous precision of statement' on his part, but in his delivery of this testimony he was 'becoming irrelevant; a question to the point cut short his speech . . . He was coming to that, he was coming to that – and now, checked brutally, he had to answer by yes or no' (23). The voice that demands more than once that Jim answer 'to the point' is the same inquisitor Conrad seems to feel over his own shoulder – twelve years after publishing the novel, still firmly within a tacit role as seamen's advocate – while writing his own testimony in the public controversy over the *Titanic*. It is as if the author is compelled to exorcise from his report the spectre raised in the *New Review* debate of the great danger to a journal's authority: a Frenchified mode of memoir-writing. Whatever authority he might otherwise wield, the realm of the literary that Conrad dangerously skirts by recounting yet another story of the sea would disqualify him from the authority governing this inquiry. In his foray into public debate he struggles to escape the status of a merely 'amusing' performance, to recall L.F. Austin, of a 'literary swordsman.'[9]

As Shoshana Felman suggests, anxiety about the contamination of the literary is endemic to legal discourse and commentary. In her study of Hannah Arendt's analysis of the Adolf Eichmann trial, Felman recalls that the prosecution sought to concentrate on the testimony of witnesses rather than documentary evidence. Despite fears that living testifiers will 'always be chargeable with bias,' as the chief prosecutor put it, his greater concern was that a document-laden trial would become 'wearisome' and would 'not get across to the people.'[10] To Arendt, this approach exacerbated a sense that the trial was mere 'theatre,' a problem aggravated by the prosecution's use of a writer as witness, the 'storyteller' Yehiel Dinoor, a Holocaust survivor who wrote under the name Ka-Tzetnik 135633 (Arendt 224). Under the sway, as Felman writes, of a 'logic that transforms testimony into a theatrical event that parasitizes the trial,' Arendt fears a 'contamination between facts and fiction – . . . the confusion and the interpenetration between law and literature' (Felman, 'A Ghost' 272).

A few years beyond *Lord Jim*, Conrad describes a certain 'advantage' of freedom peculiar to the literary author. 'Where a novelist has an advantage over the workers in other fields of thought is in his privilege of freedom – the freedom of expression and the freedom of confessing his innermost beliefs' (*Notes* 7). Freedoms of expression and confession, in harmony; but in *Lord Jim* and the 'Reflexions,' these mark the poles, rather, of untraceable anonymity and personal responsibility. Expression: it is unclear at first glance why a novelist would have greater freedom here than writers in other 'fields of thought.' Jacques Derrida helps to delineate the conception of literature at work here:

> Literature [as opposed to 'belles-lettres or poetry'] is a modern invention, inscribed in conventions and institutions which, to hold on to just this trait, secure in principle its *right to say everything* . . . The possibility of literature [is conjoined] – politically – with the unlimited right . . . to analyze every presupposition, even those of the ethics or the politics of responsibility. (*On the Name* 28–9)

This right to say everything includes the right, too, to an absolute dialogism: the right to release not just some, but any and all voices in the novel from the jurisdiction of the author. It is a right of the novel, therefore, to its own absolute schizophrenia. Derrida follows the consequence of this freedom:

> But this authorization to say everything paradoxically makes the author an author who is not responsible to anyone, not even to himself, for whatever the persons or the characters of his works . . . say and do, for example . . . This authorization to say everything . . . acknowledges a right to absolute nonresponse, just where there can be no question of responding, of being able to or having to respond. (28–9)

It is against this author – anonymous, unlocatable, and in narratological terms at the outermost 'level' of narration – that *Lord Jim* and the 'Reflexions' explicitly strain. But although Conrad thus takes on the responsibility of the testifier in his essays, he cannot escape the persona of the littérateur, the non-responsible 'play' of literature. The literary author is thus kept at a remove from authority, historiographic and otherwise, in a way that no other pundit or public speaker can be.

The author of *Lord Jim* is compelled to revisit in *The English Review* the stage of public inquiry scripted in the novel, but this time he renders explicit its socio-political dimension, naming institutional names. My insistence on the historical co-implication of *Lord Jim* with the *Titanic* essays is meant to challenge prevailing evaluations of the social dimension of Conrad's oeuvre, one of the most influential of which is Fredric Jameson's reading of the novel in *The Political Unconscious*. My attempt to so 'open the frame' of *Lord Jim* is nevertheless exactly what Jameson calls for in his desire to permeate, expose, and properly historicize all such formal or aesthetic containers. But Jameson sees no historical condition or discourse to which the novel's trial scene affixes, or by which it is informed; indeed, his conclusion that it is nothing more than an 'aesthetic rehearsal of . . . the feudal ideology of honor' – bespeaking a critical eye that has not strayed an inch from the broadest of the episode's themes – seems only to sustain its inviolability as an aesthetic container (217). The complications that arise in Jameson's reading of *Lord Jim* are considerable if we allow Jim's trial to be informed by such things as the author's later projection into the *Titanic* defence box 'the masses of men who work, who deal in things and face the realities – not the words – of this life,' and who are interrogated by a Board of Trade into which converge so many juridical and mercantile interests (*Notes* 217). Further on I will return to Jameson's critical overview and look closely at his own use of 'aesthetic containment' to elide what he calls the 'authentic content' of Conrad's work.

As have other intellectual authorities throughout the novel's history, the Lukácsian critical tradition that Jameson refines puts the novel as a genre on trial, calls it to the stand partly for its audacious challenge to historiography as another mode by which history and society might be understood. As Conrad's testifier is condemned to silence and irrelevance in *Lord Jim*, the climactic tribunal scene in that novel recreates this trial. From Defoe's defence of *Robinson Crusoe* to Conrad's own suggestion that 'fiction is nearer truth' than history, the novel has contended that 'facts' alone can never adequately render a scene, historical or otherwise.[11] Michael McKeon's penetrating historical analysis of this challenge reveals the purely negative genealogy of 'romance,' whose primary denotation by the eighteenth century was any story whose form or content seemed to echo those of conventionally acknowledged fiction. Becoming in this way a rather broad name for narrative falsehood, romance became useful to the early novelists' attempts to define, demarcate, and accredit their work. The seeming absence of formal precedent in the novel kept it free of the 'romantick.' As in most analyses of these seventeenth- and eighteenth-century apologias, the climax of McKeon's overview is a reprobation of the sleight-of-hand by which the novel, elevating itself above the romance, seems to keep at arm's reach, or to have rendered irrelevant, the fact of its ahistoricity.

Yet McKeon's *The Origins of the English Novel* does not delineate the more foundational critique within many of these early inquiries, the object of which was historical narrative, not fiction. It is an omission that ultimately serves a common critical strategy of protecting the category of historiography from the various contagions of trope and interpretation that we generally prefer to contain safely within fiction.

McKeon looks closely, for instance, at Defoe's *Serious Reflections*, wherein the essay 'On Lying' asserts that 'nothing is more common, than to have two Men tell the same Story quite differing one from another, yet both of them Eye-Witnesses to the Fact related' (Defoe 113). Defoe goes on for several pages tracing this phenomenon to various causes, but McKeon implicitly subsumes the remark within the next section of the essay, which is devoted to the separate 'case' of fiction. Here Defoe defends his initial presentation of *Robinson Crusoe* as historical fact with the argument that the universal truths it expresses renders moot the question of its historicity, and that the ahistoricity of his tale is much less pernicious than a historically true tale that becomes warped through inept or misleading presentation.

> Others make no Scruple to relate real Stories with innumerable Omissions and Additions: I mean, Stories which have a real Existence in Fact, but which by the barbarous Way of relating, become as romantick and false, as if they had no real Original. (Defoe 117)

Defoe ultimately recognizes, McKeon argues, that this critique of fact-based narratives 'would appear to deny the responsibility of narrative to a standard of truth that is separate from and higher than its own inventions' (*Origins* 121). To prove this recognition, however, McKeon reaches back to the previous section of the essay, to a sentence that appears long before Defoe introduces the subject of fictional narrative: '[The] supplying a Story by Invention is certainly a most scandalous Crime . . . It is a sort of Lying that makes a great Hole in the Heart' (113). This 'Invention' and 'Lying' does not, as McKeon asserts, refer to the false claim to historicity made by a novel like *Robinson Crusoe*; it refers entirely to the false 'Addenda' to history, the 'frequent Addition put to it in the Relation, till not only it comes to be improbable, but even impossible to be true' (113). The lies to which Defoe points in his defence of the novel are those proceeding from 'Omissions and Additions' to any narrative, from a 'barbarous Way of relating' and faulty presentation, not from a false claim to historicity. McKeon rightly points out that Defoe's discussion could put under suspicion all narrative apparatus as such; but even this extremity would not, as he suggests, sweep novels and histories alike into the black hole of fiction. Nowhere does Defoe loose the 'facts' of his hypothetical stories from the mooring to which that term is anchored, such as the personal and cartographic names that would be common to both of his hypothetically divergent

'Eye-witness' accounts of an event. Early in the essay, for instance, Defoe discusses the use of the personal name in a narrative as a bid for historicity; its legitimizing power is eagerly abused by lying reporters, who will often 'vouch also, that they knew the Persons who were concerned' in their accounts (115). Reference to historical fact is a prerequisite for historicity, but it will in no way protect the related history from the falsehood of 'romantick' presentation. McKeon nevertheless depicts the *Reflections* as at an impasse produced by the 'absolute dichotomy' between '"true history" and "romance,"' whereby 'romantick' falsification could only occur in fiction (121).

McKeon's blunt dichotomy, which would obviate Defoe's concerns about presentation in historical narrative, continues to rule many discourses about truth and historicity to this day. Faced, for instance, with a controversial biography of Ronald Reagan that included several playful and fictional 'additions,' as Defoe might have called them, and which were clearly marked as such in the book, the *New York Times Book Review* asks, 'Where's the Truth of Him?' – as if this question would have been unproblematically answered by a traditional biography in which the spectre of fiction never appears.[12] It is a truism that the claims of causality and the narrative-driven demarcation of events in any historiography, which allow a mere chronicle to be knit into historical narrative, are acts of judicious interpretation. No historian would suggest such narrative could achieve the status of unquestionable Truth. When the term 'fiction' appears in discourses about history writing, however, the fact of this interpretive condition suddenly disappears. Fiction becomes a scapegoat, the single name for everything that keeps historical truth from view. Fiction becomes a veil before history, and truth is now simply a matter of unveiling. When the category of fiction is then cast out, bearing all sins of falsehood and indeterminacy, the historiography that remains behind in the settling dust seems to emerge as unobscured truth. A rhetoric of history as revelation replaces history as production.[13] We will see later how literary criticism unwittingly measures the novel's commitment to truth by whether or not it figures within itself this movement of veiling and unveiling. Consistently, the modernist novel's purported rejection of the real is traced to its failure to establish or complete this circuit.

It would be difficult to exaggerate how much our conception of the modernist novel has been shaped by the rhetoric of narratology. Conrad's work is said to be an avatar of modernism in England largely by virtue of its narrative structure. It is a familiar and still-venerated truth that these novels despair at the insurmountability of subjectivity, and consequently effect a retreat 'inward,' away from the real. This truth is usually presented as an inevitable consequence of these works' narrative structure alone, regardless of whether it is also expressed in their thematics or explicit discourse. Ursula Lord's formulation is paradigmatic:

> Heart of Darkness and Lord Jim disclose in narrative structure the relativism of modern epistemology . . . Conrad's creation of Marlow and his embedding of Marlow's narrative within another acknowledge that we always perceive the world many times removed, filtered through our own consciousness and that of others, as through a glass darkly. (63–4)

What I want to demonstrate through the case study of Conradian criticism is that this embrace of subjectivity and this retreat inward, purportedly the necessary consequences of Conrad's narrative arrangements, are in fact critical phantasms. These inside/outside tropes are consistently projected onto the novelistic scene of writing, necessary only to the narratological structuralism that deploys them, and ultimately serve a very particular authoritarianism, what one might call an antitestimonial ideology. As we will see, however, this structuralism can be traced back at least to Henry James, and its usefulness in maintaining bedrock orthodoxies about modernist narrative – that it is inward-looking, ahistorical, trapped in its own formalism and subjectivity, etc. – has penetrated, in fact, the entire field of literary criticism, inhabiting projects that are indifferent or even inimical to narratology.

That the operations of attestation, deposition, and confession are primary subjects of Conrad's scrutiny has been both a truism and an impossibility for literary criticism. Although we no longer follow Henry James in pulling Conrad's scenes of narration out of the realm of a novel's proper 'content' and into an externality of 'treatment,' the still-active rhetoric of epistemological 'filtering' that we see in Lord owes a great deal to this long-standing banishment. James had gotten the ball rolling in his 1914 summation of Conrad in 'The Younger Generation,' which focuses exclusively on the author's staged narration, and is, rather remarkably, the only formal study of Conrad he would ever articulate. Purely 'the exhibition of method,' according to James, and therefore external to content, Conrad's investigation of Marlow's investigations cannot possibly be conceived as a subject under treatment. 'What shall we most call Mr. Conrad's method,' James writes, 'but his attempt to clarify [his subject] *quand même* . . . steeping his matter in perfect eventual obscuration' (157).[14]

Behind James's judgment in 'The Younger Generation' is a theory of narration that had already been infused with the logic to which Lyotard draws our attention: Attestation, once it is framed or made visible as such, is necessarily untrustworthy. In a 1911 letter to H.G. Wells, James had written:

> . . . I make my remonstrance – for I do remonstrate – bear upon the bad service you have done your cause by riding so hard again that accurst autobiographic form . . . Save in the fantastic and the romantic . . . it has no authority, no persuasive or convincing force – its grasp of reality and truth isn't strong and disinterested . . . There is, to my vision, no authentic . . . report of things on the novelist's . . . part unless a particular detachment has operated, unless the great stewpot or crucible of the imagination, of the observant and recording and interpreting mind in short, has intervened and played its part . . . (*Henry James* 500)

The authority of a novelistic statement hinges at the outset on a disavowal of its status as testimony, even as that authority retains its own 'interpreting mind' that would 'intervene' in our quest for the 'reality and truth' it grasps. Hence the axiom in 'The Younger Generation' that the lack of true authority in Conrad's Marlow is entirely due to his status as 'a reciter, a definite responsible intervening first person singular.' Authority can reside only in a non-responsible narrator, a 'single . . . impersonal and inscrutable . . . omniscience, remaining indeed nameless' ('Younger' 157).

As it pretends to cite but actually inscribes into orthodoxy 'the general law of fiction' that Conrad disobeys, James's essay begins by explaining that the scene of deposition Conrad habitually keeps in view should rather be suppressed; the reader should remain unconscious of the interrogative or confessional arrangements that are the precondition of testimony.

> It has been the course . . . of [Conrad's] so multiplying his creators or, as we are now fond of saying, producers, as to make them almost more numerous and quite emphatically more material than the creatures and the production itself in whom and which we by the general law of fiction expect such agents to lose themselves. We take for granted by the general

> law of fiction a primary author . . . [who] works upon us most in fact
> by making us forget him. Mr. Conrad's first care, adversely to this, is ex-
> pressly to posit or set up a reciter, a definite responsible intervening first
> person singular. (157)

The language of law serves to preempt inevitable questions about why we should 'take it for granted' that the 'primary author' of, say, *The Ambassadors* remains 'nameless' and non-locatable. In fact this refusal in Conrad to let his 'projected' storyteller disappear as a responsible intervener confronts James with something that inevitably precludes his law: the inescapable possibility that what a reader takes for granted is precisely a historical determination of this author, e.g., a determination of a Mr Henry James, of various facts and lore constituting his public persona. To ensure that we 'forget' this author, and to establish that its 'observant and recording and interpreting mind' is categorically distinct from Marlow's – that 'beautiful and generous' interpreter of events (157) – what is available to James is no law, but only his own decree.[15] As we will see, however, it is a decree that will become the foundation of later narratologies, the only means of establishing both the discretion and totalization of a given 'structural' schematic for a novel, as well as that structure's independence from 'content.'

As are later narratologists, James is careful not to play the trump card of 'omniscience' to establish a difference in authority that would exist between Marlow and the proper Jamesian narrator to which he is necessarily opposed; rather, he gives the term to Marlow himself.

> Marlow's omniscience . . . is a prolonged hovering flight of the subjec-
> tive over the outstretched ground of the case exposed. We make out this
> ground, only through the shadow cast by the flight . . . to the no small
> eclipse of intrinsic colour and form and whatever, upon the passive
> expanse. (157)

James does not allow his all-important 'methodological' distinction to be based on a godly power that, if achieved merely by avoiding the 'first person singular,' an author could so easily and arbitrarily give himself, and which Conrad would thus have austerely renounced. Instead, the essay achieves its abjection of the Conradian testimonial by strategically grafting onto its narrative agents designations of subject and object. Marlow is said to be effectively omniscient, but he also allows himself to be 'seen' as an object of study, which places him merely 'within' the comprehension that ought always to 'enclose and confine' determined objects (158). In contrast, the unacknowledged Jamesian narrator is perforce freed from all qualities and effects attributed to an object, such as the inevitability of casting a 'shadow,' the shadow of his own 'subjectivity.'

To pick just one point of its entry into the subsequent history of critical thought, the imaginary comprehension that would 'enclose' all objectified narratives reappears in narratology's conception of 'external focalization.' As Gérard Genette writes in *Narrative Discourse*, this externality becomes evident when a literary hero 'performs in front of us without our ever being allowed to know his thoughts or feelings.' Ernest Hemingway's 'Hills like White Elephants' is said to be an exemplary case, 'which carries circumspection so far as to become a riddle.' Genette continues:

> But we should not limit this narrative type to a role only in works at the highest literary level. Michel Raimond remarks rightly that in the novel of intrigue or adventure, 'where interest arises from the fact that there is a mystery,' the author 'does not tell us immediately all that he knows.'[16] (190)

There is an epistemological contract peculiar to the whodunit, which first promises then unveils a predetermined answer to a mystery. Genette identifies the mystery of this determined truth with the mysteries supposed to belong to Hemingway's fiction. The answer to these mysteries would apparently include the truth of a fictional hero's consciousness and the 'riddle' of the story as a whole, the encoded truth it ultimately speaks. Despite Genette's ostensibly gratuitous movement toward the subgenre of the mystery as if toward another illustrative case, the activity peculiar to such stories – of manufacturing a screen behind which secrets are said to lie, thereby assuring the advent of truth in the mere drawing of the curtain – has been presumed all along to belong to fiction in general. There would then always have been an answer to the riddle of fiction, and the truth that literature speaks will be identical to the establishment and completion of such circuits of veiling and unveiling.[17] In order to establish what, exactly, would constitute full disclosure in a story such as 'Hills like White Elephants,' the critic must draw up a contract to designate the question(s) whose answer shall be the ultimate revelation.[18] In the pact Genette would impose on Hemingway's story, the designated question is of the 'thoughts and feelings' of the hero. If an answer to this question had been provided by the fiction, the author would reportedly have given us 'all that he knows' – despite the fact that there remain countless other possible questions, pooled from the psychological knowledge-systems Genette faintly evokes, that could just as easily have been the designated one: questions about the hero's childhood, sexual habits, relationship with his mother, etc.

In *The Political Unconscious*, Fredric Jameson verifies that the act of projecting into Conrad an epistemological hermeneutic – which exists, in reality, only through the operation of the critic – does not require allegiance to any formal narratology.

> Conrad's elaborate narrative hermeneutic [in *Lord Jim*] – what really did happen? who knows it all? what impressions do people have who possess only this piece of the puzzle, or that one? – tends to reinforce and supply powerful narrative demonstrations of . . . [an] ideology of the relativity of individual monads. (222)

The precedent for this formulation is so extensive and familiar that we might pass right over it without verifying whether the questions it ventriloquizes could possibly be evoked by this novel. Yet from the perspective of the 'individual monads' to which Jameson alludes – Marlow, Stein, the French lieutenant, etc. – we have to ask: Is there any fact about Jim's 'story' or his desertion of the *Patna* that Conrad leaves in question? In the 'elaborate' narrative environments of *Lord Jim*, *Chance*, *Nostromo*, or *Under Western Eyes*, does there ever remain for the reader any mystery about 'what really did happen'? Do not these fictions rather stage as their primary conflict the pathetic attempt of an embattled conscience to breach the inviolability and irreducibility of a fact that is known by all? As Marlow reminds us repeatedly about Jim's story, '[t]here was no incertitude as to facts' (56). What we see in Jameson is another case of forging the signature of modernism on the epistemological contract of the whodunit.[19] The trope of the scattered puzzle is vital to this purpose. The succession of narrative 'impressions' that could adequately be depicted, and with the greatest simplicity, as superadditions – a purely productive vision of Conradian narrative which Jameson himself had conjured three pages earlier[20] – are instead designated as 'pieces' or fragments, thereby importing into the text Jameson's own lamentation for the lack of a designated univocal authority. With respect to the diegetic facts and the 'history' that is *Lord*

*Jim*, Jameson's structural principle must attribute to each character's narrative a historiographic inadequacy that, ultimately, does not exist. We cannot conclude, of course, that the traditional Marxist critique of the modernist's failure to replicate the proper grand narrative of history is thus undermined. But Jameson's reading does make clear that even the most supple and reportedly post-poststructuralist Marxism can anchor itself in pseudoscientific certainties about the structural and espistemological consequences of testimonial narration.

In *Lord Jim*, Marlow recites and comments on narratives he obtained from Jim. As there is no controversy or incertitude 'as to facts' between these two, the differences that might exist between their narratives could only be those of interpretation, of their judgments about those facts. All of the novel's questions, whether they be called existential, ethical, or political, would have remained questions without Marlow's participation, even if we had obtained these stories from Jim himself, and even if the entirety of the novel had been voiced in third-person omniscience. The persistence into contemporary criticism of the opposing notion, that a staged narrator necessarily keeps us from certain 'answers' to which we would otherwise have had access, can be attributed partially to the narratological metaphor of 'embedded' narration. Onto the narrative series that constitutes a Conradian novel, this image superimposes an activity of receding 'inward' with each new embedding. Although Marlow's discourse is actually no further from the facts than Jim's or a third-person's hypothetical narration, this imaginary movement of ever-greater 'enclosure' enables the critic to posit an immediacy that has been left behind.

The metaphysical baggage within the critical tropes of fragmentation and embedding is largely ignored in its almost universal application to the modernist novel. It has facilitated a broad portrayal of staged narration, especially in Conrad, as the expression of a pathology, a sceptical retreat inward – ostensibly from the impasse of a late nineteenth century whose centres cannot hold. In his influential critical biography of the author, Frederick Karl understands Marlow to be the means by which Conrad 'descends narcissistically into his own world.'[21] Karl sees this use of a 'surrogate narrator' as a symptom of what Mallarmé called 'angelism,' a composite of 'hermeticism and narcissism, the first indicating the closed system of the artist and the latter the absorption of his self in his work, to the extent that he is himself always the subject of his work, disguised though he may be' (451).[22]

As I suggested above, literary criticism's selective application of the 'embedding' metaphor is evident in its treatment of a novel such as *Pamela*. Although the relation between Pamela's and Mrs Jewkes's speech is identical to that between Marlow's and Jim's narrative, critics have never felt compelled to apply tropes of embedding to the epistolary novel. We allow Richardson what we do not allow Conrad: the possibility of unproblematic citation, of 'clean' and absolute succession from the reporter's discourse to the testimony she reports. *Lord Jim's* narratives, by contrast, are conceived in three dimensions, according to a psychic depth model. Jim's speech, reported by Marlow, is said to be embedded within the mariner's testimony, and therefore within his 'consciousness.' As received by the reader, Jim's narrative has been 'filtered' through Marlow's consciousness as through a cheesecloth, and thus has been uniformly altered or transformed.

With its attendant figure of 'internalization,' of an inside and outside of a fictional consciousness, and with its assurance that a character's reiteration of another's narrative is always compromised, the trope of embedding necessarily initiates a psychological or characterological reading of the fiction. Yet the major attraction of these narratological models is their supposed independence of the vicissitudes of interpretation. As Genette writes, 'That which has to do with interpretation does not lie within the province of narratology.'[23] Although some of Genette's successors do not embrace this categorical statement, they tend to hold at least to some version of Jonathan Culler's conception of narratology as concerned with '"story" – a sequence of actions or events' as opposed to 'discourse' (or *fabula* over *sjuzhet*, in Russian Formalist terms; see Culler 189). However narratology isolates the objective features and effects of a given text, the coherence of the project is fatally undermined the moment it depends on a diagnosis of a character's psyche or a general theory of human psychology asserting that no person can reiterate the words of another without 'colouring' them.

Metaphors, as Paul de Man says, are much more tenacious than facts, and they retain the upper hand in narratological vocabulary even where the analyst, such as the astute Seymour Chatman, is determined to get out from under them:

> 'Focalization,' for all its scientific aura, is of course no less metaphoric than 'point of view.' It seems difficult or impossible to avoid optical metaphors when we try to name the narrator's use of a character's consciousness as the screen or filter through which the events of a story are perceived, conceived and so on. (Seymour, 'Characters' 191)

Figures of vision must be understood as such, but those of 'filtering' remain foundational, unseen. 'Focus of Character means restriction to the I-character as the central one, while Focus of Narration means a filtering of all story-experience through some character's consciousness, rather than an unmediated presentation by the narrator' (196).

There are doubtless any number of fictions within and without modernism whose imbrication of narrated narrators actually does encourage the epistemological worries that critics since James have seen in Conrad. However, once we acknowledge that presumptions about filtering will always have derived from conjectures about fictional characters and events, as opposed to objective features of narrative structure, the relevant question for *Lord Jim* or *Heart of Darkness* is whether or not the novel really does sculpt 'unreliable narrators,' and whether the work as a whole – or any larger discourse in which it might participate – really does assert, as Lord puts it, 'the relativism of modern epistemology.' Does the fiction really conceive subjectivity as an inescapable enclosure? Does it put the 'problem' of subjectivity at the top of its philosophical agenda? I have been arguing that, in Conrad's case, the answer is clearly no, and neither are such a concerns a logical consequence of his narrative arrangements. I hope to make it apparent below that narratology must nonetheless read Conrad's testimonial narration in these terms because it is crucial to the very foundation of its structuralism. This structuralism then becomes a useful tool for other critical projects that would seem to be indifferent to narratology but which are ideologically invested in portraying modernism as a retreat from the real and a champion of relativism.

My argument, however, does not suggest that critical tropes of 'embedded' narration cannot play an illuminating role in interpretation. In the case of a novel whose various narratives are arranged with the rigorous symmetry and regularity of nesting dolls, that arrangement becomes a gesture, a theme, and just as much an object of attention as anything in the fabula. For this reason critics have been eager, in Conrad's case, to reinforce the trope of subjective enclosure they have imported into his work by demonstrating therein an operation of narrative nesting. For his instructive narratological analysis of *Heart of Darkness*, for instance, Peter Brooks depends heavily on a diagram of symmetrical brackets, and yet he acknowledges that upon close examination 'we realize that the diagram is false: the inner frame of Kurtz's narrative has no such shapely coherence, and – perhaps as a consequence – neither Marlow's narrative nor the first narrator's appears to "close" in satisfactory fashion' (*Reading* 351 n 8). Lacking brackets, these narratives are said to be ruled nevertheless by a bracketing structure – more precisely, by the failure of Kurtz's narrative to achieve such structure. This absence, according to Brooks, is something that might even have 'consequential' power over the other narratives. Structure is no longer just a way to describe a particular text; it is an external regulator to which the text is subject. The pervasive depiction of Conrad's narrative design in primarily negative and reactive terms, as a rebellious destroyer of structural coherence, portrays this writing as something that does, in fact, orient itself according to the rules of structuralism, although its project just happens to be a perverse thwarting of those rules. Almost never is the possibility entertained that the reason Conrad's fiction is inimical to these structures and figures is that they are inventions of the critic imposed from without.

After a half century of criticism has thoroughly anatomized Conrad's failure to construct 'the neat pattern of nested boxes . . . we should have,' as Brooks puts it, we can now begin to investigate the injunction behind this 'should' (*Reading* 256). The nature of Conrad's obligation to narrative nesting is not clear. Brooks might simply be referring to a nineteenth-century tradition to which we might expect the author to be bound; but with a broader survey of the literary criticism that consistently reiterates Brooks's formulation, it becomes clear that 'should,' in this discourse, is indistinguishable from 'ought': that Conrad's failure to make certain orderly formal arrangements is a slap in the face to rationality and good philosophical hygiene, and has dire consequences for the work itself. In his programmatic *Narrative Discourse*, for instance, Genette proclaims that the 'entanglement' caused by *Lord Jim*'s narrated narrations threatens 'the bounds of general intelligibility' (232). In the later *Narrative Discourse Revisited*, however, Genette recognizes his 'blunder' in imputing such confusion to a story in which there is 'nothing, after all, but a first narrator, a second narrator (Marlow), and . . . some narratives in the third degree' (94–5). Yet he insists that the source of his confusion turns out to be the novel after all, and he reaffirms the affront to intelligibility that had formerly been said to stem solely from *Lord Jim*'s narrative entanglement: 'I must have displaced onto narrative structure an obscurity of another order' (*NDR* 95). For warping his clear narratological lens, Genette blames Conradian 'obscurity' – an epithet that has achieved in critical discourse the unquestionability of a structural principle precisely by such unexplained 'displacements.'

Since Genette, of course, narratology has significantly evolved, and subsequent theorists have attempted to expunge its more troubling metaphysical and epistemological assumptions. Mieke Bal's 1997 *Narratology*, for instance, raises questions about the vocal dislocation normally attributed to the 'external focalizer.' 'From a grammatical point of view,' she argues, all narration stems from 'a "first person." In fact, the term "third-person narrator" is absurd: a narrator is not a "he" or a "she"' (22). Hence, 'where the focalization level is concerned, there is no fundamental difference between a "first-person narrative" and a "third-person narrative"' (157). Yet it remains in Bal's narratology a structural certainty that a 'character-bound focalizer . . . brings about bias and limitation' (146).[24] As exemplary proof of this categorical statement, Bal points to the in-the-dark detective of a mystery story, albeit a 'literary' one: in Henry James's *What Maisie Knew*, the child hero is besieged by signals difficult for her, but easy for us, to decode. The epistemological contract here is distinct from the whodunit only in the reader's position in the circuit of veiling and unveiling. We the readers are in the know, backstage during the magician's performance, and we watch Maisie all alone in the auditorium struggling for comprehension. The essential, relevant truth of the fiction, identified by Bal as 'what is actually going on,' is then easily determined: it is comprised of whatever facts of the fabula that have become clear to us but which Maisie evidently does not know (147). Reminding us that 'the narrator and focalizer' are not to be conflated in this or any novel, Bal confirms a more general narratological principle: 'When an external focalizer [EF] seems to "yield" focalization to a character-bound focalizer [CF], what is really happening is that the CF is being given within the all-encompassing vision of the EF' (157–8). For each bit of knowledge that has been produced for the reader by a stretch of Maisie-bound focalization, Bal requires the positing of a further 'external focalizer' that had been extant, somewhere, during each such passage, existing independently of the 'focalized' text. Thus, even if each and every prepared and encoded signal of what Maisie does not know had been generated through a focalization 'bound' to the girl, the total knowledge thus produced for the reader is necessarily exceeded and 'encompassed' by the other, external focalization, since otherwise the two would be identical. Loosed from the finite sum of the encoded signals that mostly fly over Maisie's head, this 'all-encompassing' vision is bound to no particular finitude whatsoever. It has remained a defining feature of narratology's metaphysics – its narrato-theology – that any imaginable nook or cranny of the fictional world left unarticulated in the text will have already been determined in the heaven of an 'external focalization.' The external fo-calizer will always be identical to this 'outside' and the impossible to-tality of its general comprehension.[25]

Other contemporary narratologists see in modernist narrative the same failure to obey an epistemological contract of comprehension. With an eye on 'internal focalization' and a rigorous policing of 'modal locutions,' David Herman alerts us to the epistemological danger of Franz Kafka's *The Trial*. Joseph K. is said to lack a reliable 'grammatical (and conceptual)' measure by which he can evaluate his own shifting conceptions of the world; from among the 'possible worlds' K. imag-ines he inhabits, he needs to choose that which will serve as the best 'model world' (137). 'In relating only the sort and the amount of in-formation immediately available from within K.'s own perspective,' *The Trial* bars us from absolute knowledge, from the determined com-prehension that ought to be our goal (100). Herman's *Universal Gram-mar and Narrative Form* offers itself as a cure for the disease of Kafka's narrative form: 'What we require are grammatical (and conceptual) re-sources for ranking possible worlds as better and worse candidates for model worlds in a given case. Such resources might help us to avoid the radical disactualizations in which Kafka's narrative form continually involves us' (137).

In a similar narratological diagnosis of *Heart of Darkness*, Diana Knight applies the term 'paralepsis' – 'the inclusion of more informa-tion than is strictly accessible to the perceiver's visual or aural view-point' – to Marlow's statement that, upon meeting Kurtz's intended, he 'perceived she was one of those creatures that are not the playthings of Time' (23). Knight writes: 'This may be presented as an act of straight perception, yet the capitalization of "Time" indicates the infiltration of an abstract noun which . . . strictly belongs to a different level of per-ception' (24). Measured against a 'level of perception' that could finally discern the truth of Time and all other such capital concepts, Marlow, and thus any witness, will always be inadequate. Even when such wit-nesses seem to acknowledge this inadequacy with what narratology calls 'modal locutions' – 'I seemed to hear,' 'I perceived,' etc. – these, ac-cording to Knight and Genette, must be read as 'unavowed paralepses' (23). Sealed inside his subjectivity, Knight suggests, the witness would do well not to pretend to achieve the 'level of perception' apparently attainable by another, unnamed perceiver.[26]

The logic by which testimony is necessarily inadequate has penetrated even into projects that would locate Conrad's fiction within the discourse of Western philosophy. Although Mark Wollaeger's *Conrad and the Fictions of Skepticism* is one of the most insightful of such works, it relies on a great shibboleth in modernist studies – originating with Ford Madox Ford, and persisting into Jameson's depiction of Conrad's 'aestheticizing strategy' – when it attributes to Conrad's prose a fundamental 'impressionism.' Wollaeger posits the 'subjectification of Marlow's narrative' in *Heart of Darkness* at the outset of his study, attributing it to the novella's 'emphasis on sensation' (8–9). What is not made clear in such criticism is the measure by which the novel's depiction of sensation is said to be 'emphasized' over its much more prevalent discourse of ideas – the like of which is, in fact, the primary object of Wollaeger's analysis – or even over its narrative incident, or its explicit historical depiction of colonial operations in Africa. By what rule or what logic can we say that the impressionistic passages in the story come to govern the entirety of Marlow's discourse, establishing the essentiality and continuity of its 'subjectification'?[27]

For a rigorous engagement with such questions we can appeal again to Jameson, who gives a name to this continuity. *Lord Jim* creates a 'sensorium' that makes its depiction of 'working life at sea . . . available for consumption on some purely aesthetic level' (213–14). The sensorium is said to be effected primarily by the text's sensory signals toward point of view. As if alerted to the inadequacy of founding the sensorium entirely on a mode of presentation – a foundation solidly in place when the narrator reports Jim 'seeing' or 'hearing' an event, but which would disappear in the absence of such terms – Jameson posits additionally an active motion of narrative 'displacement.' The novel's 'intermittent vision of the sea's economic function,' which exhibits both the 'reality of production' and 'Conrad's unquestionable and acute sense of the nature and dynamics of imperialist penetration,' is an authentic 'content' occluded by the aestheticized content in the interstices of this intermittence (215). The trope of displacement seems to locate the otherwise elusive activity of aestheticization – the exhibition, then derealization of 'content' – in the temporal progression of narrative; that is, over the course of 'the nonstop textual production' of 'the first half of *Lord Jim*' (214, 219). Jameson thus protects the working reality of aestheticization by affixing it to the reality of textual production; he rescues its operation from the very 'abstract structure of temporality' he claims to be endemic to modernism itself (261). Hence the authentic content of Jim's relation to the production of imperial capitalism, the like of which appears in the early rendition of the firemen aboard the *Patna*, is said to be displaced by the subsequently rendered 'vision of the ship' (214).

Jameson carries us to the question: If authentic content in a narrative is placed, then displaced, can it be re-placed upon further textual production? In its wide-ranging appeal to other works 'in Conrad' wherein displacement takes place, *The Political Unconscious* answers affirmatively: displaced from one text in the Conradian arena, authentic content can be re-placed in a subsequent work. If we were to allow this re-placement across works, but disallow it 'within,' we would have a critical project governed by precisely the strategy of 'aesthetic containment' that Jameson would expose in Conrad. The questions that inevitably ensue, about the attribution of comprehensive governance to one but not another 'place' in this chain of textual displacement – i.e., to the aestheticization that appears in one passage, but not to the 'authentic content' that will inevitably arise in a subsequent one, whether within this or the 'next' Conradian text – are too many for us to host here. They must be submitted ultimately to the ongoing debates within Marxist thought about the univocality of ideology, about its place or *khora*. For Jameson's reading of *Lord Jim* and Conrad in general, these questions are posed rather insistently by the 1912 *Titanic* essays, which angrily name specific corporate and industrial interests that Conrad sees poised against sea labourers. Given the chain of content-displacement that had begun (again) in a novel of 1900, what could halt that chain – and suspend it finally in the purgatory of 'aestheticization' – before it reaches the depiction of labour and capital in these *English Review* essays?

Situating historically Conrad's use of personal statement, critics have not been eager to trace it through eighteenth-century epistolary fiction, whose strategies of testimonial narration were so crucial to the novel's development. Tony Jackson's astute *The Subject of Modernism* represents an exceptional case, but he makes the connection, ultimately, only to implicate the epistolary form with Conrad in a general ploy to manufacture authority through the posture of the witness. The authority established by the 'face-to-face' relationship of 'oral narrative' is said to be the hidden desire of any and all first-person novels.

[The early novel] stands apart from the time-proven classical literary genres, and so is missing the ready grounding of an already authorized and authorizing readership. Consequently, we find, especially in earlier novels, writers feeling the need to establish the truth and value of their work from within that work . . . One of the most common means of self-authorization is the attempt to imitate the immediate personal presence of the oral storyteller . . . The first novelists who consciously strive for some form of realistic representation seem acutely aware of what they might lose in not having the face-to-face, teller-listener relationship of oral narrative, and they take pains to establish their authority in storyteller fashion. Thus, we find the first-person narration of Defoe and the very personal voice of the epistolary novel. (35–6)

As it posits in the epistolary novel a gambit for 'face-to-face' authority, and as it denies third-person narration and its readers the effects and consequences of a 'teller-listener' relationship, Jackson's literary-historical map begins to lose conceptual coherence. Yet what remains intact is the more important and fundamental assumption, not at all peculiar to Jackson, that the predominating first-person mode of the new prose form had always constituted a circumvention, a turning away from a narrative ordinance to which the novel would have held itself if not for its historically contingent need for an aura of authority. The evaded ordinance, of course, could only be some form of detached third-person presentation. We thus find ourselves having posited a norm for the novel that has nothing to do with its actual, historical instantiation.

Despite its presumption that first-person presentation throughout the novel's history has always been a deviation from another, more primary practice, literary criticism has not detected in early epistolary and travel fiction the thicket of philosophical problems it sees in the testimonial narration of modernism. It is only when we turn our eyes to the twentieth century that we discover the dangerousness of the first-person novel, its purported capacity, as Samuel Hynes writes, to raise 'uncertainty about the nature of truth and reality to the level of a structural principle' (55). This historically selective emphasis on epistemological problems that would have to inhere in any and all testimonial structures is the trace of a philosophical and cultural program, one that seeks to define the modernist novel in terms of an unprecedented psychic withdrawal and retreat from the real. For some critical discourses, however, the perfection of this move inward is also the means by which an aging modernism finally fulfils a contract of comprehension. Although it has failed to construct a circuit by which 'the nature of truth and reality' would be unveiled, modernism finally answers the question to which Hemingway had been contracted – about the 'thoughts and feelings' of a fictional persona – with its perfected forms of interior monologue. In the 'immediate speech' of a Molly Bloom, for instance, narratology sees, in Genette's words, an unprecedented 'emancipation,' a means of 'obliterating the last traces of the narrating instance' that would normally come between a character's consciousness and ourselves (*ND* 173–4).

Even as it places a premium on character-bound narration, however, the narratology that declares this victory for modernism remains fully dependent on the abjection of personal testimony. Modernist innovations in 'psychonarration' are said to show that a character's consciousness can be borne faithfully in iteration – more faithfully, at least, than ever before. Yet the structural law that denies the power of comprehension to any framed or testimonial narration requires it to be impossible that the character herself could ever accomplish that iteration. It becomes a categorical truth that although a character might testify about her own psyche, '[o]nly a narrator can provide language' to convey 'the deepest of all [her] internal experiences' (Chatman, 'Ironic' 125).[28] The self-expression of a Pamela, these critics suggest, could never under any circumstance achieve the immediacy in relation to her own consciousness that 'Penelope' achieves in relation to Molly Bloom's. If Molly's discourse had been introduced in *Ulysses* as a radically freeform entry in her diary, we would no longer be allowed to call it an unadulterated glimpse into her mind, even if its text were identical to the final chapter of the novel as it exists now. It would take only the minute addition of a single set of quotation marks at the beginning and end of the chapter to mark the discourse as testimony, and thus transform it from something immediate and emancipated into a fallen 'narrating instance.'

As the herald of a narrating instance, quotation marks are functionally indistinguishable from a novel's title page, or from its position as a bound volume in the fiction section of a book store – from all the features that variously objectify the literary text, and without which a narratological mapping of *Ulysses*, or any novel, could not begin. What are the criteria by which narratology selects some but not other of these features to be operative signals of a narrating instance? For narratology, legitimate signals must have been authorized as such, demonstrably asserted by the text either in explicit statement or through conventional signs like quotation marks. We might want to ask what it means to say that the objective, structural features of the novel are constituted not by any and all operative framing effects, but by a selection thereof established by decree, by a mere assertion of the novel? Yet even this question will always have been precluded by another: Did not the same kind of authorizing intentionality also inscribe the novel's title, and often a signature beneath, thereby intending and announcing that what follows is an instance of narration?

Jacques Derrida has already demonstrated why the frame that would be established by a fiction's title must, for any structuralism, remain invisible as such, or just outside critical consciousness.[29] For narratology, as for Henry James, the power to frame can belong only to a designated 'outer' narration that must never itself be subject to even the possibility of framing. The frame of the outermost narration takes on a unique spectrality, for if it were fully visible as such, it would be an object, and we would have to acknowledge the new framing standpoint, even further 'out,' that we now occupy. The hermeneutic would dissolve, and it would be impossible for there ever to have existed an autonomous structure that could disable the framing effect of a title, banishing it to an 'outside' of the novel, and neither could there have been a 'law of fiction' to determine the illegitimacy of this frame.

Just as James had been compelled to draft such legislation as modernism began its emphasis on testimony, Genette's seminal work updates the ordinance to better police its post-Edwardian development. In *Narrative Discourse*, he writes:

> [N]othing claims that Meursault or The Unnamable wrote the texts we read as their interior monologues, and it goes without saying that the text of the *Lauriers sont coupés* cannot be anything but a 'stream of consciousness' – not written, or even spoken – mysteriously caught and transcribed by Dujardin. It is the nature of immediate speech to preclude any formal determination of the narrating instance which it constitutes. (230)

Here is a logocentrism that does not privilege speech, for even if the monologue had been 'spoken,' it would not have escaped its iterability, its participation in 'writing in general.' This speech would have been implicated with writing in its distance from present consciousness, from an 'immediate speech' prior to speech. Speech and writing, once determined as such, could only be a report, mere testimony about presence. In order to transcend *the testimony that is writing in general*, the writing that is said to articulate consciousness cannot be writing.

'Nothing claims' that 'the texts we read' as stream of consciousness exist as writing within their respective fabulas, but does this mean that these novels therefore 'claim' that their prose renditions are not an attempt to represent consciousness with the peculiar medium of writing? That a certain high modernism pretends to have revealed consciousness itself, beyond or behind writing in general, is a thesis belonging to Genette and many others. That the work in question makes such an assertion, however, is not at all clear. Just as there is no evidence in Conrad that his testimonial narration keeps us removed from diegetic facts, nothing suggests that the text of 'Penelope' is supposed to be a radical 'not-writing' indistinguishable from Molly's consciousness. Such assumptions would be required only by a prior commitment to a determined comprehension imagined to enclose any and all novels. Whereas Conrad was said to have suspended that comprehension in an unreachable outside, Joyce is said to have exposed it in a writing that is not writing – the negation being required to prohibit any movement of zooming out from the discourse in question.

Taking it as given that writing in general is an obstacle to comprehension, Jameson explicitly subsumes 'the alienation of the printed book' into the historical emergence of Conrad's narrated narrators. In its strongest Lukácsian register, *The Political Unconscious* hearkens back to 'that older concrete social situation' of bards and storytellers, wherein the spoken signifier was never subject to the possibility of diversion, misreading, or ungoverned reiteration. In the 'communicational situation' of precapitalist narrative practice, the signifier is said to have always arrived at its proper destination. In his account of Marlow as a literary phenomenon, Jameson thus appeals to Plato's *Phaedrus*.

> It is clear that to return from the primacy of the Jamesian narrative category of point of view to the older fiction of the storyteller and the storytelling situation is to express impatience with the objective yet ever intensifying alienation of the printed book, those bound and portable novels which 'when they have been once written down . . . are tumbled about anywhere among those who may or may not understand them, and know not to whom they should reply, to whom not: and, if they are maltreated or abused, they have no parent to protect them; and they cannot protect or defend themselves.' (219–20)

The role assigned here to Conrad in a literary-historical dialectic is all the more startling considering the near impossibility of finding any body of work that demonstrates with as much force and repetition that no 'storyteller situation' could ever secure the testifier's ability to protect, defend, or otherwise govern the career of his testimony. Jim is given the floor at his public inquiry, but no matter: in that forum, 'speech was of no use to him any longer' (33). And even the monologist aboard the *Nellie* in *Heart of Darkness* must ask his 'concrete' listeners, half-asleep and hidden by shadows, 'Do you see the story? Do you see anything? It seems to me I am trying to tell you a dream . . .' (172).

Having confidently left behind almost all debate about the effect of such critical logocentrism on our conception of the modernist novel, we might reasonably expect our fresh post-postmodern eyes to have perceived anew, and finally in positive terms, the significance of Marlow's emergence in the English novel. Conrad, after all, remains crucial to what Douglas Mao and Rebecca L. Walkowitz call the 'transnational turn' of the 'new modernist studies,' which expands a process that began in the 1990s of absorbing the study of modernism almost entirely into postcolonial criticism (737–8). As anybody on the academic job market in recent years can attest, a postcolonial specialist is assumed to be a competent scholar of modernism, but not so the reverse. This is partly a consequence of the wider purview of postcolonial studies and its greater attention to historical contexts that had long been neglected. Hence, 'one could do worse than light on *expansion*' to sum up in a single word the 'transformations in modernist literary scholarship over the past decade or two' (Mao and Walkowitz 737). Prepared, however, by the contemporaneous institutionalization of European modernism with global literatures in English, the rapprochement of the two fields is not merely a response to an arbitrary call for greater inclusiveness. As they expand outward, some new modernist studies suggest there is good reason to keep a peculiarly European modernism within reach as a touchstone. Simon Gikandi even goes so far as to argue that 'it was primarily – I am tempted to say solely – in the language and structure of modernism that a postcolonial experience came to be articulated and imagined in literary form' (420).

Like the present work, postcolonial criticism initially emerged as a multiform blend of poststructuralist and historicist approaches. As pertains to modernism, however, there has been in recent years a general tendency away from poststructuralism in literary studies, whether as the result of critical opposition, or, more frequently, from a stance of having beneficially digested it before moving on. This transition may be a continuation of what Paul de Man saw in 1979 as a repeated cycle in which a critical period that is perceived to address only formal or structural concerns is followed in the next generation by a demand for 'external' or historical reference. It is telling that new modernist studies can reach comfortably and uncritically back to Lukács in an effort to find counter-modernisms within modernism: texts that thwart its '"opaque, fragmentary, chaotic and uncomprehended" aestheticization of everyday experience,' as Urmila Seshagiri writes.[30] Holding up Jean Rhys's *Voyage in the Dark*, a title that recalls *Heart of Darkness* in order to oppose and remedy its ahistoricity (its purported disengagement with its 'immediate historical context'), Seshagiri reinstates the Lukácsian narrative wherein Conrad represents a regression from the historical grounding of nineteenth-century realism. As ever, it is a narrative that requires us to understand Conrad's rendition of colonial operations in central Africa as having, by necessity, less historical purchase than *Daisy Miller, Can You Forgive Her?* or *Jude the Obscure*. In tandem reaction to a mode of rhetorical analysis that merely brackets historical questions, as poststructuralism is rightly or wrongly conceived, the manifold illuminations of contemporary postcolonial, historicist, and 'new modernist' approaches to Conrad have inevitably orbited, even if at widely different distances, around the one issue that does not seem to shirk political and historical responsibility; namely, the question of how Conrad's fiction reinscribes an imperialist apologia, even and especially where it seems to attack it.

Those who share a desire for a clearer global perspective on Conrad and a more rigorous historicism overall still have reason to be troubled that our critical view generally has not moved beyond poststructuralism as much as it has merely sidestepped it. Postcolonial and cultural criticism has not interrogated the narratology with which it frequently discerns the 'deep structure' of modernism's relation to colonialism, race, and empire. Michael North's *The Dialect of Modernism*, to look at one example, is one of the most penetrating recent revaluations of race and its representation in key modernist works. For North, Conrad's famous introduction to *The Nigger of the 'Narcissus,'* in conjunction with the novel itself, is a genuine 'preface to modernism' because '[r]acial and cultural difference is both constitutive and radically disruptive of the work announced in Conrad's preface' (40). It is a thesis that *Dialect* as a whole admirably bears out. Yet North's crucial project of inscribing race into our understanding of modernism in general, however, is undermined where he traces the dynamics of racial and cultural difference to the chimerical problems of epistemology Conrad is said to have inaugurated. Anxieties of racial and cultural 'solidarity' are of course very real in Conrad and throughout modernism, as North demonstrates, but the theoretical foundation of *The Dialect of Modernism* locates these anxieties in the problem of communication supposedly introduced by the 'innovations and intricacies' of Conrad's 'modernist clangour' (40).

> *Lord Jim*, to take just one example, degenerates from an omniscient and all-seeing account into Marlow's version, told 'audibly,' and then into the packet of written documents left for the 'privileged man' in chapter 36, declining from the seen to the heard to the written as the story compounds its mysteries. The aesthetic attempt to conjure out of some sensually unrewarding marks on paper a full sensory experience is constantly qualified in this way by Conrad's sense of its structural impossibility. (38)

The idea that Conrad's testimonial scenarios put us at a remove from a reality and a truth that would have revealed themselves in 'an omniscient and all-seeing account' appears to be as indispensable as ever. The ritual evocation of inevitably unspecified 'mysteries' in *Lord Jim* suggests that post-poststructural literary criticism has only streamlined the procedure by which the whodunit's contract of comprehension dovetails with a metaphysics of presence ('full sensory experience') to produce the 'structural' truth, reportedly 'confessed' by Conrad himself, of the degenerate nature of testimony.

If we leave behind such externally imposed tropes of epistemological 'degeneration,' so curiously reserved only for instances of embedding and letter-writing in modernist literature, what emerges in a novel like *Lord Jim* is not a helpless mourning of lost comprehension, but an assertion of testimony in a culture of anonymous authority. Anticipating Franz Kafka's modernity, Conrad's is one in which testimony will always be on trial, in which the traveller's tale will always be more or less defensive, subject to a dislocated but ever-effective 'proceeding.' The 'public inquiry' depicted in the novel, as in the later essays, takes place in a virtual auditorium made possible by a journalism whose site is nowhere and everywhere. As we will see, Conrad is a sensitive and articulate subject of a disciplinary society, and at the same time a nomad seeming to mourn the lost home of a ship with its accountable – and autocratic – captain. As such, he conjures a demon of modernity whose depiction will reach its greatest intensity in Kafka: a world of potent authority without centre, unlocalized; the jurisdiction of a bodiless and anonymous Judge to which the personal name and its 'case' is held accountable.

The tribunal scene of *Lord Jim* is remarkable in the history of staged narration in that it clearly ties the traditional promise of such a scene – the promise of comprehensive disclosure – to that of the anonymous third-person narrator who opens the novel, sets up the scene of deposition, but virtually disappears thereafter. In a letter to Conrad defending the *Titanic* inquiry, after the author had lambasted the whole 'journalistic enterprise' in the *English Review* – a letter to which Conrad's second essay is in fact a response – John Quinn asks Conrad to have faith in the inquiry as that which reveals everything. '[T]he inquiry was a Godsend,' Quinn writes, 'in that it lifted the cloud of mystery that shrouded the whole thing . . .' It made people 'more or less satisfied that they had got to the bottom of things.'[31] One could have anticipated Conrad's disagreement given *Lord Jim*'s treatment of the omniscient posture to which it binds the *Patna* inquiry. If we listen carefully in the novel to the transition from omniscience to testimony as the novel actually presents it, we would have to evaluate 'Marlow's version,' as North calls it, in a way that is quite at odds with the picture of 'degeneration' he draws above. The posture of epistemological comprehension struck by the 'omniscient and all-seeing' narration of the opening chapters does not fare well in relation to Marlow's voice. What Conrad stages is, in fact, a narratological coup over an anonymous authority he has set up precisely for this purpose.

*Lord Jim* implicates this anonymous omniscience with the institutional powers depicted in the fiction, specifically, with the forces mobilizing the public inquiry that triggers the narrative transition. The shift takes place between two chapters but right in the middle of Jim's deposition, as he answers questions about his abandonment of the crippled, pilgrim-laden steamship, the *Patna*. Following the climax of the episode at the close of the fourth chapter, both the theatre of deposition and the anonymous narrator heretofore governing the novel are simultaneously ousted by Marlow's voice. Aside from a few momentary resurfacings, the omniscient narrator will never regain the reins of the novel, not even to provide the symmetry of a narrative 'end bracket.'[32] Far from a degeneration, it is a succession that takes its mandate from the fiction itself. Marlow takes over at precisely the moment when Jim's testimony is revealed to be irrelevant within the frame of a spectral, corporate authority. The statement Jim hopes to make, with its 'shades of expression' and 'complicated aspect,' has been precluded by a well-circulated story already established before he took the stand, a 'tale that was public property,' but which the novel does not depict (31, 41). The authorless tale of the *Patna*'s latest voyage and its scandal, pointedly unpronounced in these opening chapters, and which a normal omniscient narrator would have articulated by now, has indeed been spelled out already to the tribunal and its audience by the likes of the *Home News* edition a stranger later hands Marlow in a café. What *is* depicted instead is the posture of diegetic removal these authorities assume. The true object of Conrad's inquiry in chapter four is not Jim, but the imaginary comprehension that renders the statement of the witness inadequate, because perspectival, and possibly corrupt, because biased.[33] As a stranger murmurs in Marlow's ear during the inquiry, speaking of the defendants: 'Of course they would lie' (135).

The novel has a long history of using the trial scene to duplicate within itself the diegetic divide between its characters and the anonymous judging reader.[34] In *Lord Jim*, however, the reader is not allowed to judge at the scene of trial. We do not know the facts of the case until the effectively diegetic divide between Jim and the anonymous inquiry has been erased by the subsequent chapters; these rewrite the scene of deposition in a blend of confession and interrogation distributed between Jim and Marlow. The disclosure we expect at the inquiry – a scene of the protagonist rendering himself intelligible to an official *prozess* – comes later, but it does so through an interlocution between subjects commonly disciplined and responsible to one another.

# 2 Theatre of Incursion and Unveiling I: Home

Conrad's insistence that Jim can be judged or evaluated only through a discourse that goes beyond mere fact-finding and by-the-book moralizing is a premise that had long been established in the novel's sentimental tradition. When the human subject becomes an object of study, for Conrad, she can be evaluated only through a sympathetic imagination that the likes of Marlow, and by extension the novel in general, have taught Western culture. 'In this age of knowledge,' according to Conrad, 'our sympathetic imagination, to which alone we can look for the ultimate triumph of concord and justice, remains strangely impervious to information, however correctly and even picturesquely conveyed' (*Notes* 84). The prime information-conveyor in this age is the 'printed page of the Press,' which 'makes a sort of still uproar, taking from men both the power to reflect and the faculty of genuine feeling' (*Notes* 90). Even at the birth of the sympathetic novel, its authors were theorizing it in its paratext. The long discussion they initiated is what ultimately prepared for James's suggestion, explicitly seconded by Conrad, that 'fiction is nearer truth' than history.[1] Yet at the same time both authors understand the sentimental tradition to be at the root of an utterly pernicious ideology, one that has paradoxically culminated in the cultural trope of 'the light of the press.' Although they ultimately do so for quite different purposes, Conrad and James together implicate the novel of sympathy, as well as the press, in a disciplinary ethos that demands articulation and accounting of all would-be 'private' spaces; an ethos, more profoundly, that will reject any claim to the right of non-articulation and non-registry. These modernists strain against the 'sentimental journey' of the confidante-raconteur who is Marlow's literary ancestor. James's narrative epistemology, however, prohibits him from following this critique to its necessary conclusion. It can deploy testimonial narration only as the sign of nefarious or unconscious concealment, and thus requires a single and exceptional sentimental authority – the 'particular detachment' of the Jamesian observer himself – to approve interiorities and expose secrets (*Henry James* 500). Conrad's narrative practice, by contrast, exists not merely in opposition to the overreaching and impertinence of 'men of feeling' and their disciplinary ethos of confession. Marlow is rather a disavowal of the very possibility of the sentimentalist's fictional achievement: a verified consistency between public and private life, outer conduct and inward conscience. For Conrad, the testifier's opacity is ultimately impossible to violate. No authority can presume to have penetrated or circumnavigated the diplomatic 'front' of testimony as a representational envoy.[2]

In the course of elucidating 'the general law of fiction' that Conrad disobeys, James had argued that the 'primary author' of a novel 'works upon us most in fact by making us forget him' ('Younger' 157). The obscuring shadow of 'the subjective' that Marlow purportedly casts over the novel would not exist without 'our' consciousness of him. Although with its 'interpreting mind' the Jamesian narrator keeps itself lawfully from view (*Henry James* 500), it is identical to Marlow in his status as a 'beautiful and generous' interpreter of events ('Younger' 157). If 'we,' the readers James imagines, were ever to become conscious of this reclusive narrator and his interpreting mind, the novel he inhabits would suddenly be overcast by the subjective. About a certain critical theory that took its cue from James, it is telling that our consciousness of the Jamesian narrator is, perforce, illegal. The prohibition is significant, too, in light of the social function and history of the novel in general. Facing Marlow, the locatable and responsible 'reciter,' in James's terms, most of his fictional listeners are silent, but some respond; Jim is not the only one to ask Marlow the first question *Hamlet* asks its audience, and which we shall see is the fundamental question about the novel's peculiarly intense participation in the historical regulation of sentiment and subjectivity: Who's there? Who demands an articulation of the 'inner life'? To whom is that interiority responsible? To what law or what authority – the like of which have claims upon body and behaviour – is this interior accountable? The confrontation between these authors over the final dispensation of a narrative comprehension, seemingly a purely literary problem, is in fact inextricable from a controversy about representing the social landscape. It is a debate over which authorities, if any, ought to remain outside the investigative frame.

As with Conrad, the social reality that makes such questions pressing for James is the 'new journalism' emerging late in the nineteenth century. In 1888, the year before Conrad would begin his writing career, James's preoccupation with the newspaper was at its apex. Having its early instantiations in *The Portrait of a Lady*'s Henrietta Stackpole and *The Bostonians*'s Matthias Pardon, the figure of the intrusive journalist seems at this time to have completely dominated James's thinking. *The Reverberator* and *The Aspern Papers*, both serialized that year, fulfil an injunction James had left for himself in his notebook:

> One sketches one's age but imperfectly if one doesn't touch on that particular matter: the invasion, the impudence and shamelessness, of the newspaper and the interviewer, the devouring *publicity* of life, the extinction of all sense between public and private. It is the highest expression of the note of 'familiarity' . . . which the democratization of the world brings with it. (*Complete Notebooks* 40)

Hence George Flack of *The Reverberator*, a man 'professionally . . . occupied with other people's affairs' (28). He is an unusually allegorical figure for James, which is simply to say that he really is nothing more or less than the personified essence of the press. To the woman he loves, early in the novella, Flack lays bare his soul, from which it is apparently impossible to extract his profession:

> It's a field for enlightened enterprise that hasn't yet begun to be worked . . . I'm going for the inside view . . . what the people want is just what ain't told, and I'm going to tell it . . . That's about played out, anyway, the idea of sticking up a sign of 'private' and 'hands off' and 'no thoroughfare' and thinking you can keep the place to yourself. You ain't going to be able any longer to monopolise any fact of general interest, and it ain't going to be right you should; it ain't going to continue to be possible to keep out anywhere the light of the Press. Now what I'm going to do is set up the biggest lamp yet made and make it shine all over the place. We'll see who's private then, and whose hands are off . . . That's a sign of the American people that they *do* want to know, and it's the sign of George P. Flack . . . that he's going to help them. But I'll make the touchy folks crowd in *themselves* with their information . . . (62–3)[3]

James is not simply suggesting that the pressman misuses or perverts the metaphor of enlightenment. Appearing everywhere he satirizes the press, this is the same knowledge-producing light revered by any healthy empiricism, and also by a disciplinary ethos that knows only a criminal avoids the light. Flack's direct analogue in *The Aspern Papers* similarly has no qualms about 'opening lights into [Aspern's] life. He had nothing to fear from [me] because he had nothing to fear from the truth' (6). Over and over again, James's writer-investigators use this 'light' to occlude the productive nature of their narrative creations, casting them instead entirely in terms of discovery and disclosure: a virtuous exhumation of salient 'facts.'

It would be overreaching to suggest that the persistent attempt in all of these novels to yank the trope of enlightenment off its rhetorical throne constitutes a critique of a historical Enlightenment.[4] Yet in their persistent attention to an 'enlightened enterprise' that creates the modern incitement to discourse – 'I'll make the touchy folks crowd in *themselves* with their information' (63) – both James and Conrad make it impossible to ignore an array of pedagogical, disciplinary, and institutional structures that are the concrete issue of seventeenth- and eighteenth-century discourses of Enlightenment. Targeting such apparatus in *The Reverberator*, for instance, is Gaston Probert's cryptic and suggestively reticent critique of the United States upon returning to Paris from his first visit there. '[W]hat didn't you like?' asks the quintessentially American patriarch Mr Dosson. Gaston replies,

'Well, the light for instance.'
'The light – the electric?'
'No, the solar! I thought it rather hard, too much like the scratching of a slate-pencil.' (194)

*The Reverberator* is the story of the Dossons, young Francie, Delia, and their father, rich Americans who have come to settle in Paris. The 'exceedingly, extraordinarily pretty' Francie becomes engaged to Gaston Probert, a member of a wealthy and reclusive family representing the 'oldest' American roots in the city (15). George Flack, whom the Dossons had befriended on their passage, is intrigued by the engagement, and only partly because Francie has rejected his love. The Proberts' low profile and social opacity strikes Flack as an ideal mystery to expose with the light of his journal, the *Reverberator*. Under the cover of airy chat, he manages to extract from the ingenuous Francie some facts about the Proberts – light gossip, but under the right editorial construction they are the traces of serious immorality, even criminality.

James's companion piece to this short novel is *The Aspern Papers*, whose inquisitive anonymous narrator, despite the difference of his high cultural credentials, is another version of George Flack. Together these fictions demonstrate that, for James, the increasing compulsion to detail and document the lives of one's neighbours permeates all strata of cultural discourse, not just yellow journalism. In *The Aspern Papers*, the vagabond investigator is now a man of letters determined to lay hands on the remaining private correspondence of his hero, the late, great poet Jeffrey Aspern. The letters are currently under the watchful guard of the elderly Juliana Bordereau, Aspern's former lover. In an opening passage that calls out the name of the other novel, which will be written later the same year, we catch a glimpse of the gentle intellectual as even more of an outright stalker than the crude George Flack. Of Bordereau's villa he writes, 'I had already been to look at it half a dozen times . . . I had besieged it with my eyes while I considered my plan of campaign. Jeffrey Aspern had never been in it that I knew of; but some note of his voice seemed to abide there by a roundabout implication, a faint reverberation.'[5] James thus implicates in his critique the biographic impulse in general, even that directed toward the most 'public' personalities. The poet, after a lifetime of calling out for public attention to his verse – to what might seem to be the most intimate mode of personal confession – would seem to be especially vulnerable to such investigation. Together these works call attention to a general ethos of documentary accountancy in this, 'the latter half of the nineteenth century – the age of newspapers' (*Aspern* 8), and they attest as well to an anxiety about its effect in a crumbling of literary hierarchies. When Francie mentions she is more likely to read a book than a newspaper, Flack responds, 'Well, it's all literature . . . it's all the press, the great institution of our time. Some of the finest books have come out first in the papers. It's the history of the age' (124).

The first argumentative step of these two cautionary tales' joint thesis is that there is a symbiotic relationship between the rhetoric of enlightenment and the incitement to inscribe, not just ourselves, but our fellows into the proliferating organs of public registry. The intensely productive generation of personal narrative, in many ways ex nihilo, is transformed by this rhetoric into an activity of pure disclosure and discovery. James's readers never lay eyes on the newspaper exposé that constitutes *The Reverberator*'s central catastrophe, but the scene in which Flack extracts his primary material from the unwitting Francie Dosson intimates much about its construction. During Flack's repeated queries, for instance, about possible religious conflict in her marriage to Gaston Probert, Francie comes to remark, 'And you know poppa ain't much on religion.' Flack responds gratefully, 'Well now that's what I call a genuine fact' (129), thus announcing his attainment of what he had called in his personal mission statement a 'fact of general interest,' the like of which the Dossons would have no right to 'monopolise.' We know Francie's statement had been a shorthand that could be used to allude to any number of people's complicated relationship to organized religion – such as Henry James's, for instance. To Flack, however, the relevant 'fact' is only the statement itself; it is salient precisely because, once it appears naked in a public forum, its seemingly arrogant dismissiveness will be shocking to Flack's readership. 'Everything *is* different when it's printed,' Flack will later acknowledge to Francie in open-eyed good conscience; 'What else would be the good of the papers?' (185). The ironic insight of the previous exchange rests in our knowledge that Francie's father, who 'ain't much on religion,' is himself the prototypical newspaper consumer, the kind of reader Flack can count on to be disgusted by the image of a newly Europeanized American with scant religious feeling. Francie will later report to her father the unexpected outcome of her conversation with Flack, which ends up focusing almost exclusively on the Proberts: 'It's all printed there – that they're immoral, and everything about them; everything that's private and dreadful.' Mr Dosson latches onto the central 'fact': 'Immoral, is that so? . . . Well, if folks are immoral you can't keep it out of the papers – and I don't know as you ought to want to' (157–9).

As he approaches the golden ring of his completed *Reverberator* article, Flack reiterates to Francie 'the sketch I gave you of my ideals.' At the threshold of his goal, however, the formerly all-important 'light' metaphor has disappeared, and seems now incommensurate with his speech: 'I want everything, as I told you . . . But I want it in the right way and of the right brand. If I can't get it in the shape I like it I don't want it at all; first-rate first-hand information, straight from the tap, is what I'm after' (123). With a metaphor of 'straight' and immediate transmission bizarrely unconscious of the 'shaping' injunction immediately preceding, it is an ultimatum that James had originally put into the mouth of George Flack's precursor, the journalist Henrietta Stackpole of *The Portrait of a Lady*. Long after her initial epistolary announcement that she's coming to England because 'the *Interviewer* wants some light on the nobility,' Henrietta expresses satisfaction with her chaperone and 'informant,' Mr Bantling:

> 'He has told me just the things I want to know . . . I can't make out that what he tells me about the royal family is much to their credit; but he says that's only my peculiar way of looking at it. Well, all I want is that he should give me the facts; I can put them together quick enough, once I've got them.' (364)

We have already seen that the interpretive and evaluative operation of any historiography can be screened from view simply by making reference to its traffic in value-free facts. As evinced by the contrast between the satirically alarming pronouncements of George Flack and the urbane, subtle, reasonable apologias of *The Aspern Papers*'s narrator, James sees the most insidious legitimization of this rhetorical abuse in the claims of biography. Rendering this narrator as a villain is difficult; his stated motive, after all, is only to augment the glory of his literary 'god' (5). He seeks the Aspern letters, which will open 'lights into his life,' only to sculpt a more accurate and revealing portrait of the man. It will be a portrait created without paint, ink, or any medium whatever, a matter of pure disclosure and revelation. Although George Flack's mission statement is bald and outrageous in comparison, it is significant that this narrator's analogous self-explanation, which sounds much more familiar and reasonable, nonetheless sharply recalls the elements of Flack's language that are used in every defence of a generalized and systematic surveillance of the individual:

> We held, justly, as I think, that we had done more for [Aspern's] memory than anyone else, and we had done it by opening lights into his life. He had nothing to fear from us because he had nothing to fear from the truth . . . His early death had been the only dark spot in his life, unless the papers in Miss Bordereau's hands should perversely bring out others. There had been an impression about 1825 that he had 'treated her badly,' just as there had been the impression that he had 'served' . . . several other ladies in the same way. Each of these cases Cumnor and I had been able to investigate, and we had never failed to acquit him . . . (155–6)

With perfect sincerity, the biographer will later describe his work – the articulation either of an 'acquittal' or of the 'dark spots' of his subject – as an expression of 'beauty,' the like of which shines from Aspern's immortal verse. The invisible and unconscious transformation of this ultimately public inquiry into a 'revealing' artistic expression is impossible without the continuity he achieves through the trope of enlightenment.

> I felt even a mystic companionship, a moral fraternity with all those who in the past had been in the service of art. They had worked for beauty, for a devotion; and what else was I doing? That element was in everything Jeffrey Aspern had written, and I was only bringing it to the light. (181)

In a climactic repetition of the narrator's self-defence, this time directly to the Aspern letters' guardian, James draws our attention to the familiar philosophical rhetoric of truth by which 'revelation' masks a production of knowledge. Facing the man who has finally identified himself to Juliana as 'a critic, an historian,' she suggests that the 'discoveries' of such investigators are 'mostly lies.' The critic disagrees:

> 'The lies are what they sometimes discover . . . They often lay bare the truth.'
> 'The truth is God's, it isn't man's . . . Who can judge of it – who can say?'
> 'We are terribly in the dark, I know,' I admitted; 'but if we give up trying what becomes of all the fine things? What becomes of the work I just mentioned, that of the great philosophers and poets? It is all vain words if there is nothing to measure it by.'
> 'You talk as if you were a tailor.' (89–90)

Juliana perceives the sticking-point – the idea that the mere act of confirming false statements of fact could establish the 'measure' of philosophical or poetic truth in general. The narrator unconsciously confirms for the second time that his enlightenment could only consist of a discourse that either affirms or denies the testimony of his subjects. Earlier he had described one of the truths he expects to establish, a mystery he hopes to resolve upon obtaining the letters:

> It was incontestable that, whether for right or for wrong, most readers of certain of Aspern's poems . . . had taken for granted that Juliana had not always adhered to the steep footway of renunciation. There hovered about her name a perfume of reckless passion, an intimation that she had not been exactly as the respectable young person in general . . . Certain it

> is that it would have been difficult to put one's finger on the passage in
> which her fair fame suffered an imputation. (48)

It is clear that the truths this narrator will extract from the hidden Aspern papers will generally be indistinguishable from the kind of truths said to be whispered by the available text of Aspern's poetry. When the narrator and his ally had 'acquitted' Aspern upon their former investigation of the way he had treated his many female admirers, they had done so by acquiring another batch of correspondence; yet even upon that successful exposure and 'bringing to light' of once-hidden papers, the absoluteness of the acquittal had flown yet again out of reach: 'I judged him perhaps more indulgently than my friend; certainly, at any rate, it appeared to me that no man could have walked straighter in the given circumstances' (7).

With the biographer's awareness that the most important discoveries he seeks are matters of interpretation and 'intimation,' how could these letters ever finalize the questions? How could they disclose, any more than the others, a previously hidden measure of truth? Against these questions the investigator's hope resides in the deceptively simple metaphysics of veiling and unveiling. As with so many other fictions, the condition of the inaccessible letter is the very engine of *The Aspern Papers*; but as we have seen, it is also the figure that has come so prominently to govern twentieth-century literary criticism in general. In his *Allegories of Reading*, Paul de Man describes a predominant 'metaphorical model of literature' in the past century 'as a kind of box that separates an inside from an outside, and the reader or critic as the person who opens the lid in order to release into the open what was secreted but inaccessible inside. It matters little whether we call the inside of the box the content or the form, the outside the meaning or the appearance' (5). The truth that the letter will reveal is inside the closed book, or locked within a lover's bureau, but when the signifier is finally exposed, the final answers fly away again, to yet another outside. So even as James's 'general law of fiction' helps to prepare a narratological structuralism, his novels persistently critique the 'inside/outside' operation de Man famously scrutinizes in various such formalisms. As we will see, however, James's scrutiny of this operation is strategically sporadic; it mirrors in function the semi-consciousness we have seen him exhibit about the objectifiability of all narrators, including the 'outermost,' and about the never-ending framability of all frames.

The letter whose inaccessibility keeps intact the promise of truth is reinforced in James's fiction by grafting itself onto a topology – a scenario of potential or frustrated physical penetration. In 'the closed windows of my hostess,' for instance, at which the *Aspern Papers* narrator gazes 'for hours . . . looking up over the top of my book' from the garden below,

> no sign of life ever appeared; it was as if, for fear of my catching a glimpse of them, the two ladies passed their days in the dark. But this only emphasized their having matters to conceal; which was what I had wished to prove. Their motionless shutters became as expressive as eyes consciously closed. (44)

The narrator attempts to underwrite his phantasm – his 'perception' of content, of explosive secrets, in a mere absence – by making reference to an empirically verifiable arrangement of walls and shutters. In the profit it reaps by foregrounding such a borderland, the narrator's apologia is not easily distinguishable from the journalist George Flack's, from the false emphasis by which the investigator manufactures a guarded secrecy. But since both fictions have been insisting all along that the final discursive productions of these investigators will never truly depend on whatever might have been unsecreted and 'unveiled,' why does the actual, successful penetration of such borders remain for these figures such a serious concern? If in the end these reporters generate 'mostly lies,' as Juliana accuses, why do they bother – indeed, why are they positively desperate – to achieve infiltration? As had been the case for their sentimental ancestors, it becomes clear that what is essential to the narratives produced by James's scribbling investigators is not the 'content' they try to extract from these imaginary borderlands of inside and outside, private and public. Rather, the only facts their prose will require are those that can construct a theatre of incursion.

In *The Reverberator*, when George Flack finally coaxes from Francie the suggestive information he will later use for his article, he happens to do so as they are making their way to the studio of a fashionable artist, Mr Waterlow, where a portrait of Francie is in progress. Flack purports to his readers that the occasion for the article is this portrait. The scandalous details flow 'spontaneously' out of this seminal object in an associative current: the portrait is said to be a sign of Francie's rapid elevation in the Parisian social scene; this is subsequently confirmed by her engagement to Gaston Probert; his family has been drawn so far into society's inner circle they have become invisible; there have been startling discoveries about this family . . . 'Didn't you understand,' Flack will later ask Francie,

> that I wanted you to know that the public would appreciate a column or two about Mr. Waterlow's new picture, and about you as the subject of it, and about your being engaged to a member of the grand old *monde*, and about what was going on in the grand old *monde*, which would naturally attract attention through that? (180–1)

In the end, nothing in Flack's article has required an act of witnessing on his part, except for the otherwise irrelevant anecdote about the portrait. The mere act of having insinuated himself into the artist's studio, of having seen with his own eyes the object originating this associative chain leading to the 'secrets' of the old world, is the only means by which Flack can establish the status and the authority of the successfully penetrating witness. As I have suggested, the early novel's confessional project established the need and the protocol for this authority right from the beginning. This particular strategy, however, of confirming that the true and the authentic has been brought back 'from the field' is something the 'new journalism' inherits from its travel-writing parentage – from a tradition of articulating the other that reaches back to antiquity, and that historians such as François Hartog have demonstrated to be the impetus of classical historiography itself. Flack must articulate his activity as one of penetration in order to stake his claim in what Hartog identifies, in *The Mirror of Herodotus*, as autopsy. The reporter, in a tone that strikes Francie as '"higher," somehow, than any she had ever heard him use,' had previously advised her: 'If I want to see the picture it's because I want to write about it . . . I wouldn't write about it without seeing it. We don't *do* that' (127). In the ability to report that he has seen with his 'own eyes,' a narrator confirms his successful penetration into what had once been veiled, and thus into truth. The truth of his 'seeing it' confirms the truth of what he will write about it. With the sequence 'I have seen, it is true,' James's investigators, like Herodotus, ensure that 'no separation is made between saying and seeing' (Hartog 251).

The investigator's preoccupation with the inside/outside division of topographical space is thus put on par in these fictions with the purely phantasmagoric dimension of the Parisian 'social landscape' that so many of James's Americans strain to discern. When Flack, for instance, had assured Francie's sister early on that the Proberts could not possibly be the hidden 'rose' of the American-Parisian social set, 'or anything near it,' because they were unknown to his long-established Parisian informant, Delia responds in 'a flash of inspiration':

> She asked if that didn't perhaps prove on the contrary quite the opposite – that they were just *the* cream and beyond all others. Wasn't there a kind of inner, very *far* in, circle, and wouldn't they be somewhere about the centre of that? George Flack almost quivered at this weird hit . . . 'Why, do you mean one of those families that have worked down so far you can't find where they went in? . . . That's the kind of family we want to handle!' (43–4)

As the sham centres, circles, secrets, and interiorities begin to pile up, we find *The Reverberator* calling into question even the 'privacy' it is supposed to be defending. When Francie's sister Delia speaks of her own privacy, it clearly corresponds on the one hand to the reality of a private room, but we also know it to be something she has manufactured as a false front in order to impress the socially elevated Proberts. When her family meets Gaston for the first time at their hotel, Delia leads them to her 'saloon, where they should be so much more private: she liked . . . to hear herself talk of privacy' (45). One is reminded of Mrs Penniman's conversation with Morris in *Washington Square*, in which she repeats the phrase 'a private marriage' because 'she liked it' (85). Delia, like so many of James's Americans, really has no use for privacy; she rather embodies Flack's ideal of a life articulated entirely in public terms, proudly and continually moulded so as to be transcribable, in its entirety, into the 'women's pages' of the *Sunday World*. As has been demonstrated by Leonore Davidoff, Catherine Hall, and other historians, the bourgeoisie of the nineteenth century is remarkable in predicating its social intelligibility on the space and the commodities that constitute its privacy.

We will recall, however, that the moral urgency behind these narratives' scathing critique rests almost entirely on the terrifying spectre of their investigators violating very real – that is, legally recognized – interior spaces. Just as the *Aspern* narrator's danger to society is ultimately measured by his compulsion to steal into the very boudoir of his hostess at the climax of the story, so too is Flack's method of 'going for the inside view' made intelligible almost entirely through the figure of the annihilated property line. Flack threatens 'the idea of sticking up a sign of "private" and "hands off" and "no thoroughfare,"' and the presumption that 'you can keep the place to yourself' (63). In this figural scheme it even becomes difficult to conceive the 'hands off' as anything less than a warning against bodily intrusion. The analogous opening note in *The Aspern Papers* is sounded by the narrator's predatory casing of the Bordereaus' villa, his 'laying siege to it' with his eyes (5). These overtures, in other words, are the manoeuvres of a work strangely at war with itself; they are preemptive strikes against the myriad assertions elsewhere in this writing about the insidious and purely rhetorical manufacture of a hidden interiority. The fictions are conflicted about what Flack had called 'the inside view,' that is, anything and everything that would be gained through the acts – and the theatre – of penetration and discovery that the narratives painstakingly construct. The competing conceptions of the inside view, as a pernicious ruse on the one hand and a fatally endangered reality on the other, revolve like propeller blades toward and away from one another; but the axis on which they turn is another term – privacy – in which the social reformism at issue in *The Reverberator*, and especially in its other sibling, *The Bostonians*, stakes an equal claim. This revolving movement in James expresses a fundamental ambivalence in the post-sentimental novel about its own role in both delineating and 'discovering' the frontiers of the private.

An honest and 'open' soul, according to James's Americans, will be one that proves at every moment there is nothing hidden within an interior; she will be consistently available and accountable to a public. It is an injunction deeply engrained even in Isabel Archer, whose ideality is so persistently confirmed in her contrast to the Flack-like Henrietta Stackpole. At one point Ralph Touchett explains to Isabel the disposition of his private space:

> 'I keep a band of music in my ante-room . . . It has orders to play without stopping; it renders me two excellent services. It keeps the sounds of the world from reaching the private apartments, and it makes the world think that dancing's going on within' . . . Isabel often found herself irritated by this perpetual fiddling; she would have liked to pass through the ante-room, as her cousin called it, and enter the private apartments. It mattered little that he had assured her they were a very dismal place; she would have been glad to undertake to sweep them and set them in order . . .

[H]er cousin amused himself with calling her 'Columbia' and accused her
of a patriotism so heated that it scorched. (113–14)

Between the literal and the figural, private space and inner self, it might
seem unquestionable that the bulk of this vignette's import is carried
by the latter. Only in that register, it would seem, could James's alarm
intelligibly sound – his warning about the potential universalization
of Isabel's command to 'sweep' and set 'in order' Ralph's interior. Yet
almost thirty years later, when, in a personification of America as 'a
motherly, chatty, clear-spectacled Columbia, who reads all the newspapers,' James obliquely recalls his Isabels, Henriettas, and Delias, he does
so with an exegesis wherein the architectural construction of interiority
is no mere figural vehicle (*American* 362). In the essays of *The American
Scene*, the expatriate James has returned after more than a generation's
absence to discover that the interior-accountability depicted in his fiction, ideologically enforced by Henrietta Stackpole and her many progeny, was now in his homeland instantiated in the very distribution of
its walls and doors. An effect of the United States' social as opposed to
merely political democracy, James writes, is an antipathy to 'the pres-
ervation of *penetralia*; so that when *penetralia* are of the essence, as in
a place of study and meditation, they inevitably go to the wall' (250).
Hence 'the most salient characteristic' of New York skyscrapers, for instance, is the window (95). Yet the eradication of private space is also
something 'the public institution shares impartially with the luxurious
"home"' (166). As he elaborates the 'universal custom of the house' in
America, James asks us to remain aware of these structures as the expression of a peculiar 'conception of life':

> The instinct is throughout . . . that of minimizing, for any 'interior,' the
> guilt or odium or responsibility, wherever these may appear, of its *being*
> an interior. The custom rages like a conspiracy for nipping the interior
> in the bud, for denying its right to exist, for ignoring and defeating it in
> every possible way, for wiping out successively each sign by which it may
> be known from an exterior . . . Thus we have the law fulfilled that every
> part of every house shall be, as nearly as may be, visible, visitable, pen-
> etrable, not only from every other part, but from as many parts of as many
> other houses as possible . . . This comprehensive canon has so succeeded
> in imposing itself that it strikes you as . . . positively serving you up for
> convenient inspection . . . [I]t takes a whole new discipline to put the visi-

tor at his ease in so merciless a medium . . . [It is] all as for the purpose of
giving his presence 'away,' of reminding him that what he says must be
said for the house . . . [H]e is beguiled by remembering how many of the
things said in America *are* said for the house . . . [It is a] conception of the
home . . . as a combination of the hall of echoes and the toy 'transparency'
held against the light. (166–8)

One can trace the terms of this discourse to those of a democratic reformism more generally and persistently within James's sights, whose
cultural manifestation owes so much to the novel of sentiment from
which his work spawns. We cannot, however, move on from this insistence on the 'signs' by which an interior might be known from an exterior – this attention to a 'comprehensive canon' reminding a visitor that
his speech will always be 'for the house' – before engaging a particular
Foucaultian strain of literary criticism that would stake a claim in every
sentence of this passage.

Like the panopticon, of course, the American house for James is the
physical manifestation of a 'political dream' of accountability (Foucault,
*Discipline* 198): a 'generalizable model of functioning; a way of defining
power relations in terms of the everyday life of men' (205). Its manifestation in the home, the last refuge of extra-disciplinary privacy, confirms that it was all along 'destined to spread' beyond the correctional
institution 'throughout the social body' (207). In light of this consciousness in *The American Scene*, and of the knowledge-production masked
as revelation that we have seen targeted in his fictions, it would seem
prudent to reconsider the influential Foucaultian analyses of this period's fiction which assert James's blindness to, and ultimate complicity
with, the operation of nineteenth-century discipline. I think we cannot
take for granted Mark Seltzer's argument, in his influential *Henry James
and the Art of Power*, that 'the almost automatic opposition' in James 'of
a creative aesthetics to a constraining politics precisely covers the "pro-
ductiveness" of modern apparatuses of power' (132) – considering that
the author's portrayal of the newspaper as just such an apparatus, in so
many fictions, exposes exactly this productivity. However James might
portray an 'autonomous (literary) discourse,' it seems impossible to rest
assured that it 'effectively screens the filiations between power and discourse in modern society' (132), especially after our confrontation with
the literary investigator of *The Aspern Papers*, which has just the opposite effect; it clearly exposes the mechanism by which his discipline,
like the journalist's, can generate a discourse of penetration to mask

the pure productivity of his biography, the registration of Aspern's life into public discourse. As he focuses on *The American Scene* in particular to demonstrate the unconscious manufacture in James of an 'outside' to politics and social discipline, Seltzer surprisingly passes over the book's many diagnoses, as in the excerpt above, of how such discipline exerts itself within – or in the name of – interiority. This is not to ignore the fact that Seltzer goes out of his way to show how *The American Scene* 'displays the panoptic and normalizing techniques' exercised by what James calls the 'hotel-civilization' of American modernity (Seltzer 115, James 438).

Seltzer's more general thesis – that James is ultimately complicit in a disciplinary 'mastery' pervading his socio-political environment – has already been subject to pointed critique. Whereas Seltzer proposes a filiation between the Jamesian narrator's mastery of his fabula and the mastery of discipline in general, Dorrit Cohn, for instance, argues that such correspondence can never be 'simple and stable' (*Distinction* 179). Gert Buelens rejects Seltzer's suggestion that Jamesian desire surmounts the chaotic and contingent 'hotel-world' depicted in *The American Scene*, arguing instead that James immerses himself in 'the metonymic contiguity' of its social and sexual mosaic (305). These critiques, however, tend to hinge on the inherent vagaries of what does or does not constitute 'control' or 'mastery' over narrative, desire, or the social world as a visual field subject to panopticism. The most compelling accounts of literature as a disciplinary agent, accomplished by Seltzer and others, still await evaluation against the more concrete mechanism Foucault keeps in view: the knowledge-producing apparatus, strictly indispensable to discipline as such, of the registry. As it produces subjects within the tables of discipline, the registry achieves legitimacy – and even invisibility, in its most efficient operation – when it appears not to have been created by the institutions that maintain it; that is, when the registry is comprised primarily of the personal testimony of the recorded subjects themselves. Often in the guise of 'private' confession, as James points out, testimony is the means by which a subject inscribes herself into public record and makes herself intelligible and accountable to power.

That the novel in general has ended up reinscribing a disciplinary ethos even when it seems to have brought discipline directly into view is an argument proposed most famously in D.A. Miller's *The Novel and the Police*. Like Seltzer, but in relation to the nineteenth-century novel in general, Miller deftly marks out the novel's contribution to a discourse that affirms a circumscribed limit to disciplinary power, a realm of privacy safely beyond its reach. Pretending to be 'set off' from worldly power by virtue of its purported supplementarity, the novel has historically asserted itself to be independent of that power and, indeed, a challenge to it. The novel shakes its artistic fist at social structures from within its own supposedly impermeable frame as an aesthetic object. Whereas Seltzer challenges the conceptual poles of 'aesthetic self-containment' versus 'the political,'[6] or art versus power, Miller's terms are the private and the police. By the end of both compelling studies, however, we find ourselves in a strange position. We have been convinced that the complete absence of the police, in a novel like *Barchester Towers*, confirms the fantasy of a bourgeois world removed from policing – but also that the presence of the police, in a novel like *Oliver Twist*, only serves to reinscribe a mystification that would locate the exercise of power only where there are buttonholing bobbies. Both the tenuousness and the virtuosity of the argument is its ability to confirm itself in the face of any and all possible representations of the police.

Adroitly, if somewhat selectively, these analyses trace the conceptual landscapes that the novel makes possible through both its discourse and its fabulous representations of subjection and freedom. The arguments weaken, however, when they claim to have discerned, from any one such novel, a totalized ideological effect. *The Novel and the Police* makes a convincing case, for instance, that *Oliver Twist* sustains the illusion that the middle class constitutes an independent 'outside' in relation to a disciplinary power wholly identified with the policeman's beat, i.e., with urban blight. Yet Miller also reveals that the demystification of this illusion is adequately accomplished by the novel's own discourse: the middle-class Brownlow, who had ostensibly rescued Oliver from the city's disciplinary institutions, is exposed by the novel as an agent 'constitut[ing] Oliver as an object of knowledge,' and thus 'assum[ing] power over him as well' (9). How is it, then, that the novel-reader's identity is 'confirmed' by the 'evidence,' as Miller puts it, of the middle class's 'constitutive "freedom"' – but that identity is not disrupted by the novel's own deconstruction of that evidence? (x). That the extra-urban family that comes to shelter Oliver is itself '"one of the family" of disciplinary institutions,' Miller writes, is an idea 'only discreetly broached by the text' (10). But by what measure and what evidence can we support the corollary assumption that the family's independence of disciplinary power is made 'obvious' by Dickens's novel, and not something that is 'only discreetly broached by the text'? As we might ask Seltzer of James: why does the novel's hidden service to a disciplinary ideology successfully engage, but the equally embedded challenge to that ideology does not? When *The American Scene* mourns the 'land of the "open door,"' and the decline of living spaces which, 'by not taking the whole world into their confidence, have not the whole world's confidence to take in return' (407), it is explicitly describing the material instantiation of a nineteenth-century incitement to discourse. In light of James's prediction that 'the desire to rake and be raked has doubtless ... a long day before it still,' it is difficult to see how this analysis of modern discipline is any less potent than Seltzer's own (168).

To achieve their goal of exhibiting an ultimately singular ideological effect of a given novel – even if the discursive forces behind that effect are not coherent – Miller and Seltzer must reach beyond their convincing demonstrations of how the panoptic eye of the omniscient narrator ensures that a character is, in Foucault's words, detailed, mapped, and 'brought to account.' They are forced to make a further claim about the assured predictability of the disciplinary effect on any and all of the novel's readers. The reader must become the interface between the fiction and the historical real, however conceived. When Miller addresses the novel's ultimate failure to perform its putatively subversive function in relation to power, he claims it does so either by 'confirm[ing] the novel-reader in his identity as a "liberal subject" ... whose private life, mental or domestic, is felt to provide evidence of his constitutive "freedom,"' or by rehearsing within itself the sham drama of its own 'scandalous' confrontation with the social order, thus 'forming ... a subject habituated to psychic displacements, evacuations, reinvestments, in a social order whose totalizing power circulates all the more easily for being pulverized' (x, xiii). Relying in both cases on a slippage between the fictional and the readerly subject, and on an undiagrammed psychological mechanism of 'habituation,' Miller claims to unveil, with Seltzer, 'a discrete continuity between literary and political practices' (Seltzer 15).

The significance of this step will not fully resolve without a brief recapitulation of Foucault's own conception of the relation between discourse and power. The rise of the human sciences, in his genealogy, fostered and refined the discourses by which the self could become knowable and accountable. Although modern society thus taught itself the terms and the taxonomies by which a subject shall become intelligible, the fulfilment of an individual's subjection takes place only through the operation of particular apparatus, at historically specific interfaces – that is, when the subject records herself (or is recorded) in a questionnaire, an affidavit, a diagnosis, profile, interview, application, trial, etc. The austerity of this vision of subjection cannot provide what Miller and Seltzer require. Impelled by what is ultimately a very old and persistent desire of literary criticism – to figure out how a fiction actually 'works' on a reader – the attempt to trace a systematic effect from any given novel will always be bound, exclusively and inescapably, to that which would enable such systematicity; that is, to the general iterability of the novel and the pure anonymity of its addressee. So conceived, the novel's effect could only be 'ideological,' and has nothing to do with subjection as Foucault finds it, in the recorded encounter between apparatus and individual.

This is why Foucaultian literary critics have so frequently been obliged to erase silently the distinction between discourses of subjectivity – their language and logic, which the novel certainly has helped to normalize – and the actual, historical subjection of individuals. A document has productive (as opposed to normative) disciplinary power only where it plays a role in mapping a historical subject, adhering the produced details to a name, and rendering her knowable and recognizable within a tabulated series of other subjects. This is not to suggest such documents have no performative effect on a readership. One need only consult Nancy Armstrong's *Desire and Domestic Fiction* or Judith Butler's *Giving an Account of Oneself* to perceive the profound normalizing effects of literary and testimonial discourse. A fiction, however, like any document that does not create and register details about its reader, cannot possibly 'produce' him as a subject. Hence the major historical thesis of *Discipline and Punish*, that although power had previously staged spectacles of punishment and rehabilitation to subject the individual – an attempt to represent to the individual a properly disciplined subject in the hopes he will 'identify' with it, or that he will take the representation 'to heart' – that strategy of discipline through representation was replaced (by the nineteenth century) with practices of self-subjection and self-registration. In this Foucault carries forward the thought of his mentor Louis Althusser, whose own portrait of the modern state had attempted to empty the term 'ideology' of all metaphysics of representation and identification. For Althusser, ideology refers to the aggregate of historical 'practices' that have the merely epiphenomenal effect of constructing for the subject an imaginary representation of his relationship to his real conditions of existence. For Foucault, the historical status of even this effect remains questionable; and since they are the practices and not the representations that are indispensable to discipline, 'ideology' itself has, conspicuously, little purchase in his later work.

Because the proper name so clearly stands at the front of any consideration of an interface between fiction and history, the reticence about this issue within seminal works of Foucaultian literary criticism is remarkable. We have yet to look closely at the disciplinary role of proper names with referents outside the historiographic archive (in its many forms), partly because of a certain politics of critical thought over the past forty years. In the aftermath of a myriad of inquiries into the rhetorical and tropological effects of discourses that are traditionally said to have transcended such effects – especially philosophy and historiography – intellectuals both within and without the academy have long attempted to portray such studies as attempting to erase differences between fictional and historical referents. Instead of arguing against this portrayal, figures like Seltzer – and even Foucault before him – have adopted it as a means of distinguishing their historicism from an apparently ahistorical and 'purely' deconstructionist subset of the poststructuralism they help to articulate. Seltzer proposes a remarkable reading, for instance, of de Man's observation that the definition of a fictional statement, as implied in Jean-Jacques Rousseau's *Confessions*, is 'the absence of any link' between the statement and a historical referent. In this Seltzer discerns an assertion that, to de Man, fiction as a genre is 'entirely free with regard to referential meaning.'[7]

The oft-cited essay on Rousseauvian confession to which Seltzer refers, and which de Man refined in the final chapter of *Allegories of Reading*, reveals in fact that nowhere is the distinction between fictional and historical reference more vexed – and yet in that vexation more productive to the confessional project – than in the writing of the sentimentalist godfather himself. Rousseau's well-known account of childish betrayal, in which he accuses an innocent girl, Marion, of pilfering a ribbon that he himself had stolen, is a narrative that excuses his behaviour with (among other things) a system of metaphorical substitutions which establishes his desire for the ribbon as an expression of his desire for the girl. Because the figural substitutions reveal ostensibly hidden 'motives, causes, desires,' Rousseau's unaccountable behaviour becomes accountable and available to understanding (De Man, *Allegories* 284). This excuse cannot fully expiate, however, because the true scope of the guilt is bound neither to the theft nor the perjury. The shame with which the confession grapples is rather its exhibitionistic desire to expose Rousseau's shame. With a convincing close reading of 'the obvious delight with which the desire to hide' is revealed in Rousseau's narrative, as when he hyperbolically prefers 'm'étouffer dans le centre de la terre' than to be caught in his lie, de Man observes that the structure of desire in the confession is based on 'exposure rather than . . . possession,' and that what 'Rousseau *really* wanted is neither the ribbon nor Marion, but the public scene of exposure which he actually gets' (285–6).

As I have suggested, it is this desire and this theatre that marks off confession as a subset of testimony, and we will see below how they instantiate themselves in the sentimental novel. Judith Butler understands this theatre to be a structural inevitability of 'giving an account of oneself' in general (10). Even where the confessing 'I' imagines apostrophe, 'every accounting takes place within a scene of address. I give an account of myself *to you*,' the other toward whom the trace is always oriented (50). Although Rousseau's desire is implicated in the performance of the confession itself, not merely in the figural 'content' of the discourse, the shame of his exhibition is reinforced in the text by a 'terminology of repression and exposure . . . entirely compatible with the system of symbolic substitutions . . . that governs the passage on possessive desire' (De Man, *Allegories* 287). Both regimes, according to de Man, are 'part of one system that is epistemologically as well as ethically grounded and therefore available as meaning.' The 'mode of understanding' the system maintains, however, is ultimately disrupted by an intrusion into the confession that Rousseau's discourse equates with 'fiction' (287). When Rousseau comes to explain why, exactly, he implicated the girl for his crime, his discourse does not seek recourse in the logic of figural displacement it had prepared, whereby the accusation can be read as a desperate consequence of his love. On the contrary, the plea 'Je m'excusai sur le premier object qui s'offrit' (I found excuse in the first thing that presented itself) introduces 'a vocabulary of contingency . . . within an argument of causality' (288), and as the introduction of the girl's name in the text appears precisely at the narrated moment of betrayal ('finally I said, blushing, that it was Marion who had given it to me'),[8] the implication that its appearance is purely the effect of chance renders the name meaningless within the figural system of intelligibility the text had created. The name 'stands entirely out of the system of truth, virtue, and understanding (or of deceit, and error) that gives meaning to the passage, and to the *Confessions* as a whole' (289). As de Man points out, this is the same irrelatión that Rousseau defines elsewhere as the occasional (but benign) intrusion of fiction into confessional discourse. In *Les Rêveries du promeneur solitaire*, Rousseau admits that certain lies inhabit his confessions, but these falsehoods are excusable because they are each 'un fait oiseux,' a useless fact, good 'neither for instruction nor in practice' (*Rêveries* 57–8). As such, 'it is not a lie but a fiction' (62). As is the case with the lie introduced by Rousseau's unaccountable nomination of Marion, fiction is that which is totally inconsequential and extraneous to the moral and philosophical economy of the confession. Fiction is defined as that which disrupts the metaphorical system that makes the text's otherwise contingent historicity intelligible – morally, philosophically, and sentimentally. Fiction is *opposed* to the artificial network of metaphor that historiographers and literary critics have traditionally identified as a literary intrusion upon an otherwise non-fictional narrative. This fictional interruption, moreover, arrives in the form of a reference to the proper name of a real historical person – a moment we would grasp, traditionally, as one thing we can count on (even if nothing else) to secure the *Confessions*'s purchase in the historical world. De Man's reading offers a glimpse at the complexities awaiting a truly rigorous treatment of the disciplinary role of the proper name and other historical lynchpins in literary discourse, and demonstrates that the upending of our contemporary expectations of what fiction and non-fiction mean to seminal discourses on testimonial and confessional narration is hardly an invention of poststructuralist criticism.

Foucaultian critics' lack of engagement with the proper name is intimately tied to their even more conspicuous diffidence about the human body as a historical entity. We have been told that any given analysis of literature and disciplinarity must bracket the body as such, either because it is an uninscribable force in a perpetual struggle with discipline, or because it is precisely the 'unthinkable' within a disciplinary regime. In *Discipline and Punish*, by contrast, the body is central: it is the surface from which discipline assigns and records so many of the details by which the subject is registered. The sustained identity of the human body – but also the body of territory, nation, property, product, 'work,' oeuvre – is guaranteed in its juridical or otherwise enforced bond to a registered proper name. The 'bodies that matter' to the tables of discipline are those that the proper name have bound to their constituent

cells. The historical inscription of the name makes a collection of attributes cohere in individuation, and reifies that individuation by affixing
it to a material entity.[9]

The strain of Foucaultian criticism that seeks to demonstrate the novel's 'efficacy in producing . . . privatized subjects' has, in short, unwittingly rejected Foucault's definition of modern discipline (D.A. Miller
82). The mechanism by which the supposedly private life of the novel's
subject 'confirms' that of the reader, or by which the reading subject
becomes 'habituated' to the disciplinary predicament of the fictional
character, could only be one of identification or internalization, and
could only have been conducted through representation. It is in service
to these terms that literary critics have so grossly over-emphasized the
single chapter in *Discipline and Punish* on Bentham's panopticon, in-
flating it to the almost complete occlusion of the book's much greater
emphasis on the mechanics of serial individuation and the documentary tactics of '"cellular" power' (149).[10] Because panopticism is read
as something that internalizes within the subject a kind of disciplinary
superego – necessarily born, as are conduct books and barracks regula-
tions, in iterability – such a systematic power is easily discerned in the
pages of fiction; hence the eagerness of literary critics in particular to re-
duce all disciplinary activity to 'the political dream' that the panopticon
represents (Foucault, *Discipline* 198). It allows Seltzer to identify panopticism, which Foucault calls 'a generalizable model of functioning'
(205), with discipline in general.[11] Despite both Miller's and Seltzer's
occasional acknowledgment that a vocabulary of 'internalization' is incoherent within Foucaultian analysis, a reader turning the last page of
*The Novel and the Police* or *Henry James and the Art of Power* would likely
be surprised by a reminder that nothing in *Discipline and Punish* suggests that surveillance is inescapable. The central tower of the panopticon, according to Foucault, has spread its easily installed mechanism
throughout the social body in a multitude of forms. These 'eyes' can
be constructed with only the slightest materials, and their effectiveness
does not require a registering brain behind the lens, although the possibility of such a hidden observer must exist in order for the subject to be
compelled to regulate himself. The person who 'assumes responsibility
for the constraints of power' and 'becomes the principle of his own subjection' through panopticism can only be 'he who is subjected to a field
of visibility, and who knows it' (202). As a mechanism of surveillance
becomes more efficient, Foucault writes, 'it tends to the non-corporal;

and, the more it approaches this limit, the more constant, profound and permanent are its effects' (203).

By a necessity established through the terms of his own analysis, Foucault must remain silent about the other side of this limit. As it pertains to the narrow subject of surveillance mechanisms, this silence simply means that we could never know what would be the status of panoptic self-discipline in relation to a subject behind closed doors who does not 'know' or consider himself to be within a 'field of visibility.' More broadly, Foucault must demur from any attempt to inscribe into intelligibility the body beyond the archive. Because Miller and Seltzer want to portray the novel as a panoptic apparatus, they must banish Foucault's prerequisite for what the reader, fantastically, would have to 'know' in such a case – that the novel in her hands is literally a portal through which the eye of power is fixing her within a field of visibility.[12]

My critique here, however, clearly cannot diminish the great accomplishment of Seltzer's study in its illumination of the problem I have been circling in these pages: the paradox by which the 'comprehensive supervision' that James takes to task in his critique of American society is deployed in 'his own techniques of representation' (Seltzer 114–15).[13] But instead of reading this tension as the effect of a 'criminal continuity' between the Jamesian novel and disciplinary power, I see it as yet another stage in the ongoing conflict in the novel between testimony and confession (57).

As we make our oblique way back to James's complaint that modern architecture is indeed the instantiation of a 'political dream' wherein all bodies are readily brought to account, it will be crucial to emphasize that the remainder 'left behind' by Foucault's demurral is no mere negativity or absence. It is a positive condition, an unarticulation without which discipline itself would be invisible and unintelligible, beyond analysis. In James's writing, this condition appears in a well-demarcated silence at work in the interstices of discipline, one whose explicit purpose is to obstruct the social forces moulding the very mortar of America, 'the land of the "open door"' (American 62). In The Portrait of a Lady, Ralph Touchett protects his own penetralia with a mask of festive music in his 'ante-room.' The undisclosed articulation of his own 'music' behind the mask – a silence for Isabel and ourselves – is thereby identified with the inaccessible yet ineluctable content of his 'private rooms,' and both are threatened by an American who 'thinks one's door should stand ajar' (Portrait 285). The synesthesia reappears in

*The American Scene,* when James mourns the decline of living spaces which, 'by not taking the whole world into their confidence, have not the whole world's confidence to take in return' (168). The filiation I suggest between this observation and the politics of portraiture in *The Portrait of a Lady* might well be emphasized, too, by a critic like Seltzer, as evidence that whatever political reverberation such a statement might inadvertently produce will inevitably be recontained in the 'removed' aesthetic world of James's fiction. Yet the certainty that such containment is the text's and not the critic's operation – in this case, that it is James's writing that is anxious to confine the political valence of his discourse on American 'confidence' within a supposedly inconsequential theatre of interpersonal relations – should be somewhat troubled by the completion of James's thought in the next sentence, which, like many in *The American Scene,* so clearly anticipates Foucault's: 'The desire to rake and be raked has doubtless . . . a long day before it still' (168).

Nancy Armstrong's *Desire and Domestic Fiction* offers a brief historical recapitulation of the 'rights to privacy' that the novel has accorded its subjects since the eighteenth century – as well as an answer to the broader question raised by the preceding critique about whether a true Foucaultian reading of the novel is actually possible. Armstrong traces the novel's contribution to a discourse instrumental in what Jacques Donzelot called 'the transition from a government of families to a government through the family.'[14] The eighteenth-century 'conduct book,' its subsumption into the 'domestic' novel, and their mutually collaborating ethos of sensibility articulated new criteria of human evaluation, competing with those based on lineage and an intricate class system. The new formulas of evaluation made popular in these books would gain currency within other socio-political forums as well. Nurtured by an Enlightenment cosmology that had centralized self and mind, the sensibility underwriting the 'individual value' of a Pamela confronts a tradition in which she has no such value. Although the untitled human subject was thus confirmed in these texts as an entity with 'rights' that existed before her identity as servant or property, the discursive reform enabling this conception harboured a self-subverting mechanism that would diffuse the incipient revolutionary danger it posed: the newly empowered self, potentially available to anyone and everyone with the proper inner sensibility, had to be emphatically marked as female to remove it from a 'sphere' wherein 'genuine' power struggles are said to take place. Yet even as the novel thus confirmed the political impotence of woman and home by aligning them with a privacy removed from 'the public,' it was just this removal that helped to create the purportedly apolitical space in which the middle class would safely construct and disseminate its competing formulas of human evaluation. The novel thus bred a contradictory fear and contempt of the effective power of femininity and domesticity. This tension winds itself tightly into a phrase that would become ubiquitous in the nineteenth-century novel: 'petticoat rule,' an expression that seeks to both ignite and assuage revolutionary fear. *Desire and Domestic Fiction* rigorously follows the traceable, historical instantiations of these discourses, and holds itself to a progression in which conduct books and novels articulate the terms by which individuals are made intelligible to power and are subsequently subjected by disciplinary apparatus. Armstrong thus achieves and draws a roadmap for a Foucaultian literary criticism that does not recruit the forces of internalization and ideology that Foucault's approach leaves uniquely behind.

Especially in his work of the 1880s, Henry James decries political reformism in general and 'women's rights' in particular as forces that seek to abolish privacy (*Bostonians* 913). The spectre of 'petticoat rule' sustains the fiction's conflicting tones of paternal condescension and plutarchical alarm. Before *The American Scene*, *The Bostonians* had shouldered the greatest burden in telling the Jamesian tale of modern social reform. In his notebooks the author reminds himself that such a 'very *American* tale' must inevitably depict 'a type of newspaper man' who would emblematize the 'extinction of all conception of privacy,' and what we have seen in the later travel essays should help to unpack this peculiar formulation, this '*conception of*.' Without preamble or even transition, however, James's prospectus for the novel immediately identifies a second subject, as if its deep implication with the first simply goes without saying – or, perhaps, as if such implication cannot easily be traced: 'the situation of women . . . the agitation on their behalf,' which is the 'most salient and peculiar point in our social life' (*Complete Notebooks* 19–20). Hence the narrator's suggestion in the novel itself that modern woman 'owes her emancipation' to the likes of the journalist Matthias Pardon (934). Although it distances itself in several ways from Basil Ransom, who embodies the antithesis to reform, *The Bostonians* speaks through him when it must finally articulate, in positive terms, the ideological basis of its relentless and unsmiling satire of a feminist-spurred urban activism. Having bent throughout the novel a charmingly condescending eye on the progressive feminist milieu he must endure to pursue the beloved Verena Tarrant, Ransom finds himself, at a climactic moment in his courtship, suddenly in the grip of a passionate and apparently well-bethought polemic that seems alien to the portrait of well-bred and politically inert Southern complacency James had heretofore been painting. 'The whole generation is womanised,' Ransom warns; 'the masculine tone is passing out of the world; it's a feminine, a nervous, hysterical, chattering, canting age . . . which, if we don't soon look out, will usher in the reign of mediocrity, of the feeblest and flattest and the most pretentious that has ever been' (1111).

For James, the two great sins of modernity, feminism and journalism, share the same root. In *The Portrait of a Lady*, the journalist Henrietta Stackpole seems to have removed herself to the Touchetts' English estate directly from a dwelling within *The American Scene*. She is a guest who not only 'walks in without knocking at the door,' but would consider any such knocker 'a rather pretentious ornament' (285). The very physiognomy of the *Interviewer* correspondent is the panoptic architecture of her homeland made flesh, ever streaming the sinister Jamesian 'light': 'Her remarkably open eyes, lighted like great glazed railway-stations, had put up no shutters.' She is also the embodiment of the newspaper itself, 'crisp and new and comprehensive as a first issue before the folding.'[15] The novel frequently reminds us that it will be impossible for the eyes of the *Interviewer* to turn away from any scene without just such a 'comprehensive' understanding of it: 'I'm not sure that I understand you,' one often hears from the reporter, 'but I expect I shall before I leave' (277). Like the power that would be increasingly attributed to the camera in the late nineteenth century, especially by journalists,[16] Henrietta insists that nothing will remain fugitive to her perception once it has entered the frame of her vision. Hence the further description of her eye as if it were a camera lens, 'particularly open' with 'remarkable fixedness . . . which rested without impudence or defiance, but as if in conscientious exercise of a natural right, upon every object it happened to encounter' (275–6).

In such alarming anthro-mechanical imagery reverberates the threat of blunt intrusion first sounded in Henrietta's written announcement of her arrival, her explanation to Isabel that she crosses the Atlantic because her periodical 'wants some light on the nobility' (274). Yet this threat is almost miraculously diffused by a simple caveat at the end of this letter, whose power of self-justification will be instantly recognizable after reading *The Aspern Papers*, and is the means by which so many of James's investigators slip through the door marked 'private' – including, we will see, the investigator James himself: 'I wish to see as much as possible,' Henrietta closes, 'of the inner life' (274). With this incantation the reporter almost invisibly slides her goal of obtaining personal histories – narratives of names and their relations – into a commendable project of maintaining a community of feeling, one whose traffic would consist only of a general, ahistorical discourse of sensibility. Unlike the mere gossip-monger's lust for universal disclosure, the archaeologist of 'inner life' carries a warrant justifying her encroachment into any privacy.

# 3 Overhearing Testimony: James in the Shadow of Sentimentalism

*Washington Square* is one of Henry James's most explicit statements about the relation between his novel and other, older forms of fiction. The meddling Lavinia Penniman, aunt of young Catherine Sloper, would love to turn James's tale into an antipaternal romance; indeed, Penniman and her brother compete as potential authors of his daughter's story. Whereas Penniman attempts to guide Catherine and her beau Morris Townsend to an illicit wedding ceremony 'performed in some subterranean chapel' (82), Dr Sloper watches Catherine's struggle somewhat as Flaubert claimed to watch his own creations sizzling and popping in the frying pan of his imagination. Curious as to whether she will 'stick' in her spirited opposition to him, Sloper may have 'hoped for a little more resistance for the sake of a little more entertainment' (79). The father has the 'big intellectual temperament' James sees in Flaubert, but also his 'dryness and coldness.'[1] The novel is too conscious of literary milieux, however, to confront Sloper's naturalism with a mere haze of 'romanticism.' Wherever Mrs Penniman 'wished the plot to thicken,' she seeks to deepen more precisely 'the sentimental shadows of this little drama' (79, 81). She will bring it to a 'sentimental crisis' by means of her 'insinuating sympathy' (79, 83). Throughout James's work, in fact, the primary weapons of his meddlers, intruders, exposers, and pressmen are the 'familiarity' of sympathy and the rhetoric of sentimentalism.

After Mrs Penniman assures Morris that Catherine's father would come to believe in his 'disinterested' motives if they eloped without hope of the doctor's fortune, Morris asks, 'Do you think he is so sentimental?' (87–8). To this fiction's progenitors in the sentimental novel, there may be no project more fundamental than the adjudication of its subjects' 'interestedness.' If James and Conrad represent the Janus face of the modernist novel, the true root of that fiction lies not in the nineteenth century but in European sentimentalism. After a century's slumber, the English novel – infiltrated as it was by what Ford Madox Ford reportedly called an 'alien cloud,' referring to Conrad and James[2] – reawoke to the realities of testimony and found itself bound to an eighteenth century that had not yet buried those realities under the machinery of omniscience. As I have suggested, the problem of testimony – as it has always been a problem for the novel – cannot be rendered fully in an ahistorical discourse of epistemology, even if our received understanding of the question has been framed almost entirely in such terms. In what follows I hope to show how this epistemology is partially grounded in the early novel's signature economy of interest, and in the ubiquitous scenes of 'overhearing' it created to conform to that economy. Mieke Bal's categorical assertion that 'character-bound' narration 'brings about bias and limitation,' for instance, is understood by narratology to be an inevitable, logical consequence of the structural mechanics of 'focalization' (146). Although this logic is partly underwritten by what I have been calling a contract of comprehension, its assumption that testimony communicates an altered, 'filtered' reproduction of the truth can also be traced to this psychologism, this a posteriori conclusion about 'human nature' and its inevitable self-interest, that was the very engine of the eighteenth-century novel.

To take a measure of this interest in the early English novel, and then to consider how it might have been conducted to Conrad and James through an exemplary nineteenth-century iteration, I want to look briefly at Henry Mackenzie's seminal *Julia de Roubigné* and Anthony Trollope's *Barchester Towers*. As it makes clear that the economy of sentimental interest-profit in these works is governed by the same mechanics and tropics of 'the frame' that maintain the negative marking of narrative testimony, this backward glance will ultimately reveal how the selectively applied logic of the supplement, which has always ruled discourses of narrative framing, has long operated within the English novel itself, designating chosen narratives as 'outside' public discourse proper and abjecting them safely into the private.

Inspired by Jean-Jacques Rousseau's *Julie, ou La Nouvelle Heloise* (1760), Mackenzie's 1777 *Julia de Roubigné* is a major artery through which the Enlightenment master's ethos of confession infused itself into the English novel of sentiment. There are two primary sets of

interlocutors in the novel: the sentimental heroine Julia and her epistolary confidant Maria, and Julia's counterpart, Savillon, who writes to
his friend Beauvaris. Like many of the era's autobiographies – Benjamin
Franklin's stands out as a particularly salient example – Julia's and Savillon's self-histories consist almost entirely of a precisely maintained
ledger of their own sacrifices and generosities. Outside of the occasions
when he acts merely as a witness to sentimentally profound subplots,
the life of the sentimental hero is comprised entirely of episodes that
culminate either in his bestowing a gift that eliminates another's misfortune or in an act of renunciation through which the hero cultivates
a patient, silent suffering. In order to achieve the all-important status
of a genuinely sentimental act of benefaction, however, these acts must
fulfil what Jacques Derrida has called the impossible promise of the gift
in general. The gift, as such, must not leave behind a memory, mark, or
ledger of the giving and taking. In order to be truly outside, or in excess
of, any future tallying between donor and donee, the gift must be completely forgotten, the memory of the giving erased as soon as it occurs.
The act of giving must not be brought into account.[3]

We might initially assume that sentimental suffering in itself, once
weaned from the sacrifice or renunciation that gave birth to it, no longer belongs to the discourse of credit and debt that tyrannically rules
not just *Julia de Roubigné* but the eighteenth-century novel in general. It
is precisely the requisite 'silence' in which the hero must suffer, however, that keeps the passion squarely within that economy – which is to
say, within economy as such. According to the rules of sentiment, the
sufferer should not exhibit the loss created by her painful renunciation;
she must not 'take credit' for her suffering. Thus Savillon implicitly reminds his reader that his own generous and self-sacrificial behaviour
on behalf of the unfortunate Roubignés is modelled on that of his friend
Herbert, whose wife has recently died. Claiming no sentimental credit
for his suffering, nor for the sentimentally profound accusations he pri-
vately levels at himself for his loss, Herbert 'disturbs not the circle of
society around him, and few . . . observe any thing peculiar in his behaviour' (2:52). Just as Savillon had previously avoided bringing his
sacrifices for the newly impoverished Roubignés into discourse among
them, Herbert remains reticent among his peers.[4]

Yet, in the end, both men ensure that their sentimental credit is in
fact brought into account – into the record that is the epistolary exchange. Like Herbert within his own 'circle of society,' Savillon does
not take credit among the Roubignés for what he gives, yet these credits

do accrue in the ledgers created between Herbert and Savillon, and Savillon and Beauvaris. 'With unwearied attention,' Savillon writes of his service to Roubigné, thus 'cashing in' the sentimental credit he has accumulated, 'I soothed his sorrows, and humbled myself before his misfortunes, as much as I had formerly resisted dependence on his prosperity' (2:8). Here again is the ghostly work of the narrative 'outside.' Just as Henry James does not bind his preferred 'outer' narrator to the epistemological problems said to inhere in the 'first person singular' – despite the fact that all narration, as Mieke Bal points out, is necessarily performed in the first person, since 'a narrator is not a "he" or a "she"' (122); and just as narratology yokes all determined instances of speech or writing with the restrictions of attestation except for the writing that lies between a novel's covers, but is still purportedly outside its fabula proper; so too does the sentimental hero, in accounting his beneficence to an addressee outside the immediate stage of his sentimental adventures, rest assured that he has claimed credit for his good deeds 'nowhere' and reap his profit precisely in the tacit non-existence of this accounting and accreditation.

Narratology will argue that it is perfectly right to leave 'out of account' that which falls outside the primary fabula – whether it be the status of the outermost narrator's writing as 'writing,' as an objectified statement, or the moral credit that inevitably accrues in the sentimental hero's account of himself – because such exclusion corresponds to the novel's own rigorous separation of the 'worlds' involved, diegetic or otherwise. We should take no heed of the fact that Savillon takes credit for his disinterested behaviour, because he does so only in the world of his epistolary rumination, a world removed from the story proper. We normally avert our eyes from his taking credit for not taking credit, because it is understood – reportedly – that the novel wants us to be unconscious of this accounting, this collecting of interest on Savillon's part, whenever it takes place at this 'outer' epistolary level, removed as it is from the main diegesis of the novel. Since the novel holds itself to a convention by which diegetic worlds or narrative 'levels' exist independently of one another, narratology tells us, so too must any responsive reading of the novel. It is, however, precisely such independence that would make the all-important claims at issue impossible: the claim, on the one hand, of a master narrative's comprehension – the possibility of which would exist for any novel, even those that perversely hide it behind never-broken clouds of attestation – and which is the precondition for establishing the 'necessarily' perspectival subjectivity *of* such attestation; and the claim, on the other hand, of the sentimental hero's epistolary narration, an accounting beyond all accounting that allows him to reap apophatically the profit he claims to have given up. These profits in sentiment and comprehension could never have been reaped if there existed a merely parallel irrelation between the diegetic worlds or narrative levels involved. They accrue only through 'vertical' commerce across these levels – between the disparate epistemological powers said to belong to embedded versus master narrations, and across the two distinct social 'circles' of the sentimental hero: the dramatis personae of his sentimental adventures and the dyad of his epistolary relationship.

What the early epistolary novel truly values, in the final analysis, is not sentiment in and of itself, but rather its exhibition as a theatrical tableau for an 'outer' audience, its existence as a scenario *of* a sentimental theatre, within which the spectral outer observer is an indispensable figure. Such is the 'private' spectacle of Herbert's grief that Savillon nevertheless exports as sentimental cargo, not just to Beauvaris, but also to the 'editor' to whom he has gladly given this private correspondence, and, consequently, to that most public of publics, the apostrophic addressee of *Julia de Roubigné*. The grief that Herbert keeps invisible from his 'circle of society,' whose constituents he continues to entertain with 'good humour,' is locked away in the private apartment by which he 'shut[s] out the world' (2:52). One of the most important signals, not just of this novel, but of the genre's argot in general, 'the world' refers especially to those economies in the public sphere that are – ostensibly – inimical to and in direct competition with an economy of sentiment, which the novel explicitly articulates *as* an economy.[5] Into the sanctum Herbert takes such pains to maintain, Savillon gains entrance by virtue of '[h]aving acquired a sort of privilege with his distress, from my acquaintance with its cause.' What the sympathetic investigator unveils in his penetration turns out to be a prototypical sentimental tableau: 'I entered his room yesterday, when he had thus shut out the world, and found him with some letters on the table before him, on which he looked, with a tear, not of anguish, but of tenderness' (2:52–3).[6] At his friend's silent invitation, Savillon discovers the letters in front of Herbert to be a collection saved from his late wife, Emily, written during a long separation when Herbert was forced to attend closely to his interests in the West Indies. Savillon reiterates to Beauvaris, 'verbatim' from memory, several long, touching excerpts from the letters that profess the writer's love and longing for her husband. 'Such was the wife whom Herbert lost,' Savillon concludes. '[Y]ou will not wonder at his grief; yet sometimes, when the whole scene is before me, I know not how, I almost envy him his tears' (2:61). Inseparable from the 'whole scene,' Savillon, replete with his own 'tears,' envies not the grief itself, but rather Herbert's figure within the tableau, now the primary sentimental object of Beauvaris's gaze.

As the newly formed domestic novel fulfils its enlightened task of articulating the interiority of its subjects, the 'private' status of this sentimental landscape, which keeps the politically dangerous ethos of sympathetic universality away from the authority of 'public discourse,' is confirmed through scenarios of transdiegetic penetration and unveiling. Yet it is precisely the fact of this interpenetration and cross-dependence that must remain outside the novel's consciousness if this primary distinction is to survive. This motivated unconsciousness, as we have seen, survives as the spectral 'frame' later maintained by the models of narratology. Although the novel cannot accomplish its task of approving interiority without confirming an 'outsider' as its ultimate addressee, narratology, which purports to reveal the purely objective, 'structural' operations of the novel, banishes from intelligibility any conception of narrative address that does not simply reiterate the fictional assertion of the novel – that we, the novel-reading public, are not the 'proper' recipients of these epistles, but have only reaped the profit of an excessive 'overhearing.' What we are overhearing in Mackenzie's novel, ultimately, is a critique first widely disseminated by Richardson's *Pamela*: the heroine's sentimental claim to an interiority that exists prior to her identity as a bought servant – or, in Julia's case, as a tribal commodity – has no currency in 'the world's' economy. Julia is thus inescapably bound to the 'wrong man' Montaubon, who, unlike Savillon, enjoys a fortune that will return her family to fiscal solvency and good public standing. The sentimental novel makes it clear that these women could never air their socio-political grievance in a 'public' forum that the novel, nevertheless, unquestionably constitutes. The novel-reading public is thus made to 'overhear' a merely private communication between women who do not speak outside their sphere, and the rights they claim need never be identified as such. The novel's very public addressee thus hears the rebellious discourse but is not obliged to acknowledge its call. The overhearer is not responsible for what he hears.

The early novel denies the inevitable contamination of private by public not only to mask the political register of its discourse, but to keep the imaginary coherence of the 'public sphere' from breaking into a disastrous multiplicity of subject-bound economies of social evaluation. In Mackenzie's novel, a portrait of Savillon's uncle contributes to this containment:

> The opinion of the world he trusts but little, in his judgment of others; of men's actions he speaks with caution, either in praise or blame, and is commonly most sceptical, when those around him are most convinced: for it is a maxim with him, in questions of character, to doubt of strong evidence, from the very circumstance of its strength.
>
> With regard to himself, however, he accepts of the common opinion, as a sort of coin, which passes current, though it is not always real, and often seems to yield up the conviction of his own mind in compliance to the general voice. (2:22)

Like any right-thinking sentimentalist, this man is wary of what passes as current. The common salvo against 'fashionable' judgment is here expressed in the possibility of a market renegade – an active trader, but one whose rates would be based on unpredictable, radically singular, and consensus-free acts of evaluation. But there is an exception: the origin of this singularity will not set his own rate when the subject under appraisal is himself. What bars such a character from competent self-evaluation is the same critical injunction that will not grant a Molly Bloom the power to articulate her consciousness, nor a Marlow the power to comprehend the story he tells. Here the seemingly alien regimes of sentimental authentication and epistemological comprehension reveal their alliance, the latter having been nourished within literary-critical discourse by the former. Among the denizens of *Julia de Roubigné*, the articulation of interiority will not be a revelation of truth without the theatre of unveiling, without a penetration into these figures as framed objects. The novel requires its non-objectified outsiders to overhear acts of sentimental disclosure for the same reason that literary criticism will much later require an 'overhearing' of consciousness in general – to avoid the distortion supposedly inherent in testimony, in any statement that has been 'prepared' for an other.[7] Just as the truth of Molly's consciousness could never be conveyed by her interested self but must be plundered from an 'outside,' neither could a figure framed within the epistolary novel, bearing forth his own sentimental heart, produce anything other than a sham interiority sculpted by self-interest. For a figure like Marlow, as we have seen, there is reportedly no hope at all of escaping the self-interested bubble of subjectivity, since no investigator arrives to penetrate and lay bare the 'opacity' he necessarily constitutes as a narrative object. What I hope will become clear in this study is an alternate view of Conradian modernism's defining break from its Enlightenment inheritances, one that sees it not as a final plunge into the subjective, 'interested' prison of testimony, but rather in its abrogation of the framing manoeuvres used to maintain such a carceral.

We must overhear conscience in the epistolary novel to confirm its disinterestedness, its full exposure, and the political impotence of its 'privacy.' Because it generally took for granted, as a reality to be incorporated into its mimetic exercise, the inevitably testimonial origin of its overheard disclosures, the novel grounded them in documents such as letters. Within the fiction these are bound to the conditions of epistolary circulation, including the 'improper diversions' by which the letter came under a fictional editor's eyes in the first place.[8] As I have suggested, however, the reality of any such record, whether or not it is intended for a 'public' eye or ear, precludes the absolute silence that disinterestedness ideally requires. Neither Savillon nor his epistolary counterpart, Julia, could ever achieve the reticence Herbert achieves as he confirms his pristine and disinterested sentiment even as he remains 'unable to speak' (2:53). Into the nineteenth century, however, the growing conventionality of omniscient narration, which had once been one of the most fantastic propositions of fiction, would guarantee for the sentimental subject a perfect silence and disinterestedness. Her interiority could be extracted and laid bare without her having to say, write, or even think a word. One might even argue that omniscient narration would largely displace the epistolary novel because it manufactures for its characters, seemingly without residue, an absolutely sealed and silent interiority, an interiority that is continually brought into discourse nonetheless. When the sentimental novel had assigned all of its constituent statements the status of testimony – by acknowledging their documentary objectivity – the novel's presentation was at odds with its discourse. The fact that interiority apparently cannot manifest itself except in the external 'mask' of testimony puts into question the continual insistence within the novel on the absolute severability of interior and exterior. Omniscient narration, once it disappears into convention, silently buries this otherwise impassable question. In the novel's cosmology, the spectrality of omniscience thus creates a new natural law, reifying the prediscursive interiorities that it produces.

We have seen that the sanctum-infiltrating agent of light in the early sympathetic novel, the heroic archaeologist of sentiment, becomes the primary antagonist in Henry James's world. We can get a rough sense of how this internal conflict came about, and a clearer understanding of both James's and Conrad's quarrel with their sentimental ancestors, with one more intermediary stop at the early nineteenth century. Just as we have seen in Jámes, the first two of Anthony Trollope's 'Barsetshire' novels locate the ethos of sensibility at the root of a democratizing, disciplinary reformism. A sequel to *The Warden*, the story of a mild, provincial official whose single desire for 'peace and quiet' is destroyed by a London newspaper's mission to bring his life to public account, *Barchester Towers* anticipates James in collapsing this journalistic disciplinarity into a single figure. The Reverend Obadiah Slope, villainous engine of the drama, has insinuated himself into Barchester society through an alliance with the existing sentiment-enforcer in the diocese, Mrs Proudie. By story's end, this woman's husband will achieve the political prize at stake in the novel – the bishopric of Barchester – but will also have 'thoroughly learnt that his proper sphere of action,' politically speaking, 'lay in close contiguity with Mrs. Proudie's wardrobe' (487). Mrs Proudie will have 'no idea of retreating' to her 'wardrobes, still-rooms, and laundries' while the bishop conducts official business during the day. She will not only be present at the bishop's various conferences, but will do most of the talking and decision-making therein. As one bewildered petitioner mutters to himself after such a meeting: 'That comes of the reform bill' (418).[9] In the meantime, this petticoat power lends itself to Mr Slope's reformist imposition on Barchester, which begins with a campaign calling for a strict observance of the Sabbath. This ecclesiasticism is portrayed as insidious, even dangerous, and yet unanswerable. It brings a parishioner's Sunday activities to account, demanding a greater articulation and detailing of his otherwise unregistered time. Slope draws attention to what Foucault might call one of the 'tolerated illegalities' by which a quiet Barchesterian avoids 'publicity' in its most general sense.

Mr Slope eventually comes under the spell of the novel's heroine, the young widow Eleanor. The moment he does so, we can see exactly how Trollope rewrites the indispensable scene of sentiment-approval in the novel of sympathy, which *Julia de Roubigné* exhibits in Savillon's movement into his friend's seclusion. Like Herbert, Eleanor is confirmed by an 'outer' narrator to be a woman 'with most singular disinterestedness' (437). In *Barchester Towers*, he who would espy and approve

Eleanor's hidden sensibility – for our benefit as well as his own – is now the villain, known as such precisely for his successful incursions. The theatre of Eleanor's exposure begins with a scene of maternal intimacy; the words opening its chapter are those of a private, inaccessible language of the mother loving her child ('Diddle, diddle, diddle, diddle, dum, dum, dum' [128]). The baby pulls Eleanor's hair from beneath her cap, and more cooing ensues. Upon Eleanor's déshabillé, Mr Slope suddenly intrudes:

> At this moment the door opened, and Mr Slope was announced. Up jumped Eleanor, and with a sudden quick motion of her hands pushed back her hair over her shoulders . . . Mr Slope . . . immediately recognized her loveliness, and thought to himself that, irrespective of her fortune, she would be an inmate that a man might well desire for his house, a partner for his bosom's care very well qualified to make care lie easy. (129–30)[10]

It is an intrusion as abrupt and apparently inexorable as ours has been. By joining us in Eleanor's seclusion, Slope is said to have gained a vantage that we might normally suppose, under a post-epistolary regime, to be available only to omniscience – instant apperception of invisible, interior qualities. The 'loveliness' that strikes him is not physical beauty. He has met her before without giving her a second look, and we had just been told two paragraphs earlier that her beauty was apparent only to 'old friends.' Having revealed to him instantly that Eleanor would be 'well qualified to make care lie easy,' the door of Slope's ingress has opened onto more than one interiority. The discovery of Eleanor's picturesque domesticity has revealed, in Armstrong's terms, 'a woman whose value resided chiefly in her femaleness rather than in traditional signs of status, a woman who possessed psychological depth rather than a physically attractive surface' (19–20). The exposure has confirmed in Eleanor the sentimental disposition required for her to become the novel's primary subject, but its particular staging as an intrusion is especially effective in maintaining a rigid distinction between public and private – again, as long as we remain unconscious of the prior incursion of omniscience itself. When at the end of the novel the narrator makes a cryptic apology for introducing the contents of an epistle into the narrative, promising that 'no further letter whatever shall be transcribed at length in these pages' (430), we might hear a certain contempt for the garrulous self-construction required by the epistolary novel, and a satisfaction that the sanctified privacy of *this* novel's denizens have to be wrenched from them by force.[11]

In *The Portrait of a Lady*, Henry James restages the same tableau, almost unchanged in form and function, by which Trollope's heroine was successfully excavated. It appears just when the novel, in its denouement, makes its surprise move in transforming Henrietta Stackpole into a sympathetic figure and feminizing her formerly unchecked masculinity. The scene takes place in the Florentine Uffizi Gallery, where Henrietta unexpectedly runs into Caspar Goodwood, the indignant, failed suitor of Isabel Archer. Having once encouraged Caspar to draw Isabel away from her European ties, back to the safety of American moral purity, Henrietta now asks him to desist, and in this way signals the humble withdrawal of her own righteousness. By itself, however, this appeal would not be enough to confirm Henrietta's formerly unsuspected sympathetic depth. Her encounter with Caspar thus begins with his accidental disruption of the first 'private moment' James has yet to give Henrietta. In the 'empty vista' of the gallery's upper chambers, 'scantily visited' at this time of year, Henrietta has sought a particular painting.

> Miss Stackpole may appear more ardent in her quest of artistic beauty than she has hitherto struck us as being, but she had after all her preferences and admirations. One of the latter was the little Correggio of the Tribune – the Virgin kneeling down before the sacred infant, who lies in a litter of straw, and clapping her hands to him while he delightedly laughs and crows. Henrietta had a special devotion to this intimate scene – she thought it the most beautiful picture in the world . . . She was about to turn into the Tribune when a gentleman came out of it; whereupon she gave a little exclamation and stood before Caspar Goodwood. (505)

Although the consummation of her bond with Correggio's scene of maternal intimacy is deferred on this visit, the passage nonetheless exhibits proleptically the theatre of Henrietta's sentimental gaze. As if to underscore that Henrietta is herself the proper sentimental subject of this recalled scene, despite her position as spectator, the novel's omniscience at the beginning of the episode effects the indispensible intrusion into her own privacy by calling unusual attention to the exercise of its 'privilege to look over her shoulder' (504).

As it had for Trollope's Eleanor, a love of maternal joy espied over-the-shoulder confirms Henrietta's newly found disinterestedness. In

*Barchester Towers*, the voice that makes explicit Eleanor's 'most singular disinterestedness' (437) is that of the cosmopolitan Madame Neroni, a figure Trollope seems to go out of his way to align with the omniscience governing the novel itself. Neroni acts primarily as a wry observer of the Barchester scene, and exercises an almost supernatural power of seeing into the hearts of men. She does so, in any given salon, from her signature position on a couch she cannot leave; like the novel, she cannot participate in the world she so perceptively surveys. Yet she is beautiful and seductive, generating 'useless' desire in others (241). She is a 'powerful spider that made wondrous webs,' but has 'no use for the victims when caught' (242). To one contemporary reviewer of the novel, she seems 'absolutely unnatural. She is an intrusion upon the stage, utterly out of harmony with the scenes and persons round her, and we cannot but think with the nature of her sex.'[12] Although Neroni is a gay but somewhat cynical and world-weary foreign outsider, she proves, in the end, to be the master of Barsetshire puppets. She determines the final dispensation of the novel's hero and villain, steering Eleanor into the right man's arms, and instigating Slope's retreat. When we are told that 'such matters were her playthings, her billiard-table, her hounds and hunters, her waltzes and polkas, her picnics and summer-day excursions,' it is difficult not to be reminded of the half-contemptuous ennui with which Trollope himself often wrote about novels and novel-writing (367–8).

Trollope's negligence in hiding Madame Neroni's function as a narrative device, a necessarily improbable agent of his own omniscience, is easily digested as another instance of his fairly regular and self-conscious winking at his audience, the like of which was fairly common and even more explicit among his forerunners in omniscient narration. Such illusion-breaking is exactly what James deplores and famously singles out in Trollope. This critique of his predecessor in 'The Art of Fiction' conspicuously exhibits the conceptual innovation that not only marks the evolution in James away from a prevailing nineteenth-century conception of narrative, but is part and parcel of the contract of comprehension that I have been suggesting reaches its peak at the end of the nineteenth century, both in the 'law of fiction' James would later articulate and in institutionalized practices of journalism and historiography. In the midst of a general analogy 'between the art of the painter and the art of the novelist,' and to make the argument that 'as the picture is reality, so the novel is history,' James draws attention to certain 'accomplished novelists' who 'have a habit of giving themselves away.'

> I was lately struck, in reading over many pages of Anthony Trollope, with
> his want of discretion in this particular. In a digression, a parenthesis or an
> aside, he concedes to the reader that he and this trusting friend are only
> 'making believe.' He admits that the events he narrates have not really
> happened . . . Such a betrayal of a sacred office . . . shocks me every whit as
> much in Trollope as it would have shocked me in Gibbon or Macaulay. It
> implies that the novelist is less occupied in looking for the truth (the truth,
> of course I mean, that he assumes, the premises that we must grant him,
> whatever they may be), than the historian, and in doing so it deprives him
> at a stroke of all his standing-room. (378–80)

Collapsing any distinction between the consequences that would follow from discovering the ahistoricity of a historian's account and
'discovering' the ahistoricity of a novelist's tale, James quite radically
rewrites the terms by which the novel's relation to truth had traditionally been debated. It would never have occurred even to a historical
novelist like Walter Scott, a major genre theorist who also was fond of
comparing novels to paintings, to conflate into a single 'truth' the two
very different questions of whether a novel makes valid historical claims
or whether its presentation effects what Scott calls 'probability' (228) –
the central term by which theorists since Richardson had measured the
truth of such fictions as James parenthetically defines it. This innovation in James has been obscured by literary historians who portray this
conflation of probability and historicity as having always been endemic
to the novel's self-conception. We have already seen, for instance, how
Michael McKeon, in his exegesis of Defoe's *Serious Reflections*, imports
into that novelist's definition of fiction the 'lying' that Defoe had, in
fact, applied exclusively to cases of distorted representations of historical events. This is the rhetoric taken up by history-writing itself whenever it desires to cast itself in the glow of an unproblematic 'truth.' It
hauls the spectre of fiction into its discourse, saddles the scapegoat with
all inconvenient questions of interpretation and narrative conjecture,
then ritually banishes it. James's famous complaint against Trollope is
thus remarkable as it manages to deploy the 'veil of fiction' ideology in
defence of fiction, and is yet another example of how James can appear
to take up a recognizably modernist challenge to certain Victorian epis-
temologies even as he unwittingly supports them.

Chastised by James as one who fails to remain in the invisibility and
ineffability of an outside to the novel, a Trollopean novelist might be
surprised to see the narrator of *The Portrait of a Lady* go out of 'his' way

to depict his declension into Henrietta's private space by taking a peek 'over her shoulder.' The otherwise gratuitous image of the god-like narrator stretching his quasi-incarnated neck close to Henrietta's ear is, after all, a monstrous theophany that disrupts the mimetic illusion just as surely as anything found in the Barsetshire novels. 'The Art of Fiction' asserts nonetheless that there is no 'standing room' for the insightful truth in a Trollopean novel without a delusion in its audience that no novelist is pulling the strings. In the end, of course, we might find it hard to believe James's incredulity that a reader's absorption in mimetic illusion exists simultaneously with her awareness that she is reading fiction. Whether we trace it to a genuine or to a 'bad faith' unconsciousness of narrative framing – either unprecedentedly sublimated or a merely useful intellectual device – James's critical thought abandons the issues of probability and presentation that had formerly ruled questions of veracity in the novel and replaces them with a strident discourse of truth and historicity. Like 'the new journalism' and the multiform historiographies increasingly born of it, James's rhetoric at the turn of the century has taken on a newly epistemological register. In these nonfictional forums, as we have seen, the 'outer' narrative frame and its constituent discourse fall into invisibility at the end of the nineteenth century, leaving in their boundless absence only a 'comprehensive coverage,' as Harold Herd had written of the new journalism (223). It becomes clear that the traditional conception of literary modernism, so often defined by its insistence on the 'fragmentary' and the subjective, would never have come into being without the various contracts of comprehension drawn up by this other modernism that James represents, the other half of its Janus face.

As is true of the dyad in *Barchester Towers* of Madame Neroni and the sentimental heroine Eleanor, in *The Portrait of a Lady* Isabel Archer is paired with an arguably stronger and more intriguing character in Madame Merle. It is remarkable that such an enormous portion of the popular and critical imagination takes from the rich mine of James's genius Isabel Archer as its ideal of novelistic portraiture. Surely one of the genre's greatest examples of character by negation, hers is a figure entirely constituted by the intricate array of her renunciations, large and small; by the exquisite tact with which she avoids a myriad vulgarities, gross and subtle; and by the 'spirit' purportedly evinced in her successive non-allegiances, her independence, and in the unarticulated, ultimately doubtful idealism for which she makes her sacrifices of speech and action. Watching this heroine's fall, precipitated by her single failure, finally, to renounce, we might rightly wonder how she could be distinguished in essence from a Pamela, from a figure almost entirely without attribute beyond the sentimentally approved perfection of her personal relations – whose rendition represents, in both cases, an apex of the author's technical mastery. As the proper subject of *The Portrait of a Lady* is established precisely in the act of penetrating inside – that is, in quickly leaving behind the merely external, and in surmounting her condition as a framed object – it appears, despite James's insistence that the novelist's mastery is identical to the painter's, that what it accomplishes is rather opposed to such portraiture, inimical to rendering the existential peculiarity of his subject's opacity.

Like Madame Neroni in *Barchester Towers*, the practically omniscient Madame Merle is wise, well-travelled, Europeanized, and perhaps just a little too experienced. Although no movement in the psychological drama surrounding Madame Merle escapes her, and although she, too, will prove to have held the puppet strings of the central heroine's fate all along, James does not exempt her, as Trollope had Madame Neroni, from the novel's ability to scrutinize her soul and hold it to account. The very trajectory of *Portrait*'s second half is governed by the penetration of Madame Merle's fascinating, well-wrought exterior, which brings to light dark intentions and a hidden agenda. Before this exposure, however, she is largely opaque, which is simply to say that she remains a dramatic figure, necessarily impenetrable as an object on stage, and no omniscience intervenes to adjudicate the honesty or hidden 'interest' of her speech. Like Madame Neroni, functionally opposed to a heroine whose sublime ignorance of the secret workings of others' hearts is an index of her sentimental value, Madame Merle presents the cautionary spectre of a future that Isabel might very well inhabit if she were to achieve the older woman's power of omniscience. Thus, when Isabel comes to a pass where she might 'look into' her friend's privacy more closely, she recoils. 'With all her love of knowledge she had a natural shrinking from raising curtains and looking into unlighted corners. The love of knowledge coexisted in her mind with the finest capacity for ignorance' (251). The propriety of Isabel's retreat from knowledge is thus confirmed through the 'enlightenment' trope that has taught us to recognize all dangerous and intrusive investigation. Yet it is precisely this vocabulary that the novel puts into the mouth of Madame Merle herself when she speaks her own veiled protest against privacy invasion. Figuring herself as a 'chipped and cracked' tea service that can 'do very well for service yet, because I've been cleverly mended,' she makes sure 'to remain in the cupboard – the quiet, dusky cupboard where there's an odour of stale spices – as much as I can. But when I've to come out and into a strong light – then, my dear, I'm a horror!' (245). As *Portrait* does eventually expose her secrets, but leaves Ralph Touchett inviolate behind the secrecy of his 'ante room,' the novel seems to take its justification from the *Aspern Papers* narrator: Ralph 'had nothing to fear' from the Jamesian lantern 'because he has nothing to fear from the truth' (*AP* 6).

Trollope, too, seeing no conflict between the interiority-accounting his novel demonizes in Mr Slope's investigations and the sentimental accountability it simultaneously demands of its heroine, can rest assured that *Barchester Towers* has nothing to do with the intrusive, feminist reformism he explicitly claims is abetted only by other novelists. With reference to a Dickensian narrative that was being serialized at the very moment of his writing, Trollope's epilogical portrait of the wife-dominated Bishop Proudie makes it clear that to give oneself over to such a novel is to submit to petticoat rule:

> And when he got home he had a glass of hot negus in his wife's sitting-room, and read the last number of the *Little Dorrit* of the day with great inward satisfaction. Oh, husbands, oh, my marital friends, what great comfort is there to be derived from a wife well obeyed! (411)[13]

As if sensitive to the paradoxical tension hovering around the issue of accountability, however, *Barchester Towers* quite remarkably does not indulge in a final 'indecent exposure' of Madame Neroni, the all-but-omniscient prototype for *Portrait*'s Madame Merle. Whereas James ultimately hauls Madame Merle, like Olive Chancellor, out of the 'cupboard' and 'into a strong light' – just as she fears – Trollope leaves Madame Neroni, the figure closest to himself as omniscient master of ceremonies, discreetly opaque. It is as if Trollope has decided not to pretend to his reader that the 'heartlessness' he associates with this legless, preternaturally observant, 'absolutely unnatural . . . intrusion upon the stage,' as the anonymous reviewer had put it, is only a figure of speech (Trollope 62).

Although James will always denounce the righteous lantern of the 'Aspern' narrator even as his narrative holds it aloft, his insistence on one's right to maintain a testimonial stance before the world intensifies in the later novels. The now-familiar satire of Americans attempting to ferret out the 'secrets' of Europeans who have the gall to maintain a public front protecting their privacy is at the heart of *The Ambassadors*. Critics such as Christopher Butler and Christophe Campos articulate, I think, a perennial misreading of James in the belief that 'at heart, he was fascinated by Europeans, and yet he always suspected them of possessing some secret that was out of reach because they would never express it clearly.'[14] It is difficult to take such a reading seriously in light of Lambert Strether's early obsession with Chad Newsome's 'secret' – a secret that would encompass much more than the banal fact of a liaison with Mme de Vionnet, and which is almost entirely the coinage of his own and of the collective 'Woollett' brain. 'Are you engaged to be married,' Strether asks of him: 'is *that* your secret?' Woollett wants to encompass the general mystery of Chad's new 'Europeanized' self into a single explosive secret. In his response, Chad attempts to disengage the metaphysical bent of his American friends from the practical fact that one always selectively represents oneself and acts as an ambassador for oneself. 'I have no *secret*,' Chad answers, 'though I may have secrets!' (227)

In Waymarsh James presents an American who cherishes his privacy and reserve as much as Chad or any other continentalized figure. But like Delia Dosson and Lavinia Penniman, who love above all to *refer* to their privacy, Waymarsh always makes sure that his 'silence' is 'charged with audible rumblings' (79). The reticence of James's Americans, including that of Mrs Newsome, is meant to speak volumes. This is represented memorably in *The Ambassadors* when Waymarsh, having to endure 'in stricken silence' an outing of shopping and touring with Strether and Maria Gostrey in the morally frivolous streets of London, suddenly and ostentatiously dives into a shop alone. Returning, he 'told them nothing, left his absence unexplained, and though they were convinced he had made some extraordinary purchase they were never to learn its nature.' Strether and Gostrey correctly interpret Waymarsh's silent gesture as a declaration of his 'different' moral standing, fairly deafening them with its 'sacred rage' (85).

True to Jamesian form, however, Strether's eventual acceptance of the European's right to testimony and his emergence from a busybody provincialism, is marred in the end by the sense that his innocence has been abused. In this novel, however, James strongly emphasizes the degree to which this innocence is almost entirely the American's own creation, and had not been crafted by an active old-world deceit. When Strether asks Little Bilham directly, referring to Chad and Mme de Vionnet, 'Then they are the virtuous attachment?' Bilham answers, 'I can only tell you that it's what they pass for. But isn't that enough?' (204). As an ambassador, Strether is simply not perceptive enough at this stage to hear Bilham's diplomatic language.

More explicitly even than Madame Neroni or Madame Merle, Fanny Assingham in *The Golden Bowl* exhibits powers of omniscience and manipulation normally reserved for the disembodied narrator. Although the novel has great fun with her attempts to act as arch-interpreter and even behind-the-scenes puppet-master, James is no longer averse to taking a serious look at what this affinity means. This 'most luminous of wives,' as Colonel Assingham observes, accomplishes a grand survey of the network of relations that is *The Golden Bowl*, and her insights are not to be dismissed (320). She clearly articulates many of the worries and possibilities to which the 'normal' extradiegetic Jamesian narrator would want to draw our attention. But James also insists, more consciously than ever, that the authorial eye presiding over his fiction cannot, or perhaps ought not, avoid merging with the projected 'public eye' Mrs Assingham represents – regulatory, normalizing, and even vulgar. As Amerigo considers the propriety of a rendezvous with Charlotte in London, he knows the American woman represents the beginning and end of all such adjudication. 'Who was there,' he asks himself, 'to raise [an objection] from the moment Mrs. Assingham, informed and apparently not disapproving, didn't intervene?' (103).

The tension that builds in Mrs Assingham's consciousness throughout the drama grows into the familiar terms of the international conflict, where James, too, is caught in the middle. She laments her burdensome knowledge of the European heart, and the responsibility of managing these transatlantic unions, both of which have put her at a distance from the 'innocence' and 'quaintness' of her American countrymen, 'from whom I've so deplorably degenerated' (318). *The Golden Bowl*, however, is peculiar among James's transatlantic tales in that it is simply impossible to know how seriously we are supposed to take this particular self-deprecation; unlike *The Wings of the Dove*, which is plunged in the definitive sentimentalist worry about the interestedness, the self-serving 'calculation' of largely opaque Europeans, the later novel unambiguously presents this worry as the product of a fatal paranoia. The Europeans whom Maggie Verver comes to see as her opponents habitually maintain behind their words the same reserve that James had championed in Ralph Touchett, he who habitually presents to the world an 'ante-room' that acts as a testimonial envoy from his 'private apartments' (*PL* 113). When Maggie perceives that Amerigo's words and actions are born of calculation, 'always from calculation,' we know that, for her, there can be nothing honest about the conscious act of representation that testimony necessarily performs – an instrumentality that Amerigo, in his sticky relational web, particularly needs (387). The American is driven to paranoid distraction by the mere existence of this testimonial reserve. Always 'believing herself in relation to the truth,' she comes to read 'symptoms and betrayals into everything she looked at . . .' (383).

For James, a non-omniscient investigator like Maggie, who is trapped within the world she investigates – a condition Conrad would simply call reality – is necessarily doomed to some form of paranoia. Without exception, every story that James hands over to first-person character-bound narration is a tale of that narrator's fatal and comprehensive delusions. For James, testimonial narration has no other purpose than to exhibit a character's utter failure to interpret and know the world around him. Although several of his short stories do so, none of James's novels present themselves in the testimonial mode – with one exception. For our purposes *The Sacred Fount* is the most remarkable exception possible. It does not just touch upon the issues at hand; the ethics and epistemology of sentimental penetration constitute *the* subject of the novel. It evokes a social world uniquely schematic for James, and does not attempt to cloak its purely conceptual agenda. Taking place entirely in a brief span at a single location – a weekend party at a country estate – *The Sacred Fount* is a parable free from all but purely intellectual constraints. The relationship on exhibit is that between the Jamesian novelist – played, as so often in the short stories, by an unnamed narrating surrogate – and the objects of his creation.

At one level, the 'fount' refers to a metaphysical force that the narrator believes he has discovered flowing among his fellow guests at a country estate. Among the romantic liaisons, secret or overt, about which he and other guests conjecture at the gathering, the narrator perceives a kind of reverse-vampirism whereby one of the lovers 'feeds' the other with a particular strength, depleting himself in the process. Although his conception of the players involved changes over time, he comes to believe that the formerly hale Guy Brissenden has transferred his youth and strength to his wife, and that the once-powerful intelligence of May Server has seeped into the newly brilliant Gilbert Long. Merely positing this condition of 'sacrifice' (35 passim) as an axiom outside any concrete scenario, James rarefies sentimental sacrifice into the purest abstraction fiction can withstand. Unlike the traditional sentimental investigator – and this difference is really at the heart of James's experiment – this narrator thinks of himself as all but literally the author of the relationships he sees before him. His fellows at the estate exist for him – and perforce for the reader as well, since she is generally bound to his consciousness – not, perhaps, as they really are, but within the elaborate 'system' created by his theory (209). Throughout the novel, he sees the scenes unfolding before him as he used to watch his own imaginative 'fairy-tales' take shape in his mind's eye. It was the 'fruit of one's own wizardry. I was positively – so had the wheel revolved – proud of my work' (97). But we are not meant to take from these signals a directive to dismiss the narrator's insights, or indeed his entire narrative, as pure fantasy. Although the narrator stands in for the creative novelist, his invention is never merely that. As is reflected in so much of his non-fiction, imagination for James is inevitably a window onto the realities of human experience. On one level, the novel's epistemological ambiguities are meant to reflect candidly on the consequence of this doubled task of inventing a world that reflects on our own.

At issue for James, however, is not just the novelist's 'interest in my fellow creatures,' which breeds observation, and observation breeds ideas,' but more important the effectively extradiegetic detachment from those creatures required by the 'omniscience' the narrator attributes to himself (123). Given the acidity with which we have seen James attack the various cousins of this investigator in his fiction, all of whom confound projection with discovery, it is extraordinary to see *The Sacred Fount* so insistently implicate the novelist himself in the same transgressions. As we will see, the surprising conclusion James comes to about his own authorial detachment does not sit easily with 'the law of fiction' he delineates elsewhere. We get a premonition of this tension in the narrator's sweeping declaration that 'one couldn't know anything without seeing all,' which almost seems a parody of the epistemological injunction James would later raise against Conrad (122). As the narrator admits, this 'all' refers to the 'perfect palace of thought' he has already constructed, which 'wouldn't have the shadow of a flaw' if it were not for 'the wretched accident of its weak foundation' (214).

The foundation is weak in this case because it is 'altogether destitute of a material clue' supporting the idea that Server and Long are lovers (57). To the narrator, however, this 'weak foundation' is what establishes his peculiar moral virtue. He refuses to intrude on the privacy of those whose disinterested sacrifice he wants to verify. Putting his only testimonial novel in the hands of this narrator and this project, James deliberately traps himself in the bind of sentiment-approval that omniscience normally avoids. The artist Obert, who accompanies the narrator along part of his investigative trail, is proud that they have restricted themselves to gathering evidence available to any social on-looker. To Obert, their inquiry into Server's love life is 'not only quite inoffensive . . . but positively honourable, by being confined to psycho-logic evidence.' The narrator remains uncertain:

> I wondered a little. 'Honourable to whom?'
> 'Why, to the investigator. Resting on the *kind* of signs that the game takes account of when fairly played – resting on psychologic signs alone, it's a high application of intelligence. What's ignoble is the detective at the keyhole. (57)

Unexpectedly, perhaps, the 'psychologic signs' refer to those that are publicly available. They are what can be gleaned from Server's out-ward behaviour and whatever clues one might draw from her speech. Because the truth they seek is encrypted by such clues, the evidence they need is opposed not only to what can be seen through the key-hole, but to the conscious self-representation of her own testimony as well – except insofar as that, too, constitutes an encrypted clue. Serv-er's speech and behaviour is 'fair game,' to use Obert's figure, as long as Server's mere appearance in public is understood to be her conscious engagement in a game whose tokens consist entirely of signals she is not conscious of transmitting, and whose stakes are the facts of her pri-vate desire and conduct.

The key moment of the narrator's hesitation – 'honourable to whom?' – would seem to mean, unavoidably, that the 'honour' of Jamesian omniscience and the hunt for its 'fair game' suffers in com-parison to an investigator like Marlow, who has access only to con-sciously crafted testimony. Although James formulated the vampirism conceit of the novel at least as early as 1894, his notebooks are appar-ently unconscious of the fact that the novel would again host the theme of the intrusive investigator, much less that it would tie the problem so firmly to the novelist himself. Insofar as the novel is a critique of the Jamesian observer who normally escapes the responsibility of the testimonial condition, it may be significant that the novel was being composed properly just after Blackwood serialized *Lord Jim*, Conrad's most profound statement on novelistic testimony and investigation. But even within James's self-critique, it is difficult to discern whether his parable's response – if it is a response – is sympathetic or antago-nistic to Conrad's proposition. As in every other instance of testimonial narration in James's short fiction, after all, *The Sacred Fount* hands itself over to the testifier partly to exhibit his profound epistemological unreliability.

In either case, this novel remains an indictment, unique in James's work, of the very thing omniscience was meant to provide – the power to simultaneously indulge and deny the desire for a theatre of incursion. In an extraordinary meditation on how the guests at the Newmarch estate digest the art of the piano – an art which, as follows James's habit, is meant to parallel his own – *The Sacred Fount* comes very close to implicating the consumer as much as the producer in this theatre. Yet this critique, too, is diffused by the narrator's caveat that it 'may just possibly have been an hallucination of my own' (120). It occurs to him that, when listening to music in a group, there is 'a certain personal grace to contribute' in one's physical attitude, one's 'posture of deference to this noble art.' The narrator is certain each guest is conscious of exhibiting her own act of reflection, a reflection, however, not just on the music, but on 'some experience . . . some indescribable thought' excited by the intriguing social intercourse taking place on the estate. This posture of reception, embodied throughout the novel in the narrator himself and the 'intensity of consciousness' his investigation requires, is itself an artistic contribution (127). This artistry, the narrator concludes, justifies his penetration into the 'private affairs' of others. '[T]o each of us was due, as the crown of our inimitable day, the imputation of having something quite of our own to think over. We thought, accordingly . . . there had as yet been for everyone no such sovereign warrant for an interest in the private affairs of everyone else' (120).

The narrator's troubled sense of honour is triggered by his growing love for May Server, and by his feeling that his 'providential supervision' of his subjects makes him 'morally responsible, so to speak,' for them (113). He imagines himself the 'natural protector' of Mr Brissenden, 'his providence, his effective omniscience' (123). Mirroring the condition of a 'real' omniscience, however, the narrator never violates the all-but-diegetic divide. He does not do so because he holds himself, perhaps without knowing it, to the same 'law' he sees governing the lovers' sacrifice. Obert asks him if Mr Brissenden can 'see how her victim loses' as her vigour grows:

'No. She can't. The perception, if she had it, would be painful and terrible – might even be fatal to the process . . . She has only a wonderful sense of success and well-being. The *other* consciousness – '

'Is all for the other party?'
'The author of the sacrifice.' (35)

Mrs Brissenden demonstrates this lack of consciousness, ironically, when she complains to the narrator about the same unawareness in Mr Long. Without knowing it, Long 'feeds' on Server; the latter 'gives the lips, the other gives the cheek.'

> 'Mr. Long finds his improvement natural . . . He takes it for granted. He's sublime.'
>
> It kept me for a minute staring at her. 'So – do you know? – are *you*!'
>
> She received to this wholly as a tribute to her acuteness . . . 'You've *made* me sublime. You found me dense. You've affected me quite as Mrs. Server has affected Mr. Long. I don't pretend to show it,' she added 'quite as much as he does.'
>
> 'Because that would entail *my* showing it as much as, by your contention, *she* does? Well, I confess,' I declared, 'I do feel remarkably like that pair of lips. I feel drained – I feel dry!' (66–7)

Although he shows little awareness of it, the narrator's condition is the same as that of the dwindling lovers. He too is 'the author of the sacrifice,' and in this way the consciousness of authorship is identified as an act of sacrifice that drains the artist as it gives life to his creation.[15] But if the object of authorial study were to become aware of the observation – a 'painful and terrible' eventuality the narrator risks in his astonished response to Mrs Brissenden – the 'process' that would be fatally disrupted is not merely the logic of diegetic independence, later to be challenged by the likes of Pirandello and O'Brien. That would be a rather facile point for James to make. At issue, rather, is the process of sentimental containment whereby the sufferers in whom the narrator takes an 'extraordinary interest' must never cash in on that interest, must not bring it publicly into account (108). It is an economy whose native condition is to always be under threat of disruption – a threat, as we have seen, that is the very engine of sentimental fiction. What this investigator wants to discover is not, ultimately, the true identity of Server's lover, but rather the sentiment approved by her unuttered renunciation. Server's consciousness of her own 'abasement' was 'all her secret' (101).

It is clearly vital for James's experiment here to deny his investigator the satisfaction of accidentally overhearing or intruding upon these secrets, thereby cashing in Server's and Brissenden's sentimental credit for them. With this restriction, according to the narrator, the only thing 'I could, after all, save from the whole business was that of understanding. I couldn't save Mrs. Server, and I couldn't save poor Briss . . .' (189). In a subtle perversion of eighteenth-century sentimental discourse, casting the man of feeling in the role of a merely reclusive, hoarding dragon, the narrator continues: 'I *could*, however, guard, to the last grain of gold, my precious sense of their loss . . .' (189). Because the testimonial condition for James is necessarily problematic in relation to knowledge, *The Sacred Fount* has no recourse even to a surreptitious theatre of sentimental penetration, as when the *Portrait* omniscience exhibits itself peeking over Henrietta's shoulder. The novel might seem to stage such a glimpse into interiority when the keyhole-eschewing investigator perceives the pain of sacrifice on Server's face, with its 'lovely grimace' that 'fluttered like a bird with a broken wing' (99). But these perceptions are undercut by the novel's persistent reminders that any and all of his impressions might merely be the projection of his own artistry. Not least of these is the entirely negative nature of the evidence he gathers, almost always taking the form of reportedly significant silences. Even as Server politely listens to his 'chatter,' to take just one of twenty examples, the narrator perceives in her silence 'a supremely unsuccessful attempt to say nothing. It said everything, and at the end of a minute my chatter . . . was hushed to positive awe by what it had conveyed' (101).

As elsewhere in the novel, the narrator's questionable perception in the scene above is said to be projected along competing vectors of intellect and feeling. Wandering the Newmarch grounds, he comes upon Server walking alone, 'exactly as if she had been there by the operation of my intelligence, or even by that – in a still happier way – of my feeling' (97). The condition of merely 'understanding' his subject as opposed to 'saving' her, because he will not cross the diegetic divide he sees between them, is said to be a relation of mere intellect as opposed to true sympathy. Resounding yet again with the sinister trope of enlightenment, the narrator's discourse recalls James's critique of Flaubert, the 'dryness and coldness' of his purely 'intellectual temperament,' which *Washington Square* had embodied in Catherine Sloper's father. The narrator's inability to 'save' his subjects is 'the price of [his] secret success, the lonely liberty and the intellectual joy' of witnessing the elaboration and unfolding of his observation and ideas (203).

[T]he special torment of my case was that the condition of light, of the satisfaction of curiosity . . . was in this direct way the sacrifice of feeling.

There was no point at which my assurance could, by the scientific method, judge itself complete enough not to regard feeling as an interference and, in consequence, as a possible check. If it had to go I knew well who went with it, but I wasn't there to save *them*. I was there to save my priceless pearl of an inquiry and to harden, to that end, my heart. (203)

The 'light' by which the investigator satisfies his curiosity returns in this fiction to smother the very promise of the sentimental project in general. The novel must 'see all' to approve sentiment – '[O]ne couldn't know anything without seeing all' (122) – but it can only do so from a cold Flaubertian mechanism that is inimical to feeling.

In this chapter I have been suggesting that the nineteenth-century novel's slowly evolving critique of what might be called a disciplinary sentimentalism reaches, in Henry James, the height of its lucidity. But there it also reaches a crisis, for even as the author insists on the individual's right to maintain the unarticulated reserve afforded by a posture of testimony, as opposed to confession, the moral import of his fiction depends on the old sentimental project of approving the disinterested interiority of the heroine and exposing the secrets of her counterparts, who inevitably use their testimonial reserve for evil purposes. It may seem far too tidy a conclusion to suggest that James's last great novel breaks through this crisis, in both its drama and narrative strategy, and emerges into what I would argue is a fully modernist consciousness of the novel's relation to testimony. Yet it is extraordinary that *The Golden Bowl* so adamantly refuses to violate European reserve, and thereby eliminates the possibility of judging what, if anything, the old-world emissaries may or may not be keeping there. It is an unprecedented restraint for James that can only leave his American heroine on the brink of madness. Even more significantly, the novel creates a proxy narrator, Mrs Assingham, who is clearly meant to embody – and even satirize – the 'observant and recording and interpreting mind' of the traditional Jamesian narrator, and plunges her into the frame of the fiction. This overseer is now among other subjects who are all perforce responsible to one another. She is now 'a reciter, a definite responsible intervening first person singular' – precisely the narrator that James bemoans in Charlie Marlow ('YG' 157). Like the sentimental investigators before her, Mrs Assingham grapples with the 'question' of Charlotte's 'sincerity,' and her husband astutely observes: 'That – I see – happens to be another of the questions you can't ask her. You have to do it all . . . as if you were playing some game with its rules drawn up – though who's to come down on you if you break them I don't quite see' (237–8). James deliberately shocks his mastermind, who would police the interior dispositions of those in the quadrangle she helped to create, with the inescapable accountability and responsibility of the testifier.

In his study of Conrad in 'The Younger Generation,' as we have seen, James insists that it is Marlow's testimonial condition as an object within the frame that irretrievably corrupts the author's narrative method. As we return to Conrad in the next chapter, which will exhibit key features of modernism's 'other face,' we will see him incorporating into the novel itself the opacity that James, too, finds sacred, but which the American must keep away from his novels – save the last – lest it betray the contract of comprehension to which he is bound. As both its operation and its thematics grapple with the enforced interior-exposures of the novel's sentimental tradition, Conrad's modernism joins James's in its increasing attention not just to privacy's 'right to exist,' as the American put it, but to its right to remain inarticulate, the right even of the testifier not to speak in a given forum. Yet Conrad's Marlow is himself the progeny of the novelistic confidante-narrator that had been born of the likes of Samuel Richardson, Laurence Sterne, Henry Mackenzie, and ultimately Jean-Jacques Rousseau, who normalized for the cosmopolitan raconteur a protocol of absolute self-disclosure, a transparent exposition of private into public life that would bring internal conscience into outer conduct. We have seen that Marlow arrived in the English novel to displace a theatre of 'external,' unframable interrogation of the subject – embodied in both the anonymous authority of the 'public inquiry' and in the depositional structure that had come to govern the novel itself – with a theatre of interlocution between commonly framed and mutually responsible subjects. Keeping in mind the particular late nineteenth-century expectations it deliberately thwarted, Marlow's emergence might seem to indicate, at first glance, an untroubled nostalgia for the much earlier sentimental hero, who also sought to rescue the personal attestation of another from the dislocated judgment and verdict of 'public opinion.' By tracing in the next chapter Marlow's immediate prehistory in The Nigger of the 'Narcissus' and his emergence into Lord Jim, I will demonstrate how and why the modernist champion of personal testimony dramatically transforms the sentimental ethos. Conrad takes it upon himself to maintain the evaluative authority of the sympathetic imagination, yet abolishes what the novel had formerly demanded of the testimony it rescued – that it trace itself back to a sentimentally approved interiority, the verification of which requires the 'exposure' of this interior into articulation. What Conrad will demand of the testifier in general – whether the sentimental journeyer himself or the subject of his tale – is rather his right to maintain the status of the emissary or prolocutor: the right to *represent*, whether the subject be himself or another, and to maintain the non-transparency necessarily implied in that term. In the case of *Narcissus*, the emissary will be Conrad himself, whose purpose is to render, on 'the public page' the 'hearts of the simple men who have for ages traversed' the solitudes of the sea (*Personal Record* 13).

# 4 'Abominable Confidence' from *The Nigger of the 'Narcissus'* to *Lord Jim*: Toward a New Sympathetic Novel

As we have seen, the innovation of unexplained, 'invisible' omniscience in the novel allows the reticence and therefore the disinterestedness of its protagonist to remain absolute – even as her admirable interior is brought continuously into discourse. Especially as the novel moved into the nineteenth century, however, some fictions took up arms against themselves, criticizing the reformist ideology that had initially inspired the sympathetic prose portrait and that tied virtue so strongly to interior accountability. *The Nigger of the 'Narcissus,'* one of the last novels of the century, keeps this self-criticism alive. On the one hand, the novel is utterly complicit with a disciplinary society and its injunction to 'expose' and register all interiority. On the other, it is the one forum in which the documented human subject can be brought to its most sympathetic and judicious evaluation. I will first explore this conflict within *Narcissus* (1897), and then how *Lord Jim* (1900) emerges as an answer to the problem, as a novel of sympathy that does not require a disciplinary exposure of its subjects. A close reading of James Wait's self-appointed caretakers aboard the *Narcissus* should also make us reconsider the postcolonial import of that novel. Here and elsewhere, Conrad depicts a 'second wave' of the European colonial project whose ideological engine is fuelled by a sentimentalism that purports to oppose it.

Long after its first appearance, *The Nigger of the 'Narcissus'* would remain, for its author, both a pinnacle and a plague. Even in 1914, just after his first popular success with *Chance*, and long since *Lord Jim*, *Heart of Darkness*, *Nostromo*, *The Secret Agent*, and *Under Western Eyes*, Joseph Conrad continued to hold out *Narcissus* as the book by which 'as an artist . . . I am willing to stand or fall' ('To My American Readers' 42).

Yet among all his fiction it also constitutes 'the bulk . . . [of] what may be called sea stuff,' which represents, for Conrad, 'barely one-tenth' of his work as a whole. *Narcissus* is thus heavily implicated in what he calls 'that obsession of my sea life' among critics and audiences, keeping his name forever bound to 'that infernal tale of ships' (Curle, *Conrad* 147).

This oft-cited complaint appears in a 1923 letter to one such critic, the author's friend Richard Curle, who had just written 'The History of Mr. Conrad's Books' as a review of the new Dent collected edition. Conrad upbraids Curle for his thesis that 'biographical matter' pertaining to the author provides the otherwise missing key to his work (Curle 148). This late-career protest against those who cannot dislodge the lore of his 'sea life' from their reception of his fiction might at first glance seem disingenuous. As he had advanced fully into the inner circle of English letters, years earlier, with the markedly geopolitical cast of *Nostromo*, Conrad nonetheless had remained perfectly willing and even eager to call attention to the credentials of his sea experience. Between 1904 and 1906, the ex-mariner published a series of memoir-essays in various periodicals, later to be compiled as *The Mirror of the Sea*. The tone of these, especially in their introductions, is not so much reminiscent as instructive. Their common goal is to translate for a land-lubbing audience the inadequate and distorted glimpses of life at sea disseminated in the press. Hence the first article in the series begins with a discussion of the terse terms by which 'Shipping Intelligence' is daily reported and of their tightly packed significance 'to a seaman'; several of the subsequent entries also cite as their impetus 'the degradation of the sea language in the daily press' (*Mirror* 183, 301).[1] The product of 'particularly benighted' mainlanders (146), this mutilated language seems to have been 'coined by landsmen to jar upon the ears of men for whom the splash of a falling anchor has been the closing sound of many phases of life' (302).[2]

The author's revulsion at Curle's literary analysis is triggered nonetheless precisely by the authority it grants Conrad by virtue of his lived experience. A year earlier, Conrad had shown the same exasperation at 'Joseph Conrad in the East,' another of Curle's journalistic projects. What Conrad bristles against in both essays is not simply the fact that a tale of his life comes to occlude his fiction, but rather the implication that such a narrative will uncover the more pertinent 'origins' of his writing (Curle, *Conrad* 113). Presuming that the value of Conrad's work lies in its proximity to a hidden historicity, Curle's second essay assures prospective consumers of the new collected edition that they will have obtained genuine goods; they will not have been cheated in the exotic import that is Conrad's fiction. In annoyed response, Conrad insists on the 'utter insignificance' of any cross-referencing between his history and fiction, and urges Curle not to cater to that 'special public . . . looking for exoticism' (153). Despite the ease with which Curle's hermeneutic flatteringly portrays his friend as a rare herald of truth because his writing has 'the basis of real experience' (Curle, 'History' 570), Conrad sees only 'its power to call attention away from things that matter in the region of art' (Curle, *Conrad* 113). 'You seem to believe,' he writes to Curle, 'in literalness and explicitness,' and that the 'facts of my life and even of my tales' should 'have that light turned onto it.' The primary argument behind Conrad's objections is clearly that his work could make no claim to art if it were reducible to its mimetic accomplishment or to the accuracy of its historicism. Yet they also show an aversion to Curle's implicit absolutism, the idea that whatever truths the fiction suggests are guaranteed and made unquestionable by their tie to real places and events. This aversion is what makes intelligible Conrad's pronouncement that 'the dogmatic, *ex-cathedra* tone' of Curle's highly flattering essay 'positively frightens me' (113).[3]

Sitting side by side with Conrad's objection, however, is the primary claim of *The Nigger of the 'Narcissus,'* articulated in its famous preface, to have painted a definitive portrait of the pre-steam mariner – a claim that would have no purchase without the popular record of his sea experience. Without the accompaniment of his biography, however variably written or conceived, *Narcissus* could not have presumed to render 'the vibration of life in the great world of waters, in the hearts of the simple men who have for ages traversed its solitudes' (*Personal* 13). In his 1912 *A Personal Record*, Conrad attributes this task of representation both to *Narcissus* and to the earlier memoir of his sea life. As it progresses, Conrad's career will become less and less dependent on the interpenetration of fact and fiction he underscores with this gesture. The growing weight of his 'artist' mantle will be enough to secure that portion of authority once gleaned, inadvertently or not, from his status as Herodotean witness – the traveller who has 'seen with his own eyes' what is invisible to a landed reading public, not least of which is the business end of its own colonial operations. At no point in Conrad's career, however, will his work fail to accumulate the profit Curle had explicitly solicited, the accrued interest of 'imported goods.' The

accumulation continues even after Conrad begins to satirize its operation within this very fiction, which so often portrays this attempt to
extract foundational truths from speculative forays into 'darkness' –
into a world far from English shores, beyond the too-familiar glow of
Western enlightenment.

Despite their vast divergences, contemporary readers from Fredric Jameson to Tony Jackson all agree on one point: that the testimonial mode of Conradian narrative is rooted, as Mark Conroy writes,
in a 'nostalgia for a situation in which a more immediate communion
between writer and public would be possible' (87). It is a consensus
founded on long-refined conclusions of narrative theory, surveyed at
the outset of this study, about the implications of 'embedded,' surrogate
narrators. Most of Conrad's contemporaries, however, being relatively
ignorant of any 'laws' of narrative structure, had a different take on the
matter. They considered Conrad's storytelling to be not enough suffused with such nostalgia – lacking, if anything, the 'immediate communion' one might expect from its apparently confessional posture.[4]
Intertwined with his explanation of the autobiographical impulse that
had led him to pen *A Personal Record*, Conrad remarks on this reception
in the preface:

> It seems to me that in one, at least, authoritative quarter of criticism I am
> suspected of a certain unemotional, grim acceptance of facts – of what the
> French would call *sécheresse du coeur*. Fifteen years of unbroken silence be-
> fore praise or blame testify sufficiently to my respect for criticism . . . But
> this is more of a personal matter, reaching the man behind the work, and
> therefore it may be alluded to in a volume which is a personal note in the
> margin of the public page . . .
>   My answer is that if it be true that every novel contains an element of
> autobiography . . . then there are some of us to whom an open display of
> sentiment is repugnant . . . In a task which mainly consists in laying one's
> soul more or less bare to the world, a regard for decency, even at the cost
> of success, is but the regard for one's own dignity which is inseparably
> united with the dignity of one's work. (13–14)

As he deliberately brings together historical and fictional biographies,
Conrad's oft-repeated concern with the role of 'sentiment' in both
genres inevitably recalls the common history of autobiography and the
early novel. From this perspective, Conrad's definition of 'confession'

elsewhere in the *Personal Record* as 'a form of literary activity discredited by Jean-Jacques Rousseau' would have to be taken more seriously than as a passing irony.[5] Conrad evokes the spectre of Rousseauvian self-writing to distance it from his own *Record* ('The matter at hand . . . is to keep these reminiscences from turning into confessions' [92]). Confession has been discredited by the Frenchman, Conrad goes on to write, 'on account of the extreme thoroughness he brought to the work of justifying his own existence' (92). As if in response to autobiography's complicity with confession, Conrad does not apply the generic term to his *Record*, calling it instead a collection of 'reminiscences,' a 'personal note on the public page.' Yet he does call attention to the 'element of autobiography' that 'every novel contains' (14).

Conrad forces us to ask how one might lay 'one's soul more or less bare to the world' without the posture of confession or self-justification that was once indispensable to autobiography. The answer to this question can begin with a consideration of what it means for Conrad to so explicitly align his life-writing with *The Nigger of the 'Narcissus.'* The author persistently draws attention to this book's function as a diplomatic envoy, on behalf of working seamen, to a landed audience. We are asked throughout the *Personal Record* to give its testimony the status of an envoy's statement on behalf of other men. As he does with Marlow's 'personal record,' which is always addressed to a group of semi-familiar strangers who happen to have gathered round him after dinner or on an idle deck, Conrad presents even his own record as a statement objectified within a public forum – a 'personal' note, perhaps, but one that has always been prepared for 'the public page,' and announced as such. Through *Narcissus*, Conrad speaks for sea labourers, represents them to the public in the role of an advocate. The novel itself figures this advocacy in how the crewmen speak for their ship. 'She was beautiful and had a weakness. We loved her no less for that. We admired her qualities aloud . . . and the consciousness of her only fault we kept buried in the silence of our profound affection' (31). At no point in the novel is the ship's hidden 'weakness' enunciated, or even alluded to again; nowhere is 'her only fault' confessed. It should go without saying that if the 'content' of this secret is nowhere articulated or even suggested, then there is no content.[6] As critics chastise Conrad for the 'obscurity' such a moment creates, they miss the whole point of the gesture as a tribute to the envoy in general, to his responsibility for creating the terms by which his client will be articulated in a public sphere. As we glimpsed in James, and will see in respect to *Narcissus*, Conrad continually draws our attention to this prerogative of representation even when advocate and client are the same person. As opposed to the confessor, who would have been obliged, in the name of transparency, to sculpt all his secrets into discourse, the testifier maintains her right to her own unarticulated secret, to what Jacques Derrida would describe as an ever-present demurral. In the testifier's relation to silence, Derrida finds not just a right, but an ineradicable dependence:

> I can only testify, in the strict sense of the word, from the instant when no one can, in my place, testify to what I do. What I testify to is, at that very instant, my secret; it remains reserved for me. I must be able to keep secret precisely what I testify to; it is the condition of the testimony in a strict sense. (*Demeure* 30)

The statements on Conrad's various stages are rarely intelligible as confessions; they are rather testimonies negotiated through an inevitably public arena. Conrad continually draws our attention to the common ground of all his portraiture in both fiction and biography, whether these representations rest on the authority of the littérateur or of the witness – the common ground that is the testimonial condition of any prolocutor. It is an emphasis that strains against the bio-critical program Curle had begun, and which is now the normal approach to the tangle of fiction and autobiography in Conrad's writing: a program of rigorously policing the discrepancies and concurrencies between the facts of the author's life as we know them and his stated recollections in fiction, letter, and memoir. When Frederick Karl, for instance, seizes upon Conrad's unusually stern lecture to Curle – against ferreting out the 'origins' of his fiction in his biography – Karl sees it only as the symptom of an 'intense secretiveness . . . almost conspiratorial in its approach to his past and his conception of it' (869).[7] Just as criticism since James has been troubled by the obscuring 'shadow' Marlow reportedly casts, as a narrated object, over his own narration, most commentary on Conrad's self-writing emphasizes, as Owen Knowles puts it, the 'unofficial and unreliable' nature of any such autobiography (2). Of course Conrad is hardly the only figure to receive continual posthumous rebuke for his failure to 'tell all.' Given the author's frequent and concentrated discourse on precisely this question, however, the modern biographer's habit of holding his subject to the ethos of Rousseauvian confession – as if none other could possibly be expected, or even conceived – is an especially telling measure of the continuing heterodoxy of Conrad's argument.[8]

Conrad attempts to distinguish the testimonial condition from 'confession' as it had been sculpted within the sentimental tradition of the novel. Yet in order to challenge the stigmas of insincerity and opacity that belong to the 'prepared statement' of the testifier, he must go out of his way to dissolve the dichotomy that sets this prepared statement in opposition to one that would come 'straight from the heart.' What Conrad demands for any of his testifying clients – Jim, Marlow, the *Titanic* crew, and even himself – is the authority given those who would deliver the 'heart' and even 'soul more or less bare,' even if they do not adopt the posture of the willing or unwilling confessor. He will not, in other words, require his testifiers to perform scenes of forced or unwitting exposure, nor pretend that a 'reading' public, in the broadest sense, was not the intended recipient of their delivery.

As a responsible yet discreet advocate, Marlow is Conrad's ideal envoy. As I will explore in detail below, Marlow represents a pinnacle in Conrad's artistry because the captain accomplishes precisely what the traditional sentimental novel could not – a sympathetic representation of other minds and other lives without enforcing confession or personal transparency. In *The Nigger of the 'Narcissus,'* however, Marlow's reign had not yet begun. The earlier novel had developed neither the discourse nor the craftsmanship that could conceive a testimonial condition that would be free of sentimental confession. Although the narrative explicitly speaks on behalf of the ship's crew, the bulk of it comes from no source locatable within the fabula. What takes over as its hero, then, is a silence, a positive unarticulation to which James, too, had appealed when he felt the weight of his era's 'desire to rake and be raked' (*American* 168). Conrad himself – whose name is an author-effect that has never escaped objectification, as Curle's efforts make clear, whether or not the author puts another testifier on stage 'within' the fiction – repeatedly draws attention to a single motive behind his creation of a voice that would be an ambassador for working sailors. He performs this service because they are a 'generation [who] lived inarticulate and indispensable.'

> They were the everlasting children of the mysterious sea. Their successors are the grown-up children of a discontented earth . . . [I]f they had learned how to speak they have also learned how to whine. But the others were strong and mute; they were effaced, bowed and enduring . . . (*Narcissus* 15)

They were 'voiceless men – but men enough to scorn in their hearts the sentimental voices that bewailed the hardness of their fate' (15). The 'sentimental voices' cited so regularly in the novel are those that cry for reform, those of '[w]ell-meaning people' on shore who 'had tried to represent those men as whining over every mouthful of food' (15). But the voice of sentiment has been mastered, too, by some of the sailors themselves, by the 'successors' of the earlier generation. In *Narcissus*, this voice belongs to Donkin, the model specimen in Conrad's fiction of the lazy, cunning, shirking, whining, would-be labour unionizer. The depiction of this 'votary of change' (9), this 'sympathetic and deserving creature that knows all about his rights' (6), seems to undercut the workman's rhetoric we saw in the *Titanic* essays. There, the targeted 'commercial and industrial interests' (commanded from offices 'with adequate and no doubt comfortable furniture') are set in class opposition to 'the masses of men who work' ('Some Reflexions' 309).

Yet the irresponsibility Conrad continually attributes to Donkin, the illegitimate working man, begins to appear rather continuous with the irresponsibility he had attributed to the Board of Trade. Just as the board had hidden behind its own spectrality – such entities having 'no souls to be saved and no bodies to be kicked . . . no limbs and no physiognomy' ('Some Reflexions' 217) – so does Donkin manage to cut the thread between his incendiary statements and the named body to which they would be traced. At the climactic confrontation between captain and crew, after the commander charges James Wait of being 'shamming sick' and relieves him of duty, Donkin stokes the fire of unrest while keeping his own 'limbs and physiognomy' safely off stage:

> There were exclamations of surprise, triumph, indignation. The dark group of men swung across the light . . . 'We've got to say somethink about that,' screeched Donkin from the rear. – 'Never mind, Jimmy, we will see you righted,' cried several together. An elderly seaman stepped to the front. 'D'ye mean to say, sir,' he asked ominously, 'that a sick chap ain't allowed to get well in this 'ere hooker?' Behind him Donkin whispered excitedly amongst a staring crowd where no one spared him a glance, but Captain Allistoun shook a forefinger at the angry bronzed face of the speaker. – 'You – you hold your tongue,' he said warningly. – 'This isn't the way,' clamoured two or three younger men. – 'Are we bloomin' masheens?' inquired Donkin in a piercing tone, and dived under the elbows of the front rank. – 'Soon show 'm we ain't boys . . .' (74)

Conrad's 'mob scene' elaborates on its model in the Shakespearean Roman play. As with the plebeians in *Coriolanus*, there is no univocality, no single trajectory of desire in this crowd. In Shakespeare, however, the Donkin-like tribunes draw the crowd aside in order to coax the disparate 'tongues o' th' common mouth' into a single appeal, moulding their discontent within a space and time 'prior' to the fully public stage that will include the ears and voices of the ruling patricians. Donkin's seduction of his mates rather takes place amidst the fully gathered society of the *Narcissus*. His body hidden behind others, behind the 'bronzed face' available and responsible to the captain, Donkin's gradual possession of the crew's voice takes place in the space between his own piercing cries ('Are we bloomin' masheens?') and the shouts that follow, whose attribution cannot be ascertained ('Soon show 'm we ain't boys'). Through this gap, both the voice and face of Donkin escape responsibility.

Two years after *Narcissus*'s publication, in an epistolary conversation with Cunninghame Graham that corners the author into a rarely visited socio-political register, Conrad makes clear again that his politics are ruled by questions of embodiment. A close, although recently found friend, Graham had asked Conrad to put his cultural weight as an artist – still quite modest, at this point – in the service of a public meeting held by the Social Democratic Federation. Although he would not join Graham on the speakers' platform, Conrad, despite his protest, did attend the socialist gathering:

> I can not admit the idea of [international] fraternity not so much because I believe it impracticable, but because its propaganda (the only thing really tangible about it) tends to weaken the national sentiment the preservation of which is my concern . . . If the idea of nationhood brings suffering and its service brings death, that is always worth more than service to the ghosts of a dead eloquence – precisely because that eloquence is disembodied.[9] (*Collected Letters* 2:158–9)

It may have been his own review of the letter, with its implication that 'the idea of nationhood' or 'the national sentiment' is of greater 'embodiment' than the same sentiment on a global scale, that led Conrad to close with: 'This letter is incoherent, like my life, but the highest logic is there nevertheless – the logic that leads to madness. But everyday worries make us forget the cruel truth. It's fortunate' (161).[10]

As evident in its treatment of Donkin, George Flack, and the *Aspern* narrator, the English novel had long passed the phase in which it required itself to infuse signs of femininity into its male enforcers of sentimental discipline. In terms of a larger geopolitical fabula, however, which Conrad will increasingly elaborate over the course of his career, there remains no ambiguity about the politicized feminism ultimately agitating Donkin and all such 'Plimsoll men.'[11] In *Heart of Darkness*, the perception Marlow discerns 'back home' that he himself is acting as an 'apostle' of reform in Africa – an 'emissary of light' who will contribute to 'weaning those ignorant millions from their horrid ways' – is said to belong not only to his aunt but to a genuine petticoat ruler, 'the wife of the high dignitary' who has given Marlow his appointment (12).

By the time he gets to *Under Western Eyes*, which finally touches on the ideology of political revolution – not merely its 'psychology' and its stratagems, as in fictions like *Nostromo* – Conrad has condensed a global 'enlightenment' into a single caricature: the world-famous revolutionary Madame de S—, said by one of her champions to be 'the quintessence of feminine intuition which will understand any perplexity . . . by the irresistible, enlightening force of sympathy. Nothing can remain obscure before that . . . inspired penetration, this true light of femininity' (151).[12]

*The Nigger of the 'Narcissus'* dignifies its labourers in their heroism but also in multiform recognitions that they are 'indispensable' to an industrial empire, 'like stone caryatides that hold up in the night the lighted halls of a resplendent and glorious edifice' (15). As in so many Victorian fictions, however, these tributes are distributed among workers as a reward for their muteness. Donkin is nothing less than an interloper in the forecastle because he 'knows nothing . . . of the *unexpressed* faith, of the *unspoken* loyalty that knits together a ship's company' (6, my emphasis); he is a counterfeit crewman because of his ability to discourse with 'filthy eloquence upon the right of labour to live' (107). Thus, when the crew debarks at the end of the story after their harrowing, death-defying trial at sea, only Donkin is comfortably in his element here on terra firma. Unlike his inarticulate comrades awkwardly awaiting their pay in the Board of Trade disbursement office, Donkin can converse 'with animation to the clerk, who thought him an intelligent man' (105).

This motif reaches a Foucaultian apex in a fevered dream of the novel's eponymous 'nigger,' James Wait. The emphatically civic images of his vision represent the milieu of the sympathetic 'landlubbers' for whom Donkin is a 'pet' (6), and in which 'he was more at home than any of us' (105). In Wait's dream, these images transform into the bars of a prison, the warden of which is apparently the sentiment-enforcer Donkin himself. Wait finds himself on land, where a reformist, civic society is indistinguishable from a penal complex:

> A place without any water! No water! A policeman with the face of Donkin drank a glass of beer by the side of an empty well . . . [Wait] expanded his hollow chest. The air streamed in, carrying away in its rush a lot of strange things that resembled houses, trees, people, lamp-posts . . . But he was in jail! They were locking him up! (69)

Everywhere else in the novel, Donkin is a creature weak and insubstantial as a 'scarecrow,' and seems perpetually 'cuffed, kicked, rolled in the mud' (5–6). The power of the police infused into him by Wait's dream is intelligible only as it has been for Henry James's Henrietta Stackpole, George Flack, and the *Aspern* narrator. Like theirs, Donkin's power rests only in his relentless attempts to 'tear the veil, unmask, expose, leave no refuge – a perfidious desire of truthfulness!' (*Narcissus* 92).

Among his fellow sea labourers, Donkin revives the sentimental voices that fill his ears on land and provide 'conscientious analysis of their unappreciated worth.' Hence the crew begins to dream 'enthusiastically of the time when every lonely ship would travel over a serene sea, manned by a wealthy and well-fed crew of satisfied skippers' (63). Here the novel silently equates the injustice that labour advocates see in the merchant marine with the inevitable 'injustice' of violent seas. This kind of caricature in Conrad's writing has rightly drawn Marxist critical attention to its naturalization of industrial labour conditions. If there is such a thing as a final or 'ruling' effect of such passages, however, it is not comprised solely of the political rationalization that they undoubtedly accomplish, especially when isolated in this way. To the reader of *The Nigger of the 'Narcissus,'* this depiction of a humanity bemoaning its 'unappreciated worth' in a violent elemental universe that does not value earth's creatures will sound, first and foremost, like yet another note in the novel's persistent harangue against humanism in general. For Conrad, humanism is the primary philosophical accomplice of a confession-enforcing sentimentalism. Yet just as the novel's sympathetic portraiture is indebted to the sentimental tradition it rebels against, so too does its antihumanism continually invert itself. As we will see, *Narcissus* makes clear that its own import is utterly void without our irrational attachment to the ship and its crew, to this piece of flotsam among all that sinks and swims in an inhuman universe.

Donkin is meant to stand for a mankind so enmeshed in the safety net of civic structure and liberal-humanist law that it imagines the churning earth itself to be beholden to the rights of man.[13] The note sounded by this character at the beginning of the novella culminates in a tyranny of humanism that Wait himself comes to represent in what is the central theme of the novel. To recall: *The Nigger of the 'Narcissus'* is the story of two seemingly unrelated catastrophes, wrought by forces external to the routine harmony of the *Narcissus*. On the ship's return voyage to England from the Indian peninsula, a typhoon nearly destroys the vessel, seizing it for one breathless night partially capsized in the water, the crew clinging all the while to masts and port rails. Emerging literally in the centre of the story, this vast movement of sea and sky nevertheless fails to hold the crew in awe of the inhuman sublime. They are already in thrall to an opposing power – James Wait, a 'St. Kitt's nigger' who had arrived on deck like a portent, enlisted at the last minute in Bombay. Almost as soon as the ship reaches deep waters early in the tale, the ominous cough that had been rattling Wait's chest makes its claim; he takes to his bed, apparently near death. The crew is more than a little suspicious that his sickness is a sham; they 'hesitated between pity and mistrust.' Yet Wait lords over his shipmates the spectre of his imminent demise, at every moment shaking 'before our eyes the bones of his . . . infamous skeleton' (22). The uncertainty about Wait's good faith ultimately enslaves the crew.

> It interfered daily with our occupations, with our leisure, with our amusements. We had no songs and no music in the evening . . . so as not to interfere with Jimmy's, possibly, last slumber on earth . . . We served him in his bed with rage and humility . . . [H]e had the secret of life, that confounded dying man, and he made himself master of every moment of our existence. (22–3)

Wait exerts a tyranny that forbids consciousness of anything outside the confines of human life. It is a tyranny that continues to hold sway over the crew even after the sardonic Conradian gods deliver their final blow, when it becomes clear to us that James Wait is indeed mortally ill, although he himself continues to believe he is fooling everyone with an act. Now, mortality itself becomes something intolerable, an affront.

He was demoralizing. Through him we were becoming highly humanised, tender, complex, excessively decadent: we understood the subtlety of his fear, sympathised with all his repulsions, shrinkings, evasions, delusions – as though we had been over-civilized, and rotten . . . (85)

Hence, 'Falsehood triumphed. It triumphed through doubt, through stupidity, through pity, through sentimentalism' (85).

It may seem perverse to insist on reading James Wait through the 'sentimentalism' particularly conceived by the early European novel. It will seem a strain to historicize the character in this way, especially in a critical field that has given us good reason to understand Wait primarily as an opportunistic colonial acquisition on Conrad's part, a casually racist means of encoding themes of abjection and perversity into black and white.[14] Unexpectedly, however, the racial imaginary of *Narcissus* also sets in motion other machinery. It helps to keep in view, for instance, the opacity necessary to the testimonial condition (Wait claims to be ill early on, but '[y]ou couldn't see that there was anything wrong with him: a nigger does not show' [27]). On an ideological level, furthermore, the novel demonstrates how Wait's blackness has also been useful to the moral apologias of colonialism, such as are commanded by Podmore, the *Narcissus*'s evangelical cook. Podmore frequently wields the conceptual instruments Conrad has been teaching us to associate with sentimentalism: 'His heart overflowed with tenderness, with comprehension, with the desire to meddle, with anxiety for the soul of that black man . . . with the feeling of might' (71). The shadow of coercion and even violence cast over Podmore's 'tenderness' is the dark side of 'comprehension,' which we have seen looming, for Conrad, in that other agent of evangelical enlightenment: the press.

In this 'mighty' evangelical tenderness toward the 'St. Kitt's nigger' is a consciousness of what the West Indies have meant to the sympathetic tradition of the novel. From *The Man of Feeling* to *Persuasion*, the new money that comes to the aid of the novel's non-pedigreed heroes habitually comes from the Caribbean. As I suggested in the previous chapter, this money quietly underwrites and justifies an economy of sentiment that purports to challenge an old 'worldly' order. The full significance of Conrad's choice of James Wait's native land reveals itself against this tradition, underscored by Jerry Allen's suggestion that the author may have deliberately altered the Georgia homeland of the real sailor who inspired the character.[15]

For a reminder of the peculiar labour the Caribbean has performed for the early novel, we can recall the example of Henry Mackenzie's

*Julia de Roubigné.* On his uncle's plantation in the West Indies, Savillon convinces the master to set his slaves free. He does so, the novel tells us, to demonstrate the effect of sentimental conscience on the Mammonist realm always within this genre's sites, 'the world.' 'I never valued wealth,' he writes typically to Julia, 'but as it might render me, in the language of the world, more worthy of thee' (2:173). Yet, strangely, this revolution will not disturb the plantation's operations, as Savillon repeatedly assures his uncle, for even 'the most savage and sullen' among the slaves 'had principles of gratitude, which a good master might improve to his advantage' (2:32). Savillon knows that the new freemen on the island will now have nowhere to turn for sustenance. They must continue to work the plantation, but now they do so happily, because their labour has been renamed 'chuse-work.' Their remuneration, which is immediately handed back for food and lodging, is now 'pay.' Each slave now knows himself, furthermore, to have his own capacity for sentiment – his own sensibility, interiority, and identity. It is a revolution that changes everything; everything, that is, except the material conditions and operations of 'the world,' where nothing has been disturbed, and where the profitability of the plantation has, in fact, increased precisely through the 'gratitude' of its labourers. Therefore, where the uncle had once lamented, in 'a language natural to the overseer,' that the value of Yambu, 'leader' of the slaves, is halved by his intractability, Savillon 'answered him, in his own style, that I hoped to improve his price some hundreds of livres' (2:32). 'I should undoubtedly profit,' Savillon writes, 'if I could establish [in the slaves] some other motive, whose impulse was more steady than those of punishment and terror' (2:31). Producing novel 'motives' with its new discursive regime, sentimentalism accomplishes the secret, smiling despotism that Savillon had earlier discovered in his love for Julia. It had 'conquered without tumult, and become despotic under the semblance of freedom' (2:6). We have no way of knowing if Conrad actually read Mackenzie's work, but in *The Nigger of the 'Narcissus,'* the crew's 'devotion' to James Wait is made fully – if not exclusively – intelligible by the sentimentalism the Scottish writer helped to define, and by its strategy of bestowing freedom and justice upon the abject of the world. As reported of one sailor, this devotion made him 'as sentimentally careful of his nigger as a model slave owner' (*Narcissus* 86).

Sentimentalism is a disciplinary device that helps to contain the most infamous of the empire's 'labour questions,' but it also carries forward the sympathetic imagination that makes the novel itself, according to Conrad, a corrective to historiography, one without which Charlie Marlow would have no reason for being. In the 'sympathetic and deserving creature' Donkin, the lone witness of James Wait's death, Conrad keeps both inheritances in view:

> And Donkin watching the end of that hateful nigger, felt the anguishing grasp of a great sorrow on his heart at the thought that he himself, some day, would have to go through it all – just like this – perhaps! His eyes became moist. 'Poor beggar,' he murmured. (95)

A possibility within all sentimentalism, Donkin's sympathy is a function of narcissism. Then, as if without contradiction to his tears, Donkin instantly moves to exploit the incapacity of this dying 'hateful nigger' by pillaging Wait's sea chest before his still-living eyes. The scene exhibits a smooth and immediate transition from a prototypical moment of sentimental epiphany to an act of looting the object of sympathy.

The extended portrait of Wait's wasting, dying body significantly anticipates the episode in *Heart of Darkness* when Marlow stumbles upon a grove sheltering several starved and fatally overworked Congolese, 'the place where some of the helpers had withdrawn to die' (17). Just as Donkin finally watches Wait's eyes 'blaze up and go out at once' (95), so does Marlow watch a 'white flicker' in a pair of African eyes as it 'died out slowly.' Those drawing their final breaths in this clearing are men who had been 'reclaimed' to the status of 'helpers' of the colonial regime. Like the slaves Mackenzie had emancipated, these 'moribund shapes were free as air – and nearly as thin' (17). Recalling Savillon's profitable sentimentalism in *Narcissus*, Donkin's act of pillaging Wait even as he weeps for him duplicates the parasitic relation Conrad sees between these agents of 'reform' and even the bloodiest colonial regimes.

The historical divide suggested by this parasitism is part of Conrad's perennial discrimination between a first and second wave of European colonialism. Throughout Conrad's oeuvre, talkative latecomers drift into outposts of empire to scrounge their subsistence among paths already forged by previous colonial adventurers. In Conrad's first fiction, for instance, the opportunistic trader Almayer finds himself stranded in a remote backwater of Borneo as a consequence not of his own intrepid

adventure but of having ridden the seafaring coattails of Captain Lingard, a true first-generation marauder. Lingard, the silent, shadowy
discoverer of lucrative sea-lanes in the Malay Archipelago and beyond,
makes repeat appearances in Conrad's fiction. He represents the forces
that had first penetrated resistant colonial interiors and increased the
flow of materials upon which the comparatively impotent members
of 'civilization' would come to depend.[16] One of the ways Almayer is
clearly marked off from Lingard is through the characteristic of his literacy. Just as the parasitic Donkin will be shown to be unusually comfortable amid the Board of Trade bureaucracy, Almayer is said to have
fallen naturally into the role of 'a kind of captain's clerk' to Lingard
during their initial voyage out. Whereas the object of the captain's desire is always the rich but repellant interior of exotic lands, the object
of Almayer's is the established comforts of Europe. *Almayer's Folly* is
the story of this second-wave colonialist's attempt to buy a better perch
for himself in the homeland of empire through one last 'big score,' one
final act of looting. Like Donkin's, Almayer's path back to England – to
a more prosperous 'level' of civilization than he has yet to attain – must
lead him, first, through a despised barbarian interior. Edward Said
points to Marlow's dramatized audience of men 'drawn largely from
the business world' as the author's 'way of emphasizing the fact that
during the 1890s the business empire, once an adventurous and often
individualistic enterprise, had become the empire of business' (*Culture* 23). Yet that emphasis is almost always borne in Conrad's fiction
by the colonial actors themselves.

Marlow, and even Conrad himself, are no exceptions. Conrad's
alter ego often acknowledges his own allegiance to the 'second wave,'
represented by an ever-expanding merchant marine that exploits the
Lingard-forged sea-paths of the world. Conrad goes out of his way
to portray Marlow's work in Africa as inevitably in the service of an
evangelism, a self-serving sentimentalism – part of what he calls 'the
new forces at work' in Africa. In *Heart of Darkness*, Marlow's berth,
his employment with 'the Company,' has been secured by his aunt. As
he takes a final cup of tea with her before leaving England, he realizes with a start that she imagines his role in Congo to be '[s]omething
like an emissary of light, something like a lower sort of apostle' (12),
and indeed Marlow's movement among colonial outposts is secured,
smoothed, and protected by the sponsorship of his aunt and the accom-
panying perception that he represents 'the new forces at work' in the

land. At his first station stop in West Africa, Marlow asks a Company employee about this Mr Kurtz he keeps hearing about, whose painting he has just glimpsed on the wall – an image of a Columbia, a woman 'draped and blindfolded, carrying a lighted torch,' whose 'sinister' glare seems to combat a 'sombre – almost black' background. We cannot help but recall the images of Columbia James evokes, in *Portrait* and elsewhere, holding aloft their sinister enlightenment. The employee responds:

> 'He is an emissary of pity, and science, and progress . . . We want,' he began to declaim suddenly, 'for the guidance of the cause entrusted to us by Europe, so to speak, higher intelligence, wide sympathies . . . [B]ut I daresay you know . . . You are of the new gang – the gang of virtue. The same people who sent him specially also recommended you.' (26)

Here Conrad directly acknowledges that the sympathetic imagination Marlow commands – which elevates the novel, according to the author, over mere historiography or journalism – is also necessarily implicated in all of the consequences of an 'interior'-seeking sentimentalism. *Heart of Darkness* looks directly at the danger of Conrad's own rapprochement, both as mariner and novelist, with a second wave of European colonialism – with decadents, deluded by sentimentalism, profiteering in the tracks of unapologetic 'adventure.'

Conrad's bisection of colonialism into distinct waves of opportunists often grafts itself onto the dichotomy we have already seen between the 'mute . . . and enduring' sailors of an earlier generation and those who have learned discontent through the forbidden fruit of speech. In *The Nigger of the 'Narcissus,'* the silence of which Donkin 'knows nothing' is fully embodied in the ancient mariner named Singleton, 'a lonely relic of a devoured and forgotten generation' (15). It is Singleton who is said to represent the 'voiceless men' of the forecastle who nevertheless know enough to 'scorn in their hearts the sentimental voices' that attempt to speak for them. He is one of the strong, 'unthinking' caryatides that have maintained the edifice of empire, and the last of his generation: 'The men who could understand his silence were gone' (15). The echo of Donkin's discursively agile sentimentalism – which helps to manufacture both the 'rights' and the 'freedom' of man – asks us to think about Singleton in relation to the 'silent sufferer' that the sentimental novel introduced. As we have seen elsewhere in *Narcissus*,

Conrad gradually and almost imperceptibly leads Singleton's scorn of sentiment to what would otherwise be a shocking antihumanism. Conrad's implied reader greets the old sailor's selfless asceticism as something familiar and English, only to discover it has inured him to something strange and continental:

> He had never given a thought to his mortal self. He looked upon the immortal sea . . . that claimed all the days of his tenacious life, and, when life was over, would claim the worn-out body of its slave . . . He radiated unspeakable wisdom, hard unconcern, the chilling air of resignation. (60, 80)

He is a being 'untouched by human emotions' (25). In the face of Wait's death, 'Singleton as usual held aloof, appearing to scorn the insignificant events of an ended life' (87). The scene of the aged seaman's final farewell to his fellows does not, surprisingly, surprise us: 'Somebody opened the door for him, and the patriarchal seaman passed through unsteadily, without as much as a glance at any of us' (105). Like Savillon, Julie, or Pamela, Singleton is deliberately conceived as a being of pure sacrifice. His disinterestedness, however, is not just alien to theirs; it actually assaults their claim to the term. Unlike his novelistic forebears, Singleton cannot 'cash in' and register his sacrifice to a letter-reading other. A man 'profound' but utterly 'unconscious' (80), Singleton can lay claim to no secret renunciation whatever, since he has no thought of sacrifice – no unspoken thought, even – to hold in reserve, to create the space of reserve.

Yet Singleton's sacrifices, in the end, *are* registered; they are brought to account in the ledger that is *The Nigger of the 'Narcissus.'* True to its purpose in the post-epistolary novel, the omniscient narrator of this tale comes to the rescue of the inarticulate Singleton. It penetrates his opacity as no mere witness could, articulating a knowledge and an evaluation of his long and secret life, past and present. More importantly, omniscience promises to bring his sacrifice to light without having to construct scenes of penetration into private ledgers – through 'overheard' conversations or 'found' letters.

But does the novel fulfil this promise? The answer is unclear because the omniscient status of this narrator suddenly, famously, collapses. It does so precisely as the novel begins to excavate Singleton's 'vast empty past' – to shine light on this 'lonely relic of a devoured and forgotten generation' (15): 'Singleton, who had sailed to the southward since the age of twelve, who in the last forty-five years had lived (as we had calculated from his papers) no more than forty months ashore' (3). The 'we' is startling not only because the narration had until now followed the conventions of third-person omniscience, which had also been the norm for Conrad's previous fiction, but because it comes immediately on the heels of a paragraph that explicitly conceives British sailors in general as a 'they.' Throughout the novel, 'they' are a collective somewhat incomprehensible to this narrator. After rendering the surprising image of Singleton reading, on deck, a copy of *Pelham; or, Adventures of a Gentleman*, the narrator explains:

> The popularity of Bulwer-Lytton in the forecastles of Southern-going ships is a wonderful and bizarre phenomenon. What ideas do his polished and so curiously insincere sentences awaken in the simple minds of the big children who people those dark and wandering places of the earth? What meaning their rough, inexperienced souls can find in the elegant verbiage of his pages? What excitement? – what forgetfulness? – what appeasement? Mystery! (3)

The sailors' precocious fascination with 'the characteristics of a gentleman' reappears in the following chapter. 'One said – "It's money as does it." Another maintained: – "No, it's the way they speak."' Their preoccupation is again said to mark them as 'children of the sea,' to recall the title Conrad chose for the first American edition of the novel. 'They disputed endlessly, obstinate and childish . . . while the soft breeze . . . stirred the tumbled hair with a touch passing and light like an indulgent caress' (19–20). One can almost hear the narrator himself affectionately mussing the collective hair of the crew. The desire and motivation of these men is sometimes pure 'Mystery!' to this storyteller, and yet it is just after this declaration that the 'we' appears, announcing that the novel's ruling voice is, in fact, one of those children. The narrator now becomes 'one of us,' to anticipate Marlow's famous pronouncement in what will be the author's next novel.

The narrator, we now know, belongs to the forecastle – a regular seaman, not an officer. But he remains shadowy throughout the story, rarely self-identified in the prose, and never a central object within the narrative frame. He often dissolves into omniscience, privy to psychic landscapes and conversations behind closed doors. Yet even if the narrator were clearly, consistently established as an individual within the fabula, that determination would not settle the question of whom he speaks for, as an envoy. Even with the arrival of Charlie Marlow in Conrad's world, it is impossible to determine whether he speaks for regular sailors, his fellow officers, or wistful ex-mariners. Does he testify on behalf of the 'children of the sea' within the forecastle, or rather for those to whom these men are a 'mystery,' and who seek sympathetic enlightenment about them? Marlow's great service is not in settling the question of whom Conrad's narrator would represent, but in concretizing the representational condition of all attestation. Through Marlow, the operation of the 'envoy' – as applicable to any writing, in the Derridean sense – becomes a major part of Conrad's drama. Although *The Nigger of the 'Narcissus'* anticipates the Marlow narratives in rejecting postures of confession and comprehension, it lacks the envoy that enables the positive alternative: testimony without confession and interpretation without a totalized comprehension.

One of the jarring consequences of this lack for *Narcissus* is an internal battle the novel must wage against the anonymous omniscience it half-heartedly embraces. The conflict works its way into an experiment the novel conducts whereby authorship itself is embodied in the figure of the captain. In a story that truly is 'A Tale of the Forecastle,' as its original subtitle announced, the commander remains largely in the background. His presence is strongest at the dramatic peak, when everything hovers at the brink of death as the ship weathers the gale half-capsized. As the men begin their rail-clinging vigil into the night, when the existence of the *Narcissus* seems to hang on the arbitrary whims of wind and water, Captain Allistoun 'seemed with his eyes to hold the ship up in a superhuman concentration of effort' (40). Even hours into the siege, 'with living eyes he was still holding the ship up heeding no one, as if lost in the unearthly effort of that endeavour' (45). The fate of the *Narcissus* seems to depend on the sustained concentration and strength of Allistoun's attention. More distinctly than most life-or-death scenarios, this one warns that if all hands disappear into the water, so will the possibility of narrative. In a letter he writes while composing the novel, Conrad encourages such a reading: 'I am going on' with the story, Conrad writes. 'Another 20 pages of type . . . will see the end, such as it is. And won't I breathe! Till it's over there's no watch below for me' (*Collected Letters* 1:321). The same metaphor appears in the author's note 'To My Readers in America' about the novel: 'I had much to do with [James Wait],' Conrad writes. 'He was in my watch' (41).

Given this language it is perhaps not surprising that the master of the *Narcissus* also seems to wield powers of comprehension and penetration that normally belong only to omniscience. His sailors often find themselves 'expectant and appeased as if that old man, who looked at no one, had possessed the secret of their uneasy indignations and desires, a sharper vision, a clearer knowledge' (79). The captain faces the crew 'with his worn, steely gaze, that by a universal illusion looked straight into every individual pair of the twenty pairs of eyes before his face' (82). Elsewhere, 'He was one of those commanders who speak little, seem to hear nothing, look at no one – and know everything, hear every whisper, see every fleeting shadow of their ship's life' (77). There is an echo in these sentences of what Henry James had required of his ideal narrator: a sense that 'a particular detachment has operated' and a 'shadowless' comprehension has been achieved.

As is demonstrated by the final moments of Allistoun's participation in *Narcissus*, however, the alignment of this captain with the literary creator ultimately demonstrates that no comprehension can be comprehensive. Allistoun's final dramatic act in the story is to step into the crew's space, across a fore-aft divide that is heavily patrolled by the narrative and that marks the respective domains of regular seamen and officers. Allistoun comes into the sailors' quarters – seems to intrude unexpectedly into this 'tale of the forecastle' – as if the problem posed by James Wait's suspect illness can no longer roil beneath his attention under the foredeck.[17] The captain-author's comprehension is now saddled with the task of mastering the problem that is James Wait. Under Allistoun's 'quiet and penetrating gaze,' which seems to expose the history of Wait's bad faith, the sailor assures the captain he is now well enough to go back on deck (73). Allistoun, however, scandalizes the crew, who themselves could never 'get rid of the monstrous suspicion that this astounding black man was shamming sick' (44–5), by commanding Wait to keep to his bed for the rest of the passage. The hovering question has been answered: '"You have been shamming sick"' – but then the captain 'hesitated for less than half a second' before adding, '"Why, anybody can see that"' (74). It is the famous paradox of this novel. We, too, are confident that Wait's former claim to perceive death just over his shoulder has been a lie, but here, seeking to escape the captain's all-seeing eyes and merge quietly into the labour on deck, Wait is now, apparently, truly ill. His feverish nightmare about the 'policeman with the face of Donkin' is the herald of his real demise; his body is now perpetually 'streaming with perspiration,' and his limbs 'heavier than lead' (69).

But if Wait has ultimately only deceived himself, then we are all so deceived in the confidence that we are not dying. 'Singleton says he will die,' someone tells Donkin, whose reply, 'And so will you,' appalls the crew in its wisdom. 'We perceived that after all Singleton's answer meant nothing . . . All our certitudes were going' (26). There has been deception, but there exists no authority that could ever confirm or locate it. Whether it is his claim to be dying when he thinks he is not or his subsequent denial of impending death, Wait's bad faith cannot be distinguished clearly from our own, and thus can never be set aside for the pillory. For ourselves as well as the crew, Wait 'would never let doubt die' (29). Through Allistoun's decree on the matter, a pronouncement of one whose omniscience and power has proven to be almost superhuman, Conrad stages an act of adjudication that would resolve this doubt. What we get, however, is a 'hesita[nt]' declaration that 'anyone can see' that this dying man is 'shamming sick.' Even as we thrill with a sense of victory when the captain severs the Gordian knot, the novel persists in drawing equal attention to the unmoored foundation of his judgment.

The author's persistent and deliberate sabotage of such foundations leaves little purchase even for the mastery implied by the notion of an ironic 'perspective.' Literary scholars have accepted rather too broadly the notion of Conrad as a master of irony – an inevitably 'corrosive' and 'pervasive' irony, as Edward Said puts it (*Culture* 188). If one were to consider only the readily decoded sentence-level irony that does indeed saturate his prose, one might grant, with Kenneth Graham, 'the omnipresence, indeed the omnivorousness, of irony in Conrad's fiction' (207). When the *Narcissus* begins to capsize, for instance, all hands clamour for the desperate last-chance remedy of cutting the masts; but the captain refuses. 'They all believed it their only chance; but a little hard-faced man shook his grey head and shouted "No!"' (36). It is an apparently ridiculous scene of many strong, healthy men held under the sway of a single, frail 'grey head.' Yet because the sentence is so easily decoded and paraphrased into a straightforward assertion – that the crew's loyalty is not shaken by its consciousness of their commander's frail mortality, or even his fallibility – it is difficult to see how such prose could ever launch the totality of Conrad's writing into 'a Flaubertian (and nineteenth-century) detachment,' as Graham and others have asserted (207). Upon sustained attention to Conrad's prose, in fact, what one finds is that his irony, like James Wait's bad faith, continually inverts itself. It rarely can be confirmed, absolutely, as irony. In its vision, for instance, of Captain Allistoun's bond with his storm-besieged ship, *Narcissus* tells us that he 'kept his gaze riveted upon her as a loving man watches the unselfish toil of a delicate woman upon the slender thread of whose existence is hung the whole meaning and joy of the world' (30–1). Teetering between the indispensability and the vain folly of a sentimental humanism, the question of Conrad's irony here reaches a peak of intensity, an unrelievable suspense.

It is a peculiarly Conradian phenomenon that such moments of undecidability ripple outward in the text and make questionable even those ironies that seem to announce themselves clearly as such. In our first wide-horizon vision of the merchant ship and its journey, for instance, we are told that 'the august loneliness of her path lent dignity to the sordid inspiration of her pilgrimage. She drove foaming to the southward, as if guided by the courage of a high endeavour' (18). Much later, however, the novel deliberately forces us to reconsider the grinning scepticism these words seem designed to evoke. The narrator resurrects them verbatim ('as though inspired by the courage of a high endeavor' [58]), but they appear this time as the shattered *Narcissus* is travelling in the opposite direction, 'foaming to the northward,' after the captain's gaze and our own have been 'riveted' on the crew's appalling battle with the storm, and on their 'unselfish toil' for the ship even in the face of personal annihilation. It is difficult here, as it might not have been at the earlier moment, to read confidently the sentence in question as a slice of healthy cynicism.

Despite an occasionally omniscient narrator and a commander sometimes aligned with an authorial god, Conrad ultimately allows no secure perch for transcendent comprehension. The same 'trouble' appears, however, at the other end of the comprehension telescope, where sentimental penetration exposes the final truth of an interiority. Whenever *Narcissus* hauls its narrator off the deck of the ship and into a transcendental ether, this speaker recoils from the position of the sentimental investigator. Although sporadic, this recoil in the novel is a nineteenth-century answer to the problem of sentimental exposure, a solution that Conrad, here, has yet to revolutionize in his writing through the emergence of Charlie Marlow. Whenever *Narcissus* reaps sentimental profit for its collective subject, each of those weighty moments vibrates with the tense question of who it is, exactly, who presumes to speak for England's sea labourers. After the storm-broken ship has fallen miraculously back on its keel, the narrator writes:

> On men reprieved by its disdainful mercy, the immortal sea confers in its justice the full privilege of desired unrest. Through the perfect wisdom of its grace they are not permitted to meditate at ease upon the complicated and acrid savour of existence. They must without pause justify their life to the eternal pity that commands toil to be hard and unceasing . . . till the weary succession of nights and days tainted by the obstinate clamour of sages, demanding bliss and empty heaven, is redeemed at last by the vast silence of pain and labour . . . (55)

Although this writer and we ourselves can 'meditate at ease' upon their plight, the sailors will never be 'permitted' to do so. Once again, the meditative 'sage' in our ear at this moment is certainly not one of these men. Conrad does not want their toil and sacrifice to have been exhumed by the sentimental 'exposure' of a private interior – by a sentimental agent that would have penetrated the forecastle and brought it to light. Instead he takes refuge, with Henry James, in a narrative agency that would recede from sight altogether and leave behind not even its own voice. The crew's life will be 'justified' and their labour 'redeemed' not in the account created by this narrative – since, in the regime of omniscience, this narrative does not exist – but in the absence of any and all accounting, in nothing but 'the vast silence' of their unrecorded labour.

Conrad persists in denying his own accountancy throughout his career, even as he reaps sentimental profit for his heroes and forges our sympathetic alignment with them. He does so, remarkably, even after his full commitment to a testimonial regime in fictions like *Lord Jim*. Hence the undeniable oddity of the quintessential Conradian storyteller: a garrulous reporter who persistently denies having any desire to iterate the tale he is now telling, and who curses the sources that have burdened him with narrative. When the wizened narrator of the 1920 'The Warrior's Soul' explains how he became the 'special confidant' of Tomassov, the romantic-minded subject of the story, he reports that the young soldier 'soon got shy of talking before the others. I suppose the usual camp-fire comments jarred his fine feelings . . . and I – I suppose you will hardly believe me – I am by nature a rather silent sort of person. Very likely my silence appeared to him sympathetic' (*Tales of Hearsay* 7–8). The story could never have emerged without the traditional

conjunction of a reluctant confessor and a silently encouraging sympathetic listener, and yet the story sneers at this necessity, insisting that
the purported silence of its talkative storyteller has been wrongly interpreted as that of an active sympathy eager for another's confession.

Tomassov and his 'reluctant' auditor represent a familiar dyad in
Conrad's writing whose first incarnation had been Jim and Marlow.
As we have seen, *Lord Jim* strictly binds its various narratives to a testimonial condition that reflects the reality of narrative in the historical
world, directly challenging postures of comprehension – assumed by
a range of public writing – that hide this reality. Now we can revisit
Marlow's emergence in that tale to see how this project propelled itself,
sometimes vexedly, in tandem with Conrad's fight for and against novelistic sentimentalism. Marlow gives Conrad's writing what the author
will call 'the intimacy of a personal communication' – which is the first
requirement of a sympathetic as opposed to doctrinal judgment of Jim's
history – but without the pretence of having transcended its reality as
a publicly negotiated testimonial. In the 1923 letter to Richard Curle,
where Conrad complains once again about his friend locating the value
of his work entirely in its connection to the real events of his life, the
author insists that Curle has a too-limited understanding of what constitutes the 'historical' reality of his tales. That reality, Conrad suggests,
necessarily involves his own negotiation with a reading public, and he
baldly asserts that his mature narrative strategy has always been in service of that negotiation:

> I am aware . . . I used the word historical in connection with my fiction . . .
> I expressed myself badly, for I certainly had not in my mind the history of
> the books. What I was thinking at the time was a phrase in a long article
> in the *Seccolo*. The critic remarked that there was no difference in method
> or character between my fiction and my professedly autobiographical
> matter . . .
>
> My own impression is that what he really meant was that my manner
> of telling, perfectly devoid of familiarity as between author and reader,
> aimed essentially at the intimacy of a personal communication, without
> any thought for other effects. (Curle, *Conrad* 148–9)

Conrad is clearly attracted to the idea that he has accomplished 'personal communication,' but without 'familiarity.' The latter is a key term
for many of his contemporaries, especially Henry James. Enforced by
the United States in particular and modernity in general, 'familiarity'

for these writers refers to a mindset that cannot in good conscience acknowledge any reserve within itself or among others, since any such reticence would bespeak a shamefully hidden interiority.

Like 'The Warrior's Soul,' *Lord Jim* refuses to establish its theatre of attestation between Marlow and Jim on the violence of 'familiarity.' Like the later story, however, the novel leaves exposed the problem of how an intimate relation between Marlow and Jim could ever have been instigated without a transition from the formal to the familiar. Like our own, Marlow's connection with Jim begins in the anonymous public relation of juror and defendant. 'My eyes met his for the first time at that inquiry' (35). Immediately after that first day's hearing, however, the strangers not only converge, but find themselves instantly face-to-face over the central question of Jim's life. As in 'The Warrior's Soul,' this rapport is forged entirely by 'mistake.' As Jim and everybody else is filing out of the courtroom, a man next to Marlow trips over a little dog that somehow got into the building. 'Look at that wretched cur,' the man says loudly, before disappearing himself. When Jim defiantly turns around to confront what he takes to be an insult directed at himself, it is Marlow who happens to be in his sights. There is a tense confrontation between them, but when Jim finally sees the dog, his face suddenly bears the traditional mark of sentimental exposure: 'The red of his fair sunburnt complexion deepened suddenly under the down of his cheeks, invaded his forehead, spread to the roots of his curly hair' (74). The relation between the men has instantly become one of 'abominable' intimacy.

> I was anxious to end this scene on grounds of decency, just as one is anxious to cut short some unprovoked and abominable confidence . . . A single word had stripped him of his discretion – of that discretion which is more necessary to the decencies of our inner being than clothing is to the decorum of our body. (72–4)

Through the deus ex machina of a little yellow dog – who is seen snapping at a fly 'like a piece of mechanism' (74) – Jim has 'given himself away' to Marlow (75). Conrad does not disguise the contrived, antinaturalist farce he must impose on the story in order to dissociate Marlow from a more traditional sentimental investigator. Marlow himself speaks of the dog's intervention as rather a diabolus ex machina:

The devil lets me in for that kind of thing. What kind of thing, you ask? Why the inquiry thing, the yellow-dog thing . . . the kind of thing that by devious, unexpected, truly diabolical ways causes me to run up against men . . . and loosens their tongues at the sight of me for their infernal confidences; as though, forsooth, I had no confidences to make to myself, as though – God help me! – I didn't have enough confidential information about myself to harrow my own soul till the end of my appointed time. And what I have done to be thus favoured I want to know. I declare I am as full of my own concerns as the next man, and I have as much memory as the average pilgrim in this valley, so you see I am not particularly fit to be a receptacle of confessions. Then why? Can't tell . . . (34–5)

We never find out, anywhere, what this 'harrowing' memory and experience might entail. These facts are kept in reserve, kept as pure reserve, since, as always in fiction, facts unarticulated have no existence whatever. They are secrets without content. To name these 'mysteries,' as literary criticism has insisted ought be done, is to efface what they do exhibit: the unarticulated 'space,' the *demeure* that the novel thus maintains.

As we will see more fully in the following chapter, Conrad reserves this space for the colonial other as well. Spiralling toward Kurtz, Marlow ruminates about cultures that must have already lived and died in the surrounding lands, people 'that are gone, leaving hardly a sign – and no memories' (36). With this consciousness of memory's dependence on the kind of trace amenable to registry, Marlow then turns his attention to the living voices and music now emanating from the forest. 'An appeal to me in this fiendish row – is there? Very well; I hear; I admit, but I have a voice too, and for good or evil mine is the speech that cannot be silenced' (37). Unlike the African's, Marlow's voice will be inscribed and disseminated, not simply because African narratives are 'unthinkable' in this text, as Edward Said suggests, but because Marlow's voice is identified here with the Western histories and anthropologies that dominate institutional registries around the world (*Culture* 24).[18]

As I have argued, the novel underscores Marlow's 'opacity' not to portray the tragic inaccessibility of truth, but to keep in view the testimonial condition that is necessarily truth's milieu. Part of the conceptual condition of testimony is that it will always be bound to a certain secrecy, to a hidden remainder that the testifier necessarily keeps in

reserve – the ever-present possibility, for instance, of a further attestation that would qualify, enhance, or negate the original. One of the remarkable revelations of the earliest recorded European witchcraft trials
is that the very act of testifying could condemn the accused because
it draws attention to the possibility that something remains unsaid
'within' the testifier. The accuser suggests that the mere act of answering 'No' to the question 'Are you a witch?' reveals a suspicious chasm
between this 'mere testimony' and the further truth that can always be
projected 'behind' it, with which it may or may not correspond.[19] The
scene of deposition is governed by what literary theorists call a 'depth
model.' Suspicion redounds doubly upon the testifier because of the
eternally reticent inward self that this rhetorical model conjures into
being.

A traditional sentimental investigator like Savillon has licence to examine his subjects partly because he does not keep secrets. He wears
his own history on his sleeve. Marlow, by contrast, testifies to a secret,
a shady past, but will not bring it into knowledge. He will always keep
inviolable this reserve or 'demurral,' as Derrida puts it, that is endemic
to the testimonial condition. In novels that follow the sentimental tradition less critically, this hidden reserve would normally constitute
the contracted truth of the character, or even of the novel itself. Under
the prevailing rules of fiction, Marlow's never-exposed reserve is a
violation of his licence both as a purveyor of truth and as an agent of
sympathy.

If Marlow's propriety as a conduit of sympathy is questionable from
a traditional perspective, then Jim's fitness as a subject of sympathy is
even more so. As in most novels of sympathy-through-interlocution,
Jim lives under a cloud of disapprobation, and the purpose of the
novel is to pierce the blind wall of persecution surrounding him with
a more insightful sympathetic evaluation. Traditionally, however, the
moral absolutism that such novels seem to be combating is never really
threatened. The reader always knows, either at the beginning or by the
end of the story, that the accused has been innocent all along – just as
the novel's initial cry against class hierarchy was often diffused by a
denouement revealing that the heroic governess of obscure origin is of
noble birth after all. In *Lord Jim*, by sharp contrast, Jim's dishonourable
act remains an uncontestable fact, even in the opening chapters when
it is not yet clear what he has done. Yet the novel insists, nonetheless,
that the subsequent sympathetic interlocution between Marlow and
Jim – which finally spells out this dishonour – will reveal something

more, and more pertinent, than the factually accurate report already articulated in the courtroom and in the columns of *Home News*.

Conrad follows the earliest sympathetic novels in his attempt to reach beyond moral absolutism, 'beyond the competency of a court of inquiry,' as Marlow says, for a means of evaluating its subject (93). As we have seen, however, the initiation of this project seems to require even the antisentimentalist Conrad to 'indecently' expose his subject through his own 'devilish' machination. Marlow himself broods on this question when he tries to discern 'the secret motive of my prying' into Jim's experience.

> You may call it an unhealthy curiosity if you like; but I have a distinct notion I wished to find something . . . some merciful explanation, some convincing shadow of an excuse. I see well enough now that I hoped for the impossible – for the laying of what is the most obstinate ghost of man's creation . . . the doubt of the sovereign power enthroned in a fixed standard of conduct. (50)

These lines, on one level, are the sympathetic novel in auto-analysis. From its inception, the genre undoubtedly fulfilled the 'unhealthy curiosity' of a public that longed to catch a glimpse of private life in action – a glimpse, further, of consciousness compromised, and therefore unguarded, 'exposed.' The role of a *Julie* or *Pamela* in this regard was almost identical to that of television 'reality' shows of the present day. Even when audiences know these productions to be essentially fictional 'set-ups,' this knowledge does not at all interfere with their voyeuristic pleasure. Unlike a real peeping Tom, audiences of prepared productions have enjoyed, historically, a pleasure over and above that which may be available through a sense of seeing unseen. They are witness not only to a public declaration of what might constitute one's privacy, but also the spectacle of how a subject might articulate and justify her private practice to a public.

It is the promise of this spectacle that creates the 'unhealthy curiosity' about Jim that Marlow hopes he has transcended, and that has attracted so many onlookers into the courtroom. As the novel makes clear, their curiosity is born of the fact that Jim is the sole officer of the *Patna* who did not take the ready opportunity to leave town and avoid the public hearing; Jim knew 'very well that if he went away nobody would trouble to run after him' (67). The tribunal audience is already aware of his guilt and of all the compelling facts of the affair. What they throng to see is the spectacle of Jim articulating his personal dishonour, voluntarily, for a public forum.

Conrad thus demonstrates the ethical bind in which *Lord Jim*, but also the novel as a genre, has always been caught. Since its inception, the novel has excused the indecent exposure of its central figures by pointing to the unique moral instruction that can only be achieved through the lifelike 'example' of such revealing narratives – a kind of instruction that the artificial 'precepts' of didactic moral tracts cannot achieve. But just as this distinction falls apart for 'reality' television when it becomes clear how rigidly the subjects have been set up and propelled toward a predetermined moral tale, the eighteenth century never really believed that the moral instruction of 'example' could reach beyond 'precept.' Even defenders of the novel like Eliza Haywood thought that the morality of fiction existed only where it could 'enforce Precept by Example' (99).

For Conrad, however, there really is something in novelistic example that creates a better ground for moral evaluation than precept. The complex singularities of scenario and circumstance in *Lord Jim* constitute a plea, a 'merciful explanation' of the subject under scrutiny that claims to have a greater wisdom than the easy dogmatism of 'a fixed standard of conduct.' The 'obstinate ghost' that a sympathetic narrative creates – that which lingers even after the tribunal has created justice, even after it is presumed to have taken everything relevant into account – is what compels Marlow to advocate for the guilty, dishonoured Jim. The young seaman 'did not want a judge. He wanted an ally, a helper, an accomplice . . . He swayed me. I own to it, I own up' (93).

Both Conrad and Marlow are accomplices to Jim's extra-juridical plot in their willingness 'to remember Jim, to remember him at length, in detail and audibly.' It is precisely this remembering that the tribunal will not allow Jim to bring into its forum:

> He spoke slowly; he remembered swiftly and with extreme vividness; he could have reproduced like an echo the moaning of the engineer for the better information of these men who wanted facts . . . [H]e had come round to the view that only a meticulous precision of statement would bring out the true horror behind the appalling face of things. The facts that those men were so eager to know had been visible, tangible, open to the senses, occupying their place in space and time, requiring for their

existence a fourteen-hundred-ton steamer and twenty-seven minutes by the watch; they made a whole that had features, shades of expression, a complicated aspect that could be remembered by the eye, and something else besides, something invisible . . . (30–1)

The statement Jim would like to produce is apparently a phenomenalist report, a detailing of time and space, but also of affect. But by launching into this report, he is 'becoming irrelevant; a question to the point cut short his speech.' He ends up 'answering questions that did not matter though they had a purpose . . . The sound of his own truthful statements confirmed his deliberate opinion that speech was of no use to him any longer' (33). In her analysis of testimony and trauma, Shoshana Felman finds courtroom witnesses to the Holocaust torn by the same forces. She considers the case of survivor and author Yehiel Dinoor, who, seemingly overcome by the task of rendering his experience in speech, fainted while testifying at the trial of Adolf Eichmann. Dinoor would later describe negotiations for his testimony:

> The prosecutor . . . said to me: 'Mr. De-Nur, this is a trial whose protocol depends on testimony to prove there was a place called Auschwitz and a description of what happened there.' . . . I said: 'Sir, describing Auschwitz is beyond me!' Hearing me, his staff eyed me with suspicion. 'You, the person who wrote those books, you expect us to believe you can't explain to the judges what Auschwitz was?' I fell silent. How could I communicate to them the way I myself burn, searching for the word to name the look in the eyes of those who would walk through me to the crematorium, with eyes that fused with mine?[20]

What Dinoor wants, Felman writes, 'is not to prove but to transmit,' to 'transmit truth as event and as the shock of an *encounter* with events, transmit history as an experience' ('A Ghost' 271, 261, Felman's emphasis). The courtroom saw '*the drama of the missed encounter*' between 'two vocabularies of remembrance' (289, Felman's emphasis). This seems precisely the missed encounter that Peter Brooks suggests is inevitable in any courtroom use of the 'Victim Impact Statement,' a relatively recent innovation in American criminal law. When Supreme Court justice Byron White points out, in his dissent in Booth v. Maryland, that the convicted defendant failed to offer any rebuttal to the VIS read at trial, Brooks finds it a significantly meaningless observation. 'How could one go about rebutting a narrative of inconsolable grief?' (*Troubling* 136). In the VIS, the American courtroom seems to have embraced and instantiated that which, in the Eichmann trial, could only intrude 'in the interstices of the law as a ghost,' as Felman observes. 'At the limit of what could be legally grasped, something of the order of K-Zetnik's mute cry – something of the order of the speechlessness and of the interminability of art – was present in the courtroom as a silent shadow of the trial' ('A Ghost' 280). As is appropriate to the category of the literary to which both Felman and Derrida bind this testimonial condition, the singular passion implied by the VIS is unanswerable, irresponsible in the strict sense of the term.

Just as the surviving witness Dinoor will later have recourse for his testimony in the alternate forum born of his literary authorship, Conrad's Jim catches the eye of one man in his courtroom audience:

> That man there seemed to be aware of his hopeless difficulty.
>     . . . And later on, many times, in distant parts of the world, Marlow showed himself willing to remember Jim, to remember him at length, in detail and audibly. (33)

It is only Marlow's narrative and commentary – a discourse largely identical with the novel itself, and which includes the 'meticulous precision of statement' that he does eventually get from Jim – that allows for the 'length' and 'detail' sufficient to re-member him. Within the extended dialogue between the men, the detailing that articulates Jim's infamous jump from the *Patna* is an appeal to what the earliest novelists called 'sensibility,' a term borne primarily by its somatic implications when applied to fiction and drama.[21] Jim's recollection of the crippled *Patna* approaches its climax – his appalling discovery of its distended bulkhead, beyond remedy and certain to implode at any moment – moving step by step through each phase by which he approached consciousness of his imminent death. As Samuel Richardson expected his own audience to be, Marlow is swayed toward fellow-feeling with Jim and his experience by being placed 'under the immediate Impression of every Circumstance which occasioned them' (*Pamela* 1:iii).

But Conrad's radical break with sentimentalism, and with the trajectory of the novel in general, lies in his exposure of the voyeuristic relation maintained even within this sympathy. Marlow reports Jim's words:

'I made up my mind to keep my eyes shut,' he said, 'and I don't care who knows it. Let them go through that kind of thing before they talk. Just let them – and do better – that's all. The second time my eyelids flew open and my mouth too. I had felt the ship move. She just dipped her bows . . . It managed, though, to knock over something in my head. What would you have done? You are sure of yourself – aren't you? What would you do if you felt now – this minute – the house here move, just move a little under your chair. Leap! By heavens! you would take one spring from where you sit and land in that clump of bushes yonder.'

. . . He looked at me very steadily . [I]t behooved me to make no sign lest by a gesture or a word I should be drawn into a fatal admission about myself which would have had some bearing on the case . . . Don't forget I had him before me . . . But if you want to know I don't mind telling you that I did, with a rapid glance, estimate the distance to [the bushes] . . . I would have landed short by several feet – and that's the only thing of which I am fairly certain. (106–7)

This episode of Marlow's reclusion with Jim – of the narrator rejecting the 'tale that was public property' (41) in favour of Jim's statement – goes out of its way to make Marlow squirm whenever he seeks protection in detachment, in the irresponsibility of the public onlooker. What Marlow must finally 'own up' to is the responsibility, in the strict sense of the term, that lurks within his voyeuristic sympathy. It is a responsibility he had previously eschewed when Conrad's 'wretched cur' of a little dog had forced him into confrontation with Jim for the first time, right after the tribunal:

'What did you mean by staring at me all the morning?' said Jim . . . 'Did you expect us all to sit with downcast eyes out of regard for your susceptibilities?' I retorted sharply . . . I was anxious to end this scene on grounds of decency, just as one is anxious to cut short some unprovoked and abominable confidence. (71–2)

Jim seizes on Marlow because he thinks he has heard the latter pronouncing judgment on him. Marlow will often prove to be 'anxious to end this scene' whenever the question of his personal evaluation of Jim comes to the fore. At such moments Marlow is like ourselves, safe behind a diegetic divide. We strain to gape at the subject under judgment, but have no desire for the responsibility of an acting judge.

It is a ready enough target for any satirist – the hypocrisy of the watcher who protests the sudden expansion of the frame so that the scene now includes the fact of his watching. But Conrad particularly highlights the comedy of the sentimental onlooker recoiling in fright when given the chance to emerge from extradiegetic shadow and make his sympathy available to the pitied and condemned object. When Jim and the other officers who had abandoned the *Patna* first report back to the merchant marine office in Singapore, they approach an official named Archie Ruthvel:

> He says that as soon as he understood who it was before him he felt quite unwell – Archie is so sympathetic and easily upset – but pulled himself together and shouted 'Stop! I can't listen to you. You must go to the Master Attendant. I can't possibly listen to you' . . . Archie's the most sensitive shipping-master in the two hemispheres. (38–9)

The alarming 'threats' of confession in all of these scenes in *Lord Jim* are dramatizations of the unresolved question in which *The Nigger of the 'Narcissus,'* with its wavering commitment to both omniscient and testimonial narration, had been rather helplessly gripped: How can a novel represent a 'silent' sea labourer without either forcing him into confession or presuming, as no envoy could, to have exposed his 'interior'? In the context of what were more common terms, culturally speaking, at the turn of the twentieth century, this anxiety stems partly from the uncertain frontiers of the public and private. *Lord Jim* continues to work out Conrad's own relation to the sympathetic traditions in the novel that have always grappled with this frontier, but which have also contributed so strongly to the modern world's conceptions of subjectivity, and to its protocols of ethical and political evaluation. Conrad would never have bothered with this 'archaic' literary milieu, and could have kept happily to the other novelistic soils he cultivated – travel-adventure, Balzacian social observation, Flaubertian naturalism, omniscient psychologism – if sympathy and sentimentalism were not inextricable from his major project of revaluing personal testimony. *Lord Jim* ultimately proposes a novel criterion by which the broader terms could be deployed. Public versus private forums could be recognized according to the presence or absence of the non-responsible onlooker. Yet the movement in *Lord Jim* away from irresponsible voyeurism, in the ostentatious act of supplanting the novel's early omniscience with the long interlocution between Marlow and Jim, reaches, in the end, a deeper conclusion: that even in the intimacy of the tête-à-tête, amid the full responsibility of both its actors, testimony will always be the envoy of the self. As Marlow's tense commiseration with Jim makes clear, testimony must negotiate as an ambassador within its private enclosures just as it must within its public forums.

# 5 Theatre of Incursion and Unveiling II: Empire

In a long 1872 letter to the *New York Herald*, a writer identified only as 'S.H.' excitedly calls attention to a peculiar arabesque within Emanuel Swedenborg's vision of the last judgment: the revelation of 'a nation of people inhabiting some portion of the interior of Africa who were in a somewhat advanced state of civilization, and were worshippers of the true and only God.'[1] S.H. had been spurred to his pen by a series of dispatches from Zanzibar that were holding the world in thrall. Henry Morton Stanley had accomplished his *Herald*-financed mission to find the famous Dr David Livingstone and was sending back reports of his conversation with the 'lost' explorer. Stanley had passed on Livingstone's description of a people west of Lake Taganyika 'so nearly approaching to white people and so extremely handsome that they eclipse anything ever seen in Africa.' To S.H., this mysterious tribe is likely to be that which had been revealed to Swedenborg. They are people, according to the mystic, to whom great spiritual secrets have been 'orally dictated by angelic spirits.'[2] The 'nearly' white skin of these Africans is the trace of a 'revelation' among them, emanating 'from the centre of their continent.'[3]

Has any place on earth attracted as much speculation and anxiety about its 'centre' as has Africa? Despite the substantial literary and historical work that has demonstrated how nineteenth-century fiction and journalism conjured both the 'centre' and the 'mystery' of Africa into being, there has been no serious study of what I argue is the sine qua non of this ideological phenomenon – Stanley's search for the secret of Africa, rhetorically embodied in the absence created by the white man swallowed into its centre, as inscribed onto the world's consciousness by Gordon Bennett and the *New York Herald*. Appalled and fascinated by this six-year-long 'newspaper stunt,' as he would later describe it, Joseph Conrad reconceives the whole scenario in 1899 through *Heart of Darkness* (*Last Essays* 17). The guns of the *Herald* expedition echoing in its background, Conrad's analysis of what we might call tales of excavation demonstrates how useful such narratives have been to a violent colonial project in which the newspaper is complicit not just ideologically but materially.

Transcending any single voice, and with an injunction to expose interiority, the *Herald* penetrates and exhumes the truth of Africa that her own testimony would never have the authority to reveal, even if European ears had any desire to translate the 'appeal' in its 'fiendish row.' As Marlow says in his intermittent embodiment of Stanley – a role he shares with the journalist Kurtz – 'for good or evil mine is the speech that cannot be silenced' (*Heart* 37). Just as George Flack had made use of Herodotean 'autopsy' to create a theatre of incursion for the *Reverberator*, so too does Stanley deploy narrative apparatus of veiling and unveiling that the novel's travel-writing heritage had perfected since Defoe. It will become clear, too, that the crackpot myth, excited by Stanley's adventure, of an ancient race of white men subsumed in Africa's heart is emblematic of a peculiar colonialist search for truth – not of the mysterious other, but rather the elusive truth of the Western world's own imperial desire.

Born John Rowlands in 1841, Henry Morton Stanley grew up in Denbigh, Wales. Abandoned early in life by his unmarried parents, and generally shunned by relatives, the penniless teenager eventually made his way to New Orleans. There he found work as a servant of Henry Stanley, a childless merchant who eventually became a father figure for the young man, and he later adopted the elder's name. In 1860, the merchant left on a short business trip to Cuba, but would die overseas. The twenty-year-old Welshman was left to work selling goods in a sparsely populated region of Arkansas. There he acquired, in Norman Bennett's words, a 'frontier familiarity with firearms that would stand him in good stead in Africa' (xvi). Civil war soon broke out, however, and Stanley was shamed into volunteering by an anonymous gift of a chemise and petticoat. Fighting for the South, he was taken prisoner at Shiloh and sent to a camp near Chicago. Later, he switched sides and enlisted in the Union army, but was discharged soon after due to illness. After a brief stint in the English merchant navy, the young man returned to the United States and joined the Union Navy in 1864. Witness to two famous attacks on Fort Fisher in North Carolina, Stanley wrote accounts of the battles which would later be published in the press. Thus begun a career whose impulse toward action and adventure is often indistinguishable from its drive to create them in print.

After further exploration of the American West in the company of a man named W.H. Cook – probably trading ventures, as were their subsequent travels – Stanley enlisted a third companion, Lewis Noe, for a voyage to Turkey. Although Stanley and Cook disputed his testimony, Noe later described the Asian voyage to the press as a trading venture that quickly devolved into the robbery and murder of at least one native at Stanley's hand.[4] Upon his return to the American West, Stanley solidified his journalistic career by publishing reports on 'the Indian problem' in papers including the *Missouri Democrat* and the *New York Herald*.

On the strength of this new work, Stanley travelled to New York in 1867 to pitch a story to *Herald* editor James Gordon Bennett, Jr. The Welshman wanted to send back reports from Africa on the current British expedition against Emperor Theodore of Ethiopia. Bennett gave Stanley the commission but would not cover his expenses. If his efforts were successful, however, the editor promised him a permanent post. Successful they were, thanks to a well-placed bribe to the Suez telegraph operator, who gave Stanley's dispatches priority over all other correspondents'. In a strange stroke of luck, the telegraph cable broke after Stanley's story was sent, and he scooped even the official British reports on the Ethiopian campaign. By 1868, Stanley had become the *Herald*'s leading correspondent.

The messianic George Flack of Henry James's *The Reverberator* – who declaims that 'it ain't going to continue to be possible to keep out anywhere the light of the Press,' and that he is destined to 'set up the biggest lamp yet made and make it shine all over the place' (63) – might strike us today as a comic exaggeration. Considering the reality of late nineteenth-century journalism, however, James's treatment is rather restrained. Early in 1872, Bennett wrote some 'reflections upon journalism as a living, present, growing power,' occasioned by 'the success of the *Herald*' in launching its African expedition (7 Jan. 1872). There were those in Britain who had been 'decrying this enterprise' because of Stanley's eagerness to overcome obstacles with violence, already evident in his first dispatch describing his trek from Zanzibar to the interior. Such complaints, Bennett writes, are merely the agitations of envious 'Cheap Jack' competitors of the *Herald*. These organs, Bennett continually reminds his readers, could never launch 'an expedition that cost money enough alone to keep all the Cheap Jacks in tobacco and bread and beer for years.' Well aware that the *Herald* has spent 'more than half a million dollars' on previous journalistic feats, 'the people know that the HER-ALD is the HERALD, just as they know that the throne is the throne. It is an institution of the country.' 'What are kings,' Bennett continues, 'and emperors and presidents and parties and administrations in compari-son? The HERALD sees them, writes their life, their death, their epitaph.' Such rhetoric was not peculiar to Bennett. That same year, for instance, *The New York Standard* proclaimed that 'in republican America our lead-ing journals have more power and far greater influence than the head of many monarchies' (3 July 1872). World leaders 'hearken to the voice of hysterical politicians,' Bennett goes on in the *Herald*. 'Why should the HERALD descend from its throne and join in the mad outcry?'

> Twelve administrations have passed in review before this throne . . . What is Grant to the HERALD? . . . What are these 'great statesmen' now in wordy conflict at Washington, that the HERALD should descend from its throne and carry their pennons? Why, it has seen a hundred statesmen . . . The HERALD did its duty by them in a royal, just, candid manner, and when they passed away it administered reward and censure to those who came, as it will to all who may come in the future. (7 Jan. 1872)

Born of the *Herald*'s new call to 'penetrate to the interior' of Africa (22 Dec. 1871), Bennett's article is a manifesto for journalism's turn against testimony. Detached not only from the newspaper's wonted al-legiance to this or that political 'pennon,' the voice of the *Herald* belongs to no mortal man whatever. Although Henry James will eagerly import Bennett-like caricatures into his fiction, the historiographic law of this 'new journalism' paves the way for the novelist's 'law of fiction.' The newspaper is no longer a collection of identifiable 'reciters,' as James would say, where each article can be traced to 'a definite responsible intervening first person singular' (James, 'Younger' 157). The *Herald* exists over and above whatever voice finally passes its 'reward and cen-sure' in the historical, mortal world, and despite the flood of ink pro-duced every day as it 'reviews' the procession below, the *Herald* retains an essential silence, removed from 'wordy conflict.'

As Bennett goes on to give a history of the press, he rejoices that its voice is no longer hobbled by its formerly persistent ties to proper

names, for with such a bond the voice must die with the name. Formerly we had 'Leggett with his pamphlets – a great man as greatness
went, but gone into oblivion with all that he did. Where are those "able
editors" and "powerful writers" and "moulders of public opinion"? . . .
All passed away . . .' Journalism was once a mess of writers and their attestation, and therefore indistinguishable from mere literature, a collection of 'gray and blind old minstrels, with their creaking harps . . .' Into
this blight arrived the *Herald* as 'a revelation, and floated over the skies
like [a] cloud.' 'What was the HERALD,' then, the article aptly asks, since
it transcended any human voice? 'Simply an idea,' Bennett answers
himself, 'and ideas have ruled the world ever since Moses climbed up
shining Sinai and wrote ten of them on his tablets of stone, so the HER-
ALD has come to be a ruler in the world.'

Bennett summoned Stanley to Paris to give him the assignment of
locating David Livingstone in the autumn of 1869. Despite the *Herald*'s
later assertions that 'unexplored' Africa is a crucial frontier for modern
science – which were inevitably followed by even louder declarations
that the *Herald* and the press in general were the primary catalysts of
progress and knowledge in the world – the true object of this venture
had little to do with Africa or even Livingstone. As Stanley's adventure
begins, Bennett rightly assures his readers that 'this expedition will accomplish something more than the solution' to the Livingstone mystery. In the guise of a search for knowledge, this 'something more' is
the mass production of an orientalist desire. As has been made clear in
postcolonial studies since Edward Said introduced the term, orientalism is valuable to colonialist discourse only so long as it does not resolve the mystery it evokes. Because it must not fully explain, expound,
or comprehend the other, colonial speculation was invigorated by the
nineteenth century's turn toward a mystery less articulated, seemingly
more profound, than the 'Eastern' orientalism it had long elaborated.
The *Herald*'s characteristic language of African penetration projects the
unarticulated mystery into an inaccessible 'centre' to which the missing
Livingstone must now be privy.

True to is ancestry, the new orientalism is not merely ideological, in both the pre- and post-Marxist conceptions of that term. It is
necessarily endemic, too, to the consumerist engine of the imperial
machine. At ease in a total conflation of the epistemological and the
mercantile, Bennett is confident that the trade routes of the new exotica
will be dominated by the press. The *Herald* promises it will go down
in history as part of 'the solution to the mysteries of the Nile,' and in

the next sentence Bennet claims that 'that our example in this African adventure can hardly fail to give new impulse to such enterprises in that . . . Continent, with its abounding resources awaiting the developments of civilization.' More such expeditions 'would soon be followed by the active development of the boundless resources of savage Africa, East and West . . . And so, from year to year, we gather in the bounteous harvest for our readers' (23 Dec. 1871).

Contrary to a popular memory of the affair that would be crafted later, with enormous help from both Stanley and the *Herald*, there had been no real clamour over the interruption of Livingstone's communiqués from central Africa. Livingstone's associates in The Royal Geographical Society had seen nothing unusual in the hiatus. Although they did eventually send out a relief expedition, and the British government allocated money for the doctor, Bennett was correct in his assertion that the Society was responding entirely to the sensation created by Stanley's initial dispatches in the *Herald*, where both Stanley and Bennett scornfully ridiculed Britain's inactivity. In October of 1869, the British consul in Zanzibar, John Kirk, had received correspondence from Livingstone that had been written in May. The doctor was calling for help because the supplies that Kirk had sent to Ujiji months earlier had dwindled from theft and negligence. The *Herald* expedition stimulated worries about Livingstone's well-being, but there was little concern about his location – it was known he would use Ujiji as a home base – and there had been no great consternation over his 'silence.' 'The Livingstone mystery,' as Bennett dubbed it on the day he announced the expedition, was given birth by the *Herald* itself, then quickly disseminated throughout the world (19 Sept. 1871).

The discursive protocol that would come to govern the story is dictated entirely by the metaphysics of veiling and unveiling, and of light penetrating darkness, which will prove crucial to the epistemological language that is always used to reshape the reality of European adventure in Africa. After Stanley finds Livingstone, the ecstatic reflections of *London Daily News* are typical:

> Dr. Livingstone has been lost for years in the mysterious centre of the African Continent; Mr. Stanley has plunged into the gloom . . . The interest felt about Dr. Livingstone is that which belongs to an enterprise carried on amid danger and mystery and darkness. For years past he has been lost to the public view behind an impenetrable veil . . . Mr. Stanley has pierced the veil. (26 July 1872)

If a drawn veil always exposes a once-hidden truth, then even a purely staged motion of 'unveiling' – a journalistic performance of eyewitness penetration into the heart of darkness – will guarantee the advent of truth. The ubiquitous but vague references to knowledge on the verge of discovery allow all of Bennett's apologias for Stanley to be cast, without exception, in the adjacent terms of science and progress. In the course of defending Stanley's habit of leaving corpses in the wake of his travel, Bennett can thus ridicule the idea that his agent 'should never pull a trigger against [the] species of human vermin that puts its uncompromising savagery in the way of all progress and all increase of knowledge' (17 Sept. 1877). Livingstone himself would later write that while Mr Stanley had led his decimated party with 'good judgment,' his treacherous native servants were 'unbearable drags to progress' (*Last Journals* 401).

We do not know how closely Conrad followed Stanley's adventures as they appeared in the *Herald*, but in the 1924 essay 'Geography and Some Explorers,' collected later in *Last Essays*, he reports that he had been devouring at that time any and all news concerning Livingstone, his favourite explorer. It was during this period, in fact, that his own desire for exploration was most inflamed; when he famously pointed to the 'blank' centre of Africa on a map to declare his intention to 'go there' (*Personal Record* 27). If he had not read translations of the sensational *Herald* articles at the time they were written, he would almost certainly have obtained French translations during his Marseilles-based seaman's apprenticeship four years later. As he refers to the expedition as 'a prosaic newspaper "stunt,"' it is unlikely that he had only read Stanley's best-selling books on the venture (17). It is difficult, in any case, not to see in his satire of the journalist Kurtz a direct response to Bennett's rhetoric. When Charlie Marlow returns to Europe, after his spiralling voyage into the Congo is over, he is beset by a journalist anxious to lay his hands on whatever discursive booty his 'dear colleague' may have left behind. Marlow hands him the pages Kurtz had written about the godlike strength the West can exert over Africa, which will inevitably 'exert a power for good practically unbounded' (51). The pressman eagerly snatches this report whose seething unconsciousness had erupted in handwritten marginalia: 'Exterminate all the brutes!' – a postscript that Marlow ultimately tears from the manuscript, re-sublimating its eruption, as part of his famous final lie to Kurtz's bride-to-be. Document in hand, the journalist 'glanced through it hurriedly, mumbling all the time, judged "it would do," and took himself off with his plunder' (74).

When Conrad had brought his first essay on the *Titanic* disaster to its climax with a bitter denunciation of the myriad forces that had scapegoated the ship's crew and captain to keep scrutiny away from powerful corporate entities, he subsumed this diffuse conspiracy into what he called a general 'outburst of journalistic enterprise' ('Some Reflexions' 315). His choice of words is illuminated by the fact that 'journalistic enterprise' was the *Herald*'s favourite phrase for its African expedition, and was eagerly reiterated by its peers, as when the Frederick (Maryland) *Herald* called Stanley's trek 'the greatest achievement of modern journalistic enterprise that has ever been recorded' (30 Dec. 1871). Conrad's conviction that journalism as an institution really was bound up with the imperial and commercial forces that had unleashed in the Congo 'the vilest scramble for loot that ever disfigured the history of human conscience' was not based on airy speculation (*Last Essays* 17). His novel *The Inheritors*, on which he collaborated with Ford Madox Ford, makes it clear that he was well aware of the fact that King Leopold II, whose Congolese slave regime is the setting of *Heart of Darkness*, had regularly purchased international support for his activities through bribery of the press.[5] *The Inheritors* features a 'Duc de Mersch,' ostensibly in the business of civilizing the Eskimo in his 'Greenland Protectorate,' 'investing' in an English newspaper to buy favourable coverage for his enterprise. For Conrad, both these and the Stanley-*Herald* ventures constitute what Edward Said calls 'colonial lobbies' who 'whether by cabal or by popular support press the nation into more scrambling for land and more natives being compelled into imperial service' (*Culture* 186).[6]

Literary criticism has long recognized, in passing, the importance of Stanley's expedition to Conrad's colonial critique. Norman Sherry, for instance, has shown connections between the opening paragraphs of the novella and one of Stanley's speeches (*Conrad's Western World* 119–21), and more recently historian Adam Hochschild has noted that 'in Kurtz's intellectual pretensions, Conrad caught one telling feature of white penetration of the Congo, where conquest by pen and ink so often confirmed the conquest by rifle and machine gun.'

> Ever since Stanley shot his way down the Congo River and then promptly wrote a two-volume best-seller, ivory collectors, soldiers, and explorers had tried to imitate him – in books, and in thousands of articles for the geographical society journals and magazines about colonial exploration that were as popular in the late nineteenth century as the *National Geographic* is in the United States today. It was as if the act of putting Africa

on paper were the ultimate proof of the superiority of European civilization. (147–8)

It is remarkable, however, that there exists only one scholarly study
of the *Herald*-Stanley enterprise in its connection to *Heart of Darkness*.
Mary Golanka devotes an essay to the subject, and her argument exem-
plifies the epistemological reading of Conrad I am attempting to revise.
Her reading of the novella is grounded in an assurance that 'Conrad
would have sympathized with Livingstone's attempt to confront the
enigmatical spectacle of Africa and with Stanley's attempt to solve the
mystery of Livingstone,' and culminates in the thesis that there is a 'pri-
mal knowledge of Africa' that has eluded Kurtz, which is why he 'cannot bear to look' when he is 'carried away from the heart of darkness'
at the end of the story (200). These formulations solidly identify Conrad's 'darkness' with Africa itself. The general, historical misperception
of the 'Livingstone mystery' as an object and not the product of the
*Herald* expedition is ideologically bound, I suggest, to this misreading
of Conrad's African 'darkness' as something native to or implicated in
the continent itself. Of this trope, and in the midst of his seminal and
otherwise brilliant reading of Conrad, Edward Said writes that Conrad
and Marlow

> are ahead of their time in understanding that what they call 'the dark-
> ness' has an autonomy of its own, and can reinvade and reclaim what
> imperialism had taken for *its* own. But Marlow and Kurtz . . . cannot take
> the next step, which would be to recognize that what they saw . . . as a
> non-European 'darkness' was in fact a non-European world *resisting* im-
> perialism so as one day to regain sovereignty and independence, and not,
> as Conrad reductively says, to reestablish the darkness. (*Culture* 30)

Conrad's precise vocabulary insists, rather, that the age-old 'blankness' of Africa in the Western imaginary should not be confused with
its 'darkness.' Foreshadowing that moment in the *Personal Record* when
Conrad recalls pointing his boyish finger at the 'blank space' in the
middle of a map of Africa and declaring '"When I grow up I shall go
*there*" . . . *there* being the region of Stanley Falls, which in '68 was the
blankest of blank spaces on the earth's figured surface' (27), Marlow
mourns at the beginning of *Heart of Darkness* that the Congo 'was not
a blank space any more. It had got filled since my boyhood with rivers
and lakes and names. It had ceased to be a blank space of delightful

mystery – a white patch for a boy to dream gloriously over. It had become a place of darkness' (8). 'Darkness,' in Conrad's lexicon, is emphatically not the essential unknowability of the other. It is a trope that emerges, rather, entirely from the theatre of imperial penetration inscribed by organs like the *Herald*, and from the myriad cartographic figures that have shaped the epistemology of empire.

This reading, of course, does not alter the fact that Conrad frequently imagines Africa to embody an animalism, helpless and cruel, that lurks beneath any veneer of civilization. 'An Outpost of Progress,' which is a clear prototype of *Heart of Darkness*, baldly posits an outlying barbarism in Africa that overtakes the weak-willed Europeans manning a coastal outpost. Yet *Heart of Darkness* is careful to maintain the logic of Marlow's distinction between the 'blankness' of the unknown and the 'darkness' deployed by Bennett, Stanley, and Kurtz – even when Marlow himself is shown to forget this distinction, becoming the dupe of these conflated tropes as his obsession for the missing journalist grows in intensity. A somewhat simplistic but still accurate reiteration of Marlow's central epiphany on his journey, which we will look at more closely in a moment, is that his compulsion to penetrate the heart of darkness – to spiral into the 'centre' of the Congo and discover the mysterious truth that the 'silence' of Kurtz must harbour – is really a fixation over a locked but empty casket. Early on, the story encapsulates this theme in a portrait of a European station manager on the banks of the river. In a passage that comically blends metaphysical interiors with anatomical ones, Conrad goes out of his way to taint the 'darkness' motif with a certain charlatanism belonging to the manager and his impenetrable smile:

> It was unconscious, this smile was . . . It came at the end of his speeches *like a seal applied on the words* to make the meaning of the commonest phrase appear absolutely inscrutable . . . He never gave that secret away. Perhaps there was nothing within him . . . Once when various tropical diseases had laid low almost every 'agent' in the station, he was heard to say, 'Men who come out here should have no entrails.' He sealed the utterance with that smile of his, as though it had been a door opening into a darkness he had in his keeping. You fancied you had seen things – but the seal was on. (22, my emphasis)

This faculty in the manager is said to inspire a singular 'uneasiness' among his cohort, and this is precisely the effect Kurtz has – that master of mysterious silence – on the administrator himself. Lest we lose the echo of this passage later in the scene, the manager begins to fidget with 'a stick of sealing wax.' He tells Marlow he is 'very, very uneasy' about Kurtz's silence and in his anxiety 'br[eaks] the stick of sealing-wax' (23).

Despite the fact that the British consulate in Zanzibar had received letters from David Livingstone in 1869 and into 1870, even the English press, in their 1872 articles praising Stanley's expedition, began to refer to a period of 'six years' during which 'the grave was not more silent to us than Livingstone.'[7] Well aware of Stanley's exhibition as a 'newspaper stunt,' Conrad would have seen that the worldwide hype over the *Herald*'s adventure had been fuelled by this conceit of the doctor's 'silence.' As one U.S. paper wrote, Livingstone had been swallowed into 'the ignorance and silence of the great Etheopian mystery' (*New York World* 8 July 1872). As the rhetoric snowballed, Livingstone came to represent a localized sphere of darkness where nothing less than the 'secret' of Africa itself was locked away. Steeped in 'ignorance,' the continent itself could never reveal its own secret. It requires a European agent whose 'disappearance' into its darkness will have transmuted him into an avatar of this secret truth. Like Kurtz, Livingstone is transformed into a lost talisman. When the fateful day of his reemergence arrives, he will have 'the last secret of Africa to impart' (LT 4 July 1872).

From silent Africa, the avatar of its secret will emerge, perforce, as a discourse. Stanley's adventure begins with his assurance that when Livingstone is found 'you shall hear what he has to say' (NYH 12 Dec. 1871), and comes to a climax after the doctor has been found with the London *Telegraph* marvelling that 'we shall have his story. What will it be?' (4 July 1872). A sudden awareness of this expectation is the true central epiphany of *Heart of Darkness*, despite our collective preoccupation with the revelation marked by Kurtz's famous final words. Marlow, figured for this purpose as Stanley himself, bent on exhuming the legendary white man engulfed by central Africa, initially imagines himself as the penetrating witness, a Herodotus out to discover for himself Kurtz's condition. It is an illusion soon shattered, and the epiphany is articulated, moreover, with a violent reaction to the trope of illumination that had been indispensable to the deceptions of each of Henry James's penetrating investigators. Winding his way toward Kurtz on the Congo, Marlow suddenly realizes why he has become depressed by the idea that Kurtz might be dead – a possibility over which Stanley, too, had brooded on his way to Livingstone. Marlow:

> There was a sense of extreme disappointment . . . I couldn't have been more disgusted if I had traveled all this way for the sole purpose of talking with Mr. Kurtz. Talking with . . . I flung one shoe overboard, and became aware that that was exactly what I had been looking forward to – a talk with Kurtz. I made the strange discovery that I had never imagined him as doing, you know, but as discoursing. I didn't say to myself, 'Now I will never see him,' or 'Now I will never shake him by the hand,' but, 'Now I will never hear him.' The man presented himself as a voice . . . [O]f all his gifts the one that stood out pre-eminently, that carried with it a sense of real presence, was his ability to talk, his words – the gift of expression, the bewildering, the illuminating, the most exalted and the most contempt-ible, the pulsating stream of light . . . (47–8)

It is remarkable that even the most profound analysts of the novella read this scene as an 'insistence on the ineffability of colonial experi-ence,' as Israel Nico puts it, suggesting that Marlow really is mourning a knowledge now lost with the death of Kurtz (50). Marlow's contempt for precisely that mourning, to which he had almost succumbed, is his contempt for the journalistic charlatan. He perceives Kurtz as a further emanation of the empty, entrail-less station manager who nonetheless had a knack for 'sealing' his discourse 'as though it had been a door opening into a darkness he had in his keeping' (22).

That which is hidden harbours the truth and exists on the order of iterability, as discourse. As James had reminded us in *The Reverberator*, and as François Hartog has exhibited in the earliest Western concep-tions of the traveller-witness's power of 'autopsy,' the self-authorization of the explorer derives from his having seen, not having heard, even when the material he collects consists entirely of verbal reports. Mar-low shares with Herodotus a struggle to extract and parse 'seeing' and 'hearing' from the composite action of the voyager-witness. 'The eyes are more trustworthy witnesses than the ears.'[8] And in the *Histories*, Herodotus recounts a story of the king of Lydia cajoling his friend: 'I think Gyges, that you do not believe what I tell you of the beauty of my wife; men trust their ears less than their eyes' (Hartog 262). The incommensurate comparisons in these formulations are significant. De-spite the insistence on the sensory organs themselves, what is being compared is not the relative value of visual and aural phenomena present to the witness. 'Hearing,' presumed at the outset to refer to the act of listening to another witness's testimony of the event in question, will always be at a remove from the 'seeing' that implies presence. Herodotus's words might very well be just a loose way of marking this distinction between being 'present' at an event (regardless of how that term would be conceived) and merely obtaining a report of it. But the insistence on the organs of perception – eyes versus ears, as opposed to one's own testimony versus another's – naturalizes the authority of the witness and effaces his own role as testifier.

The language of African penetration allows Stanley and the *Herald* to seize the authority of the witness even as it occludes their testimonial condition. From the perspective of the *Herald*, furthermore, Livingstone's exclusive claim to witness helps to confirm not just the truth of what he will write about it, but the status of his discourse as the exhumed truth of Africa. It will be apparent that the Herodotean conception of the eyewitness to which *Heart of Darkness* draws our attention is one that grants him the ghostly privilege of the nineteenth-century anonymous narrator. As with the 'external focalizer' I examined in the opening chapter – a concept, I have argued, that could ultimately be traced to James – the historiographer-as-witness might reiterate the testimony of another, but whereas that testimony is suspect as hearsay, the historiographer's own eyewitness report is presumed to be free of the 'problem' of testimony, as if it existed beyond the order of iterability. As I hope is evident, however, the peculiar divided consciousness in James that I have examined in the chapters above dovetails with Conrad's critical analysis of the transtestimonial authority available to the witness-journalist. It is the metaphysics of autopsy that had grounded the *Aspern Papers* biographer, and the Jamesian journalist in general, in a perception that is essentially paranoid, a conviction that the inaccessible iteration is the voice of truth. Chad Newsome of *The Ambassadors*, extracted from an interior of which Americans normally keep to the periphery, will emerge with a 'secret,' the dark truth of Europe, whatever it may be. As we will see in Conrad as well, the investigator ultimately learns that his real expectation all along has been an answer to the question of his own desire.

I divert here briefly to point out that literary criticism traditionally pairs James and Conrad for a purpose opposite of my own. Jamesian realism is said to contrast Conrad 'making the descent into the irrational jungle of himself,' as Leon Edel puts it, as if Conradian modernism is not conscious of such interiors as orientalist fabrications and as provisions in a contract of truth and comprehension (5:51). Edel's comparison of *Heart of Darkness* to 'The Beast in the Jungle' is one of the seminal statements of this orthodoxy:

> The two stories speak for the two temperaments. Conrad making the descent into the irrational jungle of himself, James fearing the irrationality, walking anxiously and warily through the dense growth of the human consciousness, on guard against the beasts that might leap – yet knowing that the beasts were those of his own mind. (Edel 5:51)

As is inevitable when Conrad is conceived in the shadow of the great nineteenth-century realist, the stock notion of his irrational descent into interiority overwhelms even James's judicious biographer. We are left yet again with the astonishing conclusion that James's tale of one man's self-delusion is somehow less absorbed in 'self' and interiority than is Conrad's account of late nineteenth-century colonial operations in Congo. In the James-Conrad critical nexus, it is essentially forbidden to see in Marlow a movement from illusion to reality, a final consciousness that the African evil that Kurtz perceives is, in fact, 'of his own mind' and born entirely of the newspaper phrases that constitute the 'discoursing being' Marlow had sought.

Following his thesis that the true inspiration for *Heart of Darkness* was probably *The Turn of the Screw*, Edel suggests that 'Conrad's excesses of indirect narration' may have been the result of learning 'too well' that story's narrative technique. In the biographer's subsequent reading of James, however, the infection appears to have gone the other way. The master himself must have been playing with the fire of 'indirect,' character-bound narration too carelessly. How else to explain Edel's conviction that James himself may be unaware that the 'evil' in *The Turn of the Screw* is of the governess's 'own mind'? As do many readers still, Edel externalizes this evil, explicitly reading the tale as Maggie Verver had read her predicament in *The Golden Bowl*: as a story of 'the horror of finding evil seated, all at its ease, where she had only dreamed of good.'[9] This now-common reading of *Turn* is startling, considering that the novella clearly and repeatedly asserts that its 'ghosts' are entirely the coinage of the governess's love-starved brain. James fairly shouts it from the moment of the first 'apparition,' a vision that appears the moment the governess fantasizes about turning a corner on her new bachelor-employer's estate and suddenly meeting 'a handsome face' who 'would stand before me and smile and approve'; just as she had hoped, in the preceding paragraph, that her service was 'giving pleasure' to the master himself; then, suddenly, lo! 'He did stand there!' – and we have our first 'ghost' of the story (174–5). Yet despite the fact that each subsequent 'apparition' is just as blatantly presented as the displacement of her repressed desire, the critical tradition persists in treating this repression as if it might not exist, as if the text is ambiguous about the ghosts as a diegetic reality. It is a reading that might be baffling had we not seen it approach over the decades hand-in-hand with the tradition – blessed, if not inaugurated by Edel – of reading this rather straightforward story of repression through a lens that implicates the later James in the modernist disease: specifically, in Conrad's purported inability to extract his own consciousness from the kind of limited 'interior view' belonging to the governess. Trapped in this modernism, a fiction cannot be conceived as taking as its subject a delusional interiority. It can only inhabit it.

As James in the literary mind becomes tainted by modernism, the opposition between the hyperconscious American and the unconscious Pole begins to dissolve. Reinforced by a desire, especially among American critics, to see another phantom ambiguity in James's progressively more pointed and unhedging critique of the American psyche, Edel extends his remarkable misreading of *The Turn of the Screw* to *The Golden Bowl*. Instead of reading Maggie Verver as the American whose distrust of privacy leads her to a governess-like delusion of persecution at the hands of her European friends – the regime of confession in violent reaction to the regime of testimony – Edel proposes that she has achieved, like none other in the novel, a penetration into 'the truth' about Amerigo and Charlotte. He cites, for this purpose, portions of the text that were clearly meant to demonstrate Maggie's absorbing paranoia. As she sits at cards with all the actors of the drama, for instance, Edel sees in James's words justification of her delusion, not an analysis thereof: 'Erect above all for her was the sharp-edged fact of the relation of the whole group, individually and collectively, to herself – herself so speciously eliminated for the hour, but presumably more present to the attention of each than the next card to be played' (qtd in Edel 5:216). Implicated in a testimony-bound modernism, the later James nonetheless escapes the epistemological calumny adhering to Conrad because he continues to pledge allegiance in his nonfiction to the contract of comprehension. It has become an indelible part of the story we tell about James – because James, in his prefaces and criticism, explicitly instructs us to tell it – that he is an agent of epistemological comprehension, in contrast to writers of the 'accurst autobiographical form' whose 'grasp of reality and truth isn't strong and disinterested' (*Henry James* 500).

As the summer of 1872 peaked, the enticing story of Dr David Livingstone's new exploration and 'disappearance' was eclipsed by that of the '*Herald* rescuer' (Oxford [Alabama] *Chronicle* July 11), the 'chief of the *Herald* exploring expedition' (Salt Lake *Herald* July 10), Henry Morton Stanley. Eventually, the voluminous collection of articles, books, and speaking tours Stanley would reap from his African adventures brought wealth and celebrity unprecedented among modern explorers. According to George Martelli, Stanley is nothing less than 'the progenitor of all the subsequent professional travel writers' (10). His succession of Livingstone on the world stage anticipates the story of first- and second-wave colonialists we have seen throughout Conrad's early fiction. The Welshman-cum-American's tale, like those of Almayer, Donkin, and the keepers of 'An Outpost of Progress,' is one of a social outcast who gambles everything on making one big score in the unpoliced outskirts of empire. Like those figures, Stanley fairly chokes on the rhetoric of science and evangelism in which he feels obliged to frame himself. One often feels 'Exterminate all the brutes!' vibrating just beyond the margin of his writing, and he sometimes fails to conceal that the true goal of his plunge into African darkness is to gather about himself a greater radiance in Western eyes. Narrating the first footsteps of his expedition from Zanzibar, Stanley writes: '[W]ith the blatant rabble of Banyans, Arabs and Beloochees I had taken my last look, and before me beamed the sun of promise as he sped toward the Occident' (NYH 22 Dec. 1871).

The desire to penetrate an African otherness that, in the end, turns out to have been a desire to uncover the mystery of the 'Occidental' heart – which we will see in the stories spawned by Stanley's famous meeting with Livingstone – is an inversion that Conrad's fiction dwells on incessantly. Almost without exception, each time Conrad's prose approaches the task of representing the colonial other, it becomes a meditation on the mystery of European desire. In *The Nigger of the 'Narcissus,'* the youthful sailor Creighton 'stood leaning over the rail, and looked dreamily into the night of the East.'

> And he saw in it a long country lane . . . He saw stirring boughs of old trees
> outspread, and framing in their arch the tender, the caressing blueness of
> an English sky. And through the arch a girl in a light dress, smiling under
> a sunshade, seemed to be stepping out of the tender sky. (13)

Conrad persistently figures his itinerant white men as trapped in a
European phantasmagoria. Even to Charlie Marlow the East is an occluded, not occluding object. Marlow first appears in 'Youth,' the autobiographical tale of the author's first contact with 'the men of the
East' (40). In a story where even the smallest gestures among the English crew of the *Judea* are elaborated at length, Marlow suddenly becomes reticent at the climactic moment of his coming face-to-face with
the people of Borneo. The *Judea* having sunk just days from the coast –
ignited by the fumes of its coal cargo – Marlow reaches the Singapore
bay in a lifeboat, ties the craft to a jetty, and falls asleep with his crew.
He is awakened by 'a silence . . . as complete as if it had never been
broken . . . And then I saw the men of the East – they were looking at
me' (40). At this moment, finally, of exhibiting the other, the being who
is inevitably at the heart of the story's romantic anticipation, Marlow's
narrative eye suddenly inverts. It turns almost entirely onto himself
and his sleeping lifeboat crew – men 'unconscious of the land and the
people' – as a marvellous object of the Eastern gaze (41). For Marlow,
'all the East is contained in that vision' when 'I saw it looking at me.
And this is all that is left of it!' (42)

'The End of the Tether,' the other bookend to *Heart of Darkness* in the
*Youth* volume, is the most insistent among these stories that the colonial
mystery haunting Europe is of the self, not the other. As the steamship *Sofala* passes a small, formerly uncharted Malaysian island along
the unique shipping route Captain Whalley had discovered some years
earlier, the narrator describes the 'outcast tribe' fishing off its shore.
Once again, although the narrative pretends nothing about the natives'
subjectivity, the point of view is theirs, and the speculated object is the
European vessel.

> Their ears caught the panting of that ship; their eyes followed her till
> she passed between the two capes of the mainland going at full speed as
> though she hoped to make her way unchecked into the very bosom of the
> earth. (245)

The passage deliberately recalls the moment in *Heart of Darkness* when
Marlow realizes at the outset of his journey that he is perceived by

influential women at home – not just his aunt, but the wife of a 'high dignitary and goodness knows . . . how many more people besides' – as an 'emissary of light' advancing on their behalf. In this role, Marlow says, 'a queer feeling came to me that I was an impostor . . . I felt as though, instead of going to the centre of a continent, I were about to set off for the centre of the earth' (12–13). Thus Conrad announces that the testimony of this fiction, of the report that is *Heart of Darkness*, is no emissary for the sentimentalists – which include, in Conrad's ideology, both 'philanthropists' and the reactionary journalism embodied by the *Herald* – who seek something inconceivable in the 'centre' of the most alien, the darkest exotic. The inscrutable and restless European 'hope' in the 'End of the Tether' passage, which winds up being the real object of wonder in this tableau of an exotic people, is here identical to that which animates Marlow's aunt. The scope and object of the *Sofala*'s desire seem unknown even to itself, overshooting its conscious mundane goal – a desire, really, to penetrate an opaque heart, the heart of hearts, the 'bosom' of the mundane itself, the secret meaning of the *Sofala*'s own worldly endeavour. This scene re-applies the language with which the merchant vessel's Malay Serang had been painted earlier, a man whose 'placid mind had remained as incapable of penetrating the simplest motives of those he served as they themselves were incapable of detecting through the crust of the earth the secret nature of its heart . . .' (228). Such scenes in the novella make us take a second look at the remarkable moment in which the angry and ambitious ship's engineer, Massy, listens with satisfaction to a loud monologue, uttered by his drunken subordinate in the adjoining cabin, praising Massy's pluck and cleverness. With a 'half smile of pride,' Massy then thinks about the lascar he knows to be on duty just outside. '[P]erhaps a youth fresh from a forest village,' the boy 'would stand . . . listening to the endless drunken gabble.'

> His heart would be thumping with the breathless awe of white men: the arbitrary and obstinate men who pursue inflexibly their incomprehensible purposes – beings with weird intonations in the voice, moved by unaccountable feelings, actuated by inscrutable motives. (224)

'The End of the Tether' ultimately makes it impossible to imagine that the question of the white man's 'inscrutable motives' belongs only to the lascar.

In each of *Youth*'s fictions, the Kiplingesque promise to excavate the secret nature of the earth beyond civilization becomes moot, unexpectedly, by a turning of tables – by our inability to know the secrets of 'our' adventuring envoy, or the truth of his investigating and civilized heart. If contemporary critical thought is now generally inured to this reversal and its implicit critique, the Western world that still seizes fondly on the moment of Henry Morton Stanley's deepest penetration – on his 'Dr Livingstone, I presume?' – is not entirely conscious that its delight is of finding the self in the land of the other, or, more precisely, in the promise that this inscrutable self has been discovered. Stanley's greeting became famous as soon as it was born. It made its first appearance in the *Herald*, on 2 July 1872, in a fast-paced synopsis of several of Stanley's letters that had arrived all at once.[10] As in Stanley's letter, the 'HISTORIC MEETING' at the centre of Bennett's story was framed by the blood Stanley shed on his way to Livingstone in Ujiji. The expedition had been held up in Unyanyembe, where tensions were rising between local Arabs and an African tribe to the west, in Kawendi. Stanley and the Arabs were outraged by the 'tributes' the African leader demanded of those who would cross his lands, and Stanley agreed to join the Arabs in an all-out war against the Africans. A veteran reporter of the United States' battles against its own indigenous people, Stanley had learned that when one must detail one's violence upon the natives, it is best to centralize the image of a single warlord or despot. Hence his focus on Mtyela Kasanda, 'Mirambo,' the villainous tribal leader. 'On the first day,' Stanley reports, 'we burned three of his villages, captured, killed, or drove away the inhabitants' (NYH 15 July 1872). Thus 'THE HERALD GOES TO WAR,' as the July 2 edition proudly proclaims in a subheading. 'The superior armament of the HERALD expedition made their assistance a matter of great importance to the Arabs . . . and the forces [marched] with the American flag flying . . .' After the first blindside against the villages, a sudden fever kept Stanley safe from further conflict. After almost a week, he was able to resume the expedition with an amended route to the west. A four-hundred-mile journey later, 'the pilgrims of progress' made 'A TRIUMPHAL ENTRY INTO UJIJI.' Stanley reports entering the suburbs 'firing away our guns as only exuberant heroes do, to the intense astonishment of the Arabs of Ujiji, who turned out en masse to know what it meant' (15 July). For an inter-title the *Herald* seizes eagerly on the image of 'THE ASTONISHED NATIVES' (2 July). Stanley continues:

> Passing from the rear of [the crowd] to the front I saw a knot of Arabs, and, in the center, in striking contrast to their sunburnt faces, was a pale-looking and gray-bearded white man . . .

> It was the dignity that a white man . . . ought to possess that prevented
> me from running to shake hands with the venerable traveler . . . False
> pride and the presence of the grave-looking dignitaries of Ujiji restrained
> me and suggested to me to say, with a shake of the hand,
>    'Dr. Livingstone, I presume?' (15 July 1872)

Even if most have never read Stanley's narrative, countless people
around the globe have smiled at this greeting. They intuit the situation
as it had been given to the *Herald*'s readers: Stanley need not 'presume,'
of course, to be addressing Dr Livingstone, the only white man to be
found in Ujiji, sticking out as he is 'in the centre' of 'a knot of Arabs . . .
in striking contrast to their sunburnt faces.' The *Herald*'s 2 July synopsis emphasizes Livingstone 'strongly contrasting with the dusky, sunburnt' faces about him. The tableau Stanley paints of the white man
discovered, finally revealed by the force of this 'contrast' to his Arab and
native milieu, was repainted by almost all of the *Herald*'s contemporaries in their own excited reports of the dispatch – reiterated as frequently and faithfully as was the utterance itself. 'Few things in the
romance of travel and adventure,' writes the London *Daily News*,
'seem to us more striking than that first meeting with the long-lost explorer among the wild crowd in the African village' (14 July). 'He was
an American,' the *London Post* wrote of Stanley, 'but "blood is thicker
than water," and among the black savages the two men who met were
truly of one race' (27 July). The *Inverness Courier* can only imagine the
odd scene of 'that Christmas dinner in Ujiji, when . . . Livingstone and
Stanley sat down together amid savage scenes and savage people'
(4 July).

As are most of Stanley's dispatches on this expedition, the famous
letter narrating his discovery of Livingstone is actually, in its bulk, a
litany of treacheries imposed on both explorers by the various natives,
Arabs and 'half-castes' in their employ. Both Stanley's narrative and his
report of Livingstone's recent travels are comprised almost entirely of
the obstacles created by the non-whites' unreliability – a feature that
the *Herald* eagerly underscores in various subheadlines and inter-titles
for the dispatch: 'COWARDLY CONDUCT OF THE ARABS,' 'AN EASTERN IN-
GRATE,' 'MY STUMBLING BLOCK.' The tenor of the narrative is succinctly
reflected in Livingstone's own synopsis of Stanley's adventure:

> Mr. Stanley has done his part with untiring energy; good judgment in the
> teeth of very serious obstacles. His helpmates turned out depraved black-
> guards . . . They had used up their strength by wickedness, and were of

next to no service, but rather downdrafts and unbearable drags to progress. (*Last Journals* 156–7)

To Stanley's jungle-hacking expedition – which had eschewed the use of roads in its final push to Ujiji – the challenges of nature were apparently nothing as compared to the devastation of cowardly Arabs and lying natives. Part of the unassailable 'presumption' that Stanley wryly shares with his reader is that Livingstone represents a singular oasis amid treacherous sands.[11]

In *Heart of Darkness*, of course, the mystery of the European self is always bound to the 'mystery' of a genocide written in the margins of its evangelical messianism, of a rubber-harvesting forced labour that would save its African victims from the tyranny of Arab slavery. In the 'journalistic enterprise' that is Stanley's expedition, this mystery bubbles just beneath the surface of its consciousness. When the *London Telegraph* proclaims that 'the day seems to have arrived when the African mystery is to be solved,' it has already reminded its readers at the beginning of the article that the mysteries it has in mind are not merely geographical:

[E]ager as we are to hear all that Livingstone will have to tell us of the great watersheds of the Nile . . . we yet are called back in a moment . . . by a sad, thoughtful sentence, full of deep meaning, which stands at the end of the Doctor's letter to Mr. Bennett. 'If,' he writes, 'my disclosures regarding the terrible Ujijian slaving should lead to the suppression of the east coast slave trade, I shall regard that as a greater matter by far than the discovery of all the Nile sources together.' (25 July 1872)

The article closes with the assurance that, now, 'the great continent must yield up its deepest secrets; and when we feel the mighty power of Livingstone's words at this moment we wonder no more that he was reached and succored . . . Heaven had need of him, and that which has been was to be.' As with Kurtz's marginalia, which, like any marginalia, and like any frame, can be selectively ignored, the *Telegraph* must immediately forget the setting that had made 'Dr Livingstone, I presume?' so thrilling in the first place – that is, the 'knot of Arabs,' where, 'in striking contrast to their sunburnt faces,' the doctor was found 'in the centre' (NYH 15 July). These are the Arabs who had been Livingstone's rescuers after his supplies from Zanzibar had been cut off, who for the last two years had been his only 'succor,' to recall the *Telegraph*'s term for Stanley's aid, but which Livingstone's journals repeatedly attach to his Arab helpers. These were precisely the Ujijian slave traders he had reproached, in the words quoted above at the beginning of the *Telegraph* article, and against whose trade his evangelical mission had always been bent. The English and American denial of the situation was pathological. Even assuming that the 'Arabs' Stanley joined to slaughter the Africans of Kawendi had nothing to do with the slave trade, it is impossible to read Livingstone's own account of his recent travels, which quickly followed Stanley's dispatches, without coming to his own conclusion: 'Who could accompany the people of Dugumbé and Tagomoio to Lomamé and be free from blood-guiltiness?' (*Last Journals* 135) Yet in the London *Times*'s synopsis of these travels, Livingstone is said to be 'at downright war with slave-dealing Sultans' (29 July). Stanley and his contemporaries must bury and rebury the question of how, exactly, the 'savagery' constantly woven into their African narrative can be detached from the Western adventurers who are the cause or coadjutors of its thrilling violence, the exporters of what the *London Daily News* calls 'one of the most exciting stories civilization has had.' That paper demonstrates the most popular way the question was scuttled: at strategic intervals, Africa becomes a cosmologically distinct realm of 'nature' where moral responsibility no longer obtains in any direction; thus the burned villages in Stanley's wake are simply proof 'that a state of nature is a state of war' (14 July).

Conrad's Western world is helplessly drawn to the opacity of the colonial frontier, to the secret that must dwell in the silence beyond, but it recoils and retreats into unconsciousness with a glimpse behind the veil at its own bloody hand. Conrad had explored this syndrome before *Heart of Darkness* and 'An Outpost of Progress' in *The Nigger of the 'Narcissus.'* The continually reiterated 'fascination' among the *Narcissus* crew about what the 'nigger,' James Wait, has not yet spoken – 'We were always incurably anxious to hear what he had to say' (45) – is the same fascination evoked by the ancient Singleton, by his ineffable knowledge of 'violences and terrors' that have taken place along the watery global network he helped to forge.

> He stopped, thoughtful, as if trying to recollect gruesome things, details of horrors, hecatombs of niggers. They looked at him fascinated. He was old enough to remember slavers, bloody mutinies . . . who could tell through what violences and terrors he had lived! What would he

say? . . . [I]ncomprehensible and exciting, [he was] like an oracle behind a
veil . . . (79–80)

Part of the doubt hovering over the *Narcissus* – unacknowledged both
by the novel and its criticism – is that the spectre of death Wait represents is not a merely universal one. The spell of 'sentimental doubt'
he casts over the crew feeds rather on their sense of being implicated
in the 'hecatombs of niggers,' the historical, pandemic 'dying off'
that his sickness and demise inevitably evoke. When Wait's illness
first becomes visible on his face, his emergence on deck permanently
annihilates the laughing camaraderie of the regular seamen, releasing 'a
subtle and dismal influence; a something cold and gloomy that floated
out and settled on all the faces like a mourning veil.' And yet again
the nature of this 'something' is locked within the object that has
excited the mystery, in an 'oracle' that is always and only about to
speak.

> The joy of laughter died on stiffened lips . . . Many turned their backs,
> trying to look unconcerned . . . They resembled criminals conscious of
> misdeeds . . . All expected James Wait to say something, and, at the same
> time, had the air of knowing beforehand what he would say. (21)

Because Conrad so frequently aligns sentimentalism with a peculiar
disciplinary reformism that ostensibly opposes colonial exploitation
even as it enables it, the 'sentimental doubt' suffusing the crew vexes
the novel itself. The novel does not, cannot posit a more enlightened
perspective from which this doubt could be dismissed. It is thus impossible to read as a mere chastisement of the crew that 'through [Wait] we
were becoming highly humanised, tender, complex, excessively decadent . . . We had the air of being initiated in some infamous mysteries;
we had the profound grimaces of conspirators . . .' (85).

If the crew's bewilderment can be traced to a semi-consciousness
of being an indispensable apparatus of the colonial machine – a monstrous engine of human civilization that their own humanity could
never derail – they are at least more conscious than the civilized landlubbers Conrad explicitly implicates. In *Heart of Darkness*, when Marlow describes the 'extravagance of emotion' he felt at the moment he
despaired of ever hearing Kurtz, his own oracle, 'speak after all,' somebody in his audience apparently rolls his eyes.

> Why do you sigh in this beastly way, somebody? Absurd? . . . This is the
> worst of trying to tell . . . Here you all are, each moored with two good
> addresses, like a hulk with two anchors, a butcher round one corner, a
> policeman round another . . . And you say, Absurd! (48)

Conrad's favourite metonyms for the unseen safety net of civic structure reappear only a few paragraphs later, as he lectures his audience
again:

> You can't understand. How could you? – with solid pavement under your
> feet, surrounded by kind neighbours ready to cheer you or to fall on you,
> stepping delicately between the butcher and the policeman, in *the holy
> terror of scandal and gallows and lunatic asylums* – how can you imagine what
> particular region of the first ages a man's untrammeled feet may take him
> into by the way of solitude – utter solitude without a policeman – by the
> way of silence – utter silence, where no warning voice of a kind neighbour
> can be heard whispering of public opinion? (50, my emphasis)

Disingenuously, Marlow imagines that a disciplined society, with no
access to the 'silence' beyond the self-policing of 'public opinion,' cannot 'understand' the mute call of the Kurtzian/Livingstonian oracle.
*Heart of Darkness* knows very well that its landed audience will be and
has been drawn to the same 'infamous mysteries'; in a remarkable passage that never made it to typescript, Marlow suggests that the truth
this mystery withholds is directly continuous with the machinery of
civic society and the violence it selectively keeps from view. Marlow
strategically begins with the 'natural,' recognized violence of the African at his wildest. Even as they 'howled and leaped and spun' themselves into a warrior's frenzy, a suspicion would 'come slowly to one'
of their 'not being inhuman' (36).

> You know how it is when we hear the band of a regiment. A martial
> noise – and you, pacific father, mild guardian of a domestic heartstone
> [*sic*] suddenly find yourself thinking of carnage . . . Not for you tho' the
> joy of killing . . . Too many things in the way, business, houses, omnibuses,
> police[,] the man next door. You don't know my respectable friends how
> much you owe to the man next door. He is a great fact. There's very few
> places on earth where you haven't a man next door to you or something of
> him, the merest trace, his footprint – that's enough. (36n)

In his reference to *Robinson Crusoe* – to the astonishing, uncanny vision of the human footprint that announces to Crusoe he is not alone in the wilderness – Conrad recalls the literary iconography that flared up around Stanley's sensational adventure: a myth of Crusoe that has been indispensable, historically, to the West's conception of the civilization machine and its relation to the colonial other.[12] On either side of the Atlantic, newspapers repeatedly described Stanley's reportage as on par with 'the best of all romance writing' (LT 29 July 1872), and as 'a tale of travel daring as Vasco di Gama's, solitary as Crusoe's, romantic as Marco Polo's' (LT 4 July 1872). The *Crusoe* nexus in the writing of Stanley's observers reveals a journalism that seeks epistemological profit from the figure of the travel-writing witness, even as it elevates Stanley's dispatches above the testimonial condition of that figure.

To this end, for instance, the *Herald* exploits the muddled, unvanquishable controversy between fact and fiction that *Robinson Crusoe* had long ago unleashed. Over the course of its frequent self-congratulation for its African adventure, the *Herald* delivers a paean to 'The Press as a Teacher of Science' and its 'Superiority Over All Other Media.' Here Bennett elaborates an assertion he makes in the leading article of the same issue that 'the great discoveries of the world' are heralded not by 'books . . . but by the press of the land' (7 Mar. 1872). He cites *Crusoe* and *Gulliver's Travels* as exemplars of the 'ineffectual' book through which students have heretofore learned about the world. In this confusion among narratives with and without a claim to historicity – a confusion quite common among all of his colleagues' comparisons of Stanley to *Crusoe* – Bennett can summon the spectres of Defoe and Swift to cast doubt on the historical reliability of any and all 'books,' and can elevate the press above the travel-writing testimonial in general, which these storytellers thus come to represent. Some journals managed to detach Stanley the witness so completely from Stanley the testifier as to obtain the logic Hartog finds in Herodotus, where 'no separation is made between saying and seeing' (Hartog 251). 'Mr. Stanley's attainment is substantial,' reports the London *Globe* upon his success: 'He has not talked or reported.' Rather, 'he has actually seen the great traveller' (3 July 1872).

Stanley himself shows the hand of a writer who has learned one of the most important lessons Defoe had to teach – to novelists, but also to travel writers and journalists – about how to infuse testimony with narrative drama, and to bolster it with what the eighteenth century called 'probability.' In his first letter from the African coast, where there is little adventure beyond the struggle to organize the expedition, the journalist creates a sense of incident by formally introducing, in the middle of his recitation, a new narrator – Stanley himself – in the form of an entry from his private journal. A tried and true movement of the epistolary novel as well, it animates Crusoe's narrative whenever the castaway creates a new scene by revealing an entry from his journal. As Stanley manufactures a 'private' testimony within his public dispatch, the testimonial nature of the surrounding report is obscured as such; it is occluded in the artificial contrast, the ultimately false dichotomy of voice within frame, testimony within comprehension. Stanley gives his reader the privilege of 'overhearing' a privacy bracketed by quotation marks, a discourse 'meant' only for Stanley's introspection, but diverted for our profit from its proper destination. Here is the transition as it appears in the *Herald*:

> As I had the success of the NEW YORK HERALD Expedition near and dear to my heart, constant thinking about it and the contingencies that might arise to prevent its success, over and over I had long sketched its march from the sea coast to Ujiji, and knew almost as well as if I had been there before what kind of difficulties I should meet. The following is one of my sketches made on board ship while coming to Zanzibar:
>
> 'One hundred pagazis will be required to convey cloth, beads and wire enough to keep me and my soldiers for one year and to pay expenses . . . In three months I will try to reach Unyanyembe . . . From Unyanyembe is one month's march to Ujiji, on the Tanganyika Lake. And after! – where is Livingstone?' (22 Dec. 1871).

In Stanley's second voice, signals of a very personal attestation are crafted with incomplete sentences, anxious rhetorical questions about the future, but also with a further removal of Livingstone into mystery, into a distance and darkness intensified by this narrative withdrawal – a removal not just into another past in relation to the present dispatch, but into the receded subjectivity of the explorer, who is now a dramatic object within the comprehension of the journalist.

The most important work accomplished by the Crusoe myth in the colonial imagination is an amelioration of the anxiety that, I have been arguing, ultimately excites the mystery of the Livingstonian-Kurtzian self that has disappeared within the African other: the helpless suspicion that the charred villages in Stanley's wake were burned by a civilization machine that we build and engage at 'home.' The emblem of this machine emerges in Defoe's novel, and is forever after suppressed in most Crusoe mythologies, in the fact of Crusoe's gun. Even today, and even in the most critical academic paraphrases of the novel, *Robinson Crusoe* is said to speak a myth of the white man as 'founder of a new world,' as Edward Said writes, and of his self-sufficiency therein (*Culture* 70). This is a myth of the European's ability to overcome both nature and man even when naked, stripped of all the apparatus on which he might seem to have become dependent. It is a conception of the story that must ignore Crusoe's gun, without which the castaway could never have corralled nature and man into service to his island kingdom. Crusoe's weapon is the product not only of centuries of research, craftsmanship, and metal refinery, but of the myriad bureaucratic, mercantile, and political apparatus that make these possible. There may be no other object into which civil society is as densely compacted, and none to whose operation and perfection it is more deeply committed. Yet how convincingly does its sleek opacity and apparent self-containment suggest that its power is triggered entirely and solely by the hand that holds it. On his bloody trail to Livingstone, Stanley sends a familiar thrill through his readers when he describes confronting a 'Sultana' who was holding some deserters from his expedition. Another Arab reportedly 'makes haste to inform the Sultana that she did not know what white people were capable of doing if they were angered.' Although this 'capability' derives entirely from the arbitrary power of the gun, which would 'kill her in her house at the distance of half a mile,' the dispatch revels in an ominous power supposedly inherent in 'white people' (NYH 22 Dec. 1871).

As in *Robinson Crusoe*, Stanley's text hides the gun and the conceptual work it accomplishes in plain sight. In Stanley's description of the equipage and provisions of the expedition, fully half of his long itemization is devoted to his 'weapons of defence' (22 Dec.). The details are elaborated, in fact, with a peculiar relish, as if to titillate the *Herald*'s readers with a kind of techno-military pornography.[13] As Stanley will persistently reiterate his loving dependence on such apparatus – including the breathtaking automatism of the six-hundred-rounds-per-minute 'Maxim gun,' which he later writes would be 'of valuable service in helping civilisation to overcome barbarism'[14] – we might expect the larger Crusoe-inflected narrative disseminated by the press to be torn between this awe of the superhuman civilization-machine, on the one hand, and the myth of the European as 'natural' overman, on the other. On the contrary, however, the gun's power to embody and announce the power of the Western civilization-machine seems, in these narratives, to rest without conflict within the Crusoe frame they attempt to construct. As he makes what the *Herald* calls his 'TRIUMPHAL ENTRY INTO UJIJI,' on the brink of Livingstone's discovery 'that Civilization has found him out' (LT 4 July 1872), Stanley enters the suburbs, as we have seen, 'firing away our guns' (NYH 15 July). This scene of what Bennett called 'THE THUNDER OF GUNPOWDER' as the herald of civilization was enthusiastically replayed by virtually all of the *Herald*'s contemporaries, rivalling in popularity even Stanley's greeting to Livingstone. In their embellished narrations of the scene, for instance, both the London *Telegraph* and *Standard* concoct a story about a 'native' counterpart to Stanley's noise, as if to place the gunfire in a dichotomy of occident and orient to which it has belonged since the decline of the Ottoman Empire. '[T]he inhabitants of Ujiji,' writes the *Standard* in pure invention, 'attempted to drown the report of Mr. Stanley's firearms in the noise of their own unearthly musical instruments' (6 July 1872). The *Telegraph*: 'The Ujijians poured out in crude shouts and beatings of their rude drums . . .' (4 July 1872).

*Heart of Darkness* was published as the second in a trilogy of stories loosely collected as a stages-of-man series that begins with 'Youth' and ends with 'The End of the Tether.' As he was writing these fictions, however, Conrad had expected the space now occupied by 'Tether' to be filled by his original, much shorter conception of *Lord Jim*. This initial plan suggests that Jim may have meant to represent another possibility, contra Kurtz, of the European 'missionary.' It becomes even more remarkable, too, that when the predatory Brown discovers Jim, long 'disappeared' from the white world, and in a country accessible, like Kurtz's domain, only by river, he sees him standing 'all white' in a 'knot of coloured figures' (379); and yet again, a 'group of dark faces with the white figure in the midst' (379). Conrad recalls the newspaper language of 1872 exactly. It is clear, furthermore, that the 'whiteness' in *Lord Jim*'s white-in-the-centre motif is not meant to be familiar, not the comforting oasis of self in the realm of the other. As we have seen elsewhere in Conrad, this whiteness is the unreadable surface of the colonial project, an enigma of motive and purpose. When Marlow's ship pulls away from Patusan for the last time, the captain watches Jim among the natives on shore and muses on the 'opportunity' for redemption the young man had hoped to find there. The language strongly recalls *Heart of Darkness*:

> Their dark-skinned bodies vanished on the dark background long before I lost sight of their protector. He was white from head to foot, and remained

persistently visible with the stronghold of the night at his back, the sea
at his feet, the opportunity by his side – still veiled . . . For me that white
figure in the stillness of coast and sea seemed to stand at the heart of a vast
enigma. (336)

This 'opportunity' is only apparently the personal redemption of a
single European, one whose complacent idealism had once been suffused with a limitless self-regard until he realized his own willingness
to abandon eight hundred Muslim pilgrims to a violent death – a mass
burial of those who had 'surrendered to the wisdom of white men' (17).
The atonement Jim achieves by routing the Bugis's slave-holding op-
pressors and bringing order to their settlement is, of course, identical to
the missionary ideal that was always supposed to have redeemed the
colonial adventure. The real motive of this adventure, and the question
of whether it truly stems from this ideal, is again lost in an inscrutable
whiteness.

Any reading of *Heart of Darkness*, or even of Conrad in general, that
concludes without ever having made reference to 'The horror! The horror!' might be seen in some quarters to be an unconscionable perversion. But I might very well have launched the whole of this study with
these comforting and attractive words – as the critical record has clearly
proven them to be – and hung everything that followed upon them.
Here at last are the words of revelation from a once-hidden oracle. They
have been hunted compulsively by a critical imagination spurred on
by a suspicion first voiced by E.M. Forster: that the 'secret casket' of
Conrad's work might contain 'a vapour rather than a jewel'; that it will
never provide an answer to its enigma. This suspicion, I have argued,
is often unaware that it has been excited precisely by the 'secret casket'
rhetoric that the work itself has deliberately conjured and lampooned.
Forster himself is apparently unaware that his figuration was both suggested and counterargued by Conrad himself in the now-famous pronouncement that, to Marlow, 'the meaning of an episode was not inside
like a kernel but outside, enveloping the tale which brought it out only
as a glow brings out a haze . . .' (5). The jewel-hunters find their quarry
at last – 'The horror! The horror!'; but then, at the moment one stumbles
upon the once-hidden prize, its secret import flies away again, as Paul
de Man has warned it would: flies not to another inside but to an outside, and we are stuck with enigma once again. The charge that Conrad
is deliberately frustrating in this way is not entirely unwarranted. At
Kurtz's end, Marlow leads us on, leads himself on, by a return to the

metaphysics of veiling and unveiling he had previously cast off in his epiphany on the river, when he realized he was expecting a comprehensive truth from an exhumed 'discoursing' oracle. 'It was as though a veil had been rent,' Marlow says of Kurtz's face, tantalizingly, at the moment before death, 'that supreme moment of complete knowledge' (70–1). Doggedly attached to this moment and this figuration, scrupulously unaware of everything else in Conrad's oeuvre that challenges them, a certain literary-critical regimen has run an inexhaustible circuit of comfort and despair, toward and away from 'The horror! The horror!'

My explication, my 'reading' – and thus my contribution to the continuing comfort of these words! – would have to acknowledge this moment in *Heart of Darkness* as indeed extraordinary in Conrad's writing, not simply because Marlow announces it with a lifting of veils – the gesture that has been the very object of his sustained and general critique – but because it represents a unique vision, in Conrad's world, of testimony transcended. The mechanism that achieves this vision, moreover, reveals Kurtz once again as a single embodiment of the Stanley-Livingstone dyad, and of the dreams and nightmares it awoke in the English-speaking world of the late nineteenth century. In the famous tableau Marlow creates as he bends his candlelight over Kurtz for the last time, it is clear that Marlow 'overhears' Kurtz's final words. A statement unprepared, or prepared for no other, it is not 'meant' for Marlow, not meant to be an emissary to anyone at all – not even, it seems, to himself. In fact, Conrad facilitates a sense that Kurtz *overhears himself* through Marlow's vision of a psychic doubling within the man, a doubling into the subject and object of his own consciousness, into a subject of the enunciation and a subject of the statement.

> Anything approaching the change that came over his features I have never seen before . . . It was as though a veil had been rent. I saw on that ivory face the expression of sombre pride, of ruthless power, of craven terror – of an intense and hopeless despair. *Did he live his life again* in every detail of desire, temptation, and surrender . . . ? He cried in a whisper at some image, at some vision – he cried out twice . . . (70–1, my emphasis)

Marlow achieves the sentimental investigator's dream of overhearing an absolutely sincere statement, void of self-consciousness or self-interest. Kurtz's peculiar cry, this addressless address, is achieved not simply through the ancient device of removing his consciousness to an otherworldly 'vision,' but through the deliberate contrast of this soliloquy against one that had just preceded it, before the 'veil had been rent.'

> He was lying on his back with closed eyes, and I withdrew quietly, but I heard him mutter, 'Live rightly, die, die, [die nobly][15] . . .' Was he rehearsing some speech in his sleep, or was it a fragment of a phrase from some newspaper article? He had been writing for the papers and meant to do so again, 'for the furthering of my ideas. It's a duty.'
>     His was an impenetrable darkness. (70)

The meaningful context of Kurtz's utterance here, I believe, is in the story Conrad had originally planned to accompany 'Heart of Darkness' and 'Youth' into his three-story *Youth* volume: *Lord Jim*. After Jim's death, an old letter from his father makes its way into Marlow's hands. Although the elder's advice to his son proves to be affectionate and sincere, Marlow judges the letter to be a document in 'easy morality.' He imagines Jim's father in a 'comfortable study, where for forty years he had conscientiously gone over and over again the round of his little thoughts about faith and virtue, about the conduct of life and *the only proper manner of dying*' (341, my emphasis). In this echo, moreover, *Lord Jim* asks us to think about this moment of Kurtz's last words in light of what Marlow has just pronounced about Jim's 'final statement' – another 'cry' – in the paragraph immediately preceding.

> You remember that when I was leaving him for the last time he had asked whether I would be going home soon, and suddenly cried after me, 'Tell them! . . .' I had waited – curious I'll own, and hopeful, too – only to hear him shout, 'No. Nothing.' That was all then – and there shall be nothing more; there shall be no message, unless such as each of us can interpret for himself from the language of facts, that are so often more enigmatic than the craftiest arrangement of words. (339–40)

Once again in this novel, as Marlow heads off a confusion between 'interpretation' and that which must be interpreted – the consensually constructed network of names and named events that he calls 'facts' – Conrad seems to anticipate the conflation of these in literary criticism, and the consequent reading of his work as a rejection of any and all knowledge. The passage inevitably directs its commentary back to Marlow himself in *Heart of Darkness*, to the 'transfixed' anticipation in which he had awaited a 'message' from the dying Kurtz (70). There, at the end of his quest for an oracle behind the journalist and colonial apologist, Marlow discovers a 'discoursing' being whose words are nothing other than newspaper cant and the 'easy morality' mouthed by Jim's father. 'The voice was gone,' Marlow says upon Kurtz's death. 'What else had been there?' (71) Whatever else it is, 'The horror! The horror!' is a grace Conrad bestows uniquely on Kurtz at his last breath, a gift of having achieved, if only once in his life, a 'cry' – not a calling to, but a calling out – that has not been prepared for the easy morality of an anonymous public.

# Notes

## 1. 'Speech Was of No Use': Conrad and the Critical Abjection of Testimony

1 See Showalter's 'The Prehistory of Omniscience' and 'Prose Fiction: France'; and for a relevant history see Davis's *Factual Fictions*, especially his chapter 'News/Novels: Undifferentiated Matrix.'

2 I will use the term 'extradiegetic' throughout to refer to the habitat of the historical author, 'this world' we share with him as readers. There are circumstances where a character within a fiction can technically be said to narrate extradiegetically, but since I will pay attention to the unequal powers and authorities narratology bestows on these two positions – i.e., the extradiegesis of 'the author,' however conceived, versus that of a character or an 'embedded narrator' – I will keep them distinct by reserving the term generally for the former.

3 The context of Conrad's phrase, in an essay on the Russo-Japanese war, makes it clear that this 'age of knowledge' refers to a propensity for documentation in the nineteenth century, as opposed to an increased historical or scientific understanding:

> We have seen [the war] only in the cold, silent, colourless print of books and newspapers . . . In this age of knowledge our sympathetic imagination, to which alone we can look for the ultimate triumph of concord and justice, remains strangely impervious to information, however correctly and even picturesquely conveyed. (*Notes* 83–4)

4 Among the essays published in the *New Review* between 1889 and 1890 are arguments in support of the 'eight hour' labour movement and an article on the progress of cooperative communities. The opposition to such innovation is regularly named 'the capitalist classes.'

5 Hopkins, 'Anonymity? I' 517. His two essays will be abbreviated hence-forth as I and II.

6 Historians of the press locate and characterize the 'new journalism' of the nineteenth century somewhat variously. As Patrick Collier points out, it is sometimes associated more narrowly with the relatively late tabloid inno-vations of Alfred Harmsworth (Lord Northcliffe) in his *Daily Mail* and its many siblings (11–13).

7 Despite the board's invisibility, Conrad can imagine nonetheless

> an office with adequate and no doubt comfortable furniture, and a lot of perfectly irresponsible gentlemen . . . with no care in the world; for there can be no care without personal responsibility – such, for instance, as the seamen have – those seamen from whose mouths this irresponsible institution can take away the bread – as a disciplinary measure. ('Some Reflexions' 216)

8 The best full-length study of dialogue and interrogation in Conrad is certainly Aaron Fogel's *Coercion to Speak*, although I disagree with what Foucault would call the 'repressive hypothesis' of the book. For Fogel, the ubiquitous scenes of 'forced speech' in Conrad are not matters of pro-ductive incitement, as I think is usually the case, but rather coerced dis-closures. The rich Kafkan comedy of Razumov's 'interrogation' in *Under Western Eyes* is an illustrative case: the phlegmatic Russian official asks nothing at all of Razumov, whose lengthy jabbering comes from a compul-sion to construct for the eyes of the state a coherent subjectivity, personal and political, that simply does not exist.

9 In a letter to Edward Garnett five years earlier, Conrad anticipated the effect of their public participation in a coordinated 'literary' protest, in the form of a letter to *The Times*, against the office of the Censor of Plays. As readers peruse the names of the forty belletristic signatories, Conrad imagines they will 'perceive dimly that we are not stockbrokers, not clerks, not manufacturers or bankers, or lawyers . . . We will in short appear to be unauthorized persons' (*Collected Letters* 3:489). It would be illuminating to consider Conrad's participation in such endeavours in light of what Aaron Jaffe calls the 'imprimature of the literary modernist' (39).

10 See prosecutor Robert H. Jackson's introduction to Whitney R. Harris's *Tyranny on Trial* xxxv.

11 Conrad goes on to recognize that although the novelist is 'the preserver, the keeper, the expounder, of human experience,' the historian, by the same token, 'may be an artist too' (*Notes* 17). Defoe's 1720 *Serious Reflec-tions* were written partly in response to Charles Gildon's 1719 *The Life and Surprising Adventures of Mr. D— De F— . . .*

12  Edmund Morris's biography, *Dutch*, in the *New York Times Book Review* 10
    October 1999.

13  It might be helpful at this point to clarify what role, if any, my project of
    'unmarking' testimony could play in theoretical debates about historiog-
    raphy. Scholars such as Hayden White have made us familiar with the fact
    that the causal relations written into history often derive solely from the
    requirements of narrative continuity, and that the authority of historiogra-
    phy cannot be based on its purported independence of 'literary' devices.
    Although I accept this as inarguable, I want to keep in view at all times the
    two distinct claims to authority that remain with history writing even if
    its rhetorical bonds to fiction are taken for granted. We have just seen the
    outline of the first claim, whereby historiography attempts to align itself
    unproblematically with the truth by opposing itself to fiction, and there-
    fore to all possible falsehood. The second claim to authority, however, is
    one that would in no way be undercut by a recognition of the testimonial
    constitution of history. The historian's achievement usually depends on a
    judicious coordination of multiple testimonies, and the resulting narrative
    can be supported or queried by others involved in the event. A historiog-
    raphy built on such endorsements and disagreements among witnesses,
    messy as they are, is distinct from one that depends entirely on a consen-
    sus among historians and other authorities. The latter is naturally more
    subject to questions about whose consensus is being achieved – questions
    that are foundational, for instance, to postcolonial studies. The historian's
    greatest authority, simply put, is achieved among responsive witnesses. A
    critical emphasis on the fact that testimony is the strongest, not weakest,
    element in our construction of history – whether or not we want to link
    that emphasis with an antifoundationalism or poststructuralism – is not at
    all inimical to this measure of authority or to the model of responsible his-
    toriography it endorses. This authority would be undermined only by the
    conceptual oppositions at issue throughout this chapter that degrade the
    competence of testimony.

14  Wayne Booth's *The Rhetoric of Fiction* is a notable twentieth-century inheri-
    tor of this insistence that a novel ought to declare unequivocally its proper
    subject. One of the authors Booth takes to task for failing to do so, ironi-
    cally, is James himself. With *The Turn of the Screw*, he writes, 'few of us feel
    happy with a situation in which we cannot decide whether the subject is
    two evil children as seen by a naïve but well-meaning governess or two
    innocent children as seen by a hysterical, destructive governess.' Booth
    hits home, however, when he adds, 'Whatever James's final view of his
    subject in such stories, we can only conclude that the relationship between

his developing narrators and the original subjects was often more complex than his own critical talk recognizes' (346).

15 Indulging in a moment of pure psychologizing conjecture, one might suspect that the tendency of this line of thought toward a direct comparison of Jamesian and Conradian narrators would have caused a certain anxiety for James at this moment. James had never been averse to the possibility of cultivating a wide base of readers, and here at the end of his career he nursed a certain bitterness as it became clear that popularity would elude him in his lifetime. Conrad's recently published *Chance*, whose surprising sales abruptly hauled the author out of the obscurity he shared with James and into popular view, was the occasion for, and the case study of, the master's overview of Conrad in the *TLS*. By mid-February of that year, the month prior to James's composition, seven printings of his former disciple's novel, about 12,000 copies, had already been sold.

16 Genette quotes from Raimond's *La Crise du roman, des lendemains du naturalisme aux années 20* (Paris, 1966), 300.

17 I am echoing here Jacques Derrida's reading of Lacan's 'Seminar on The Purloined Letter'; see 'La Facteur de la Vérité' in *The Post Card*.

18 The opposing thesis – that this contract is not imposed, but rather structures narrative itself – is explicitly articulated in Roland Barthes's *S/Z*.

19 I stress that this 'forgery' is nothing peculiar to Jameson or to a Marxist strategy of philosophically discrediting modernism; it is often accomplished even within the most illuminating defences of modernism. In *The Concept of Modernism*, for instance, Astradur Eysteinsson examines the 'ideological disadvantage' modernism supposedly suffers in relation to postmodernism; yet he deploys one of the crucial metaphors sustaining this disadvantage when he reminds us to think of the modernist hero as 'a detective who never solves the crime' (120). One of the novels Eysteinsson has in mind could very well be *Heart of Darkness*, a work that takes investigation and penetration as central themes. At issue in this fiction, however, is not an existential insolubility, nor the unattainability of a longed-for comprehension: what the novel puts on display is precisely the man-made epistemological circuit that manufactures such longing. Marlow in his hunt for Kurtz imagines him to be a purely 'discoursing' being, an oracular voice that will uncover not only the mystery that is Kurtz, but the supposed mystery of Africa, and even the mystery of the story itself, its 'riddle.' As my final chapter will demonstrate, the emptiness of Kurtz's discourse, composed as it is of the familiar colonialist chaff of the English press, exposes the positing of these mysteries, the contract of truth itself, as an artificial production.

20 'Certainly the first half of *Lord Jim* is one of the most breathtaking exercises in nonstop textual production that our literature has to show, a self-generating sequence of sentences for which narrative and narrator are mere pretexts, the realization of a mechanism of well-nigh random narrative free association, in which the aleatory and seemingly uncontrollable, unverifiable generation of new detail and new anecdotal material out of the old . . . obeys a logic of its own' (Jameson 219). Aside from the confusion of a productivity that would obey 'a logic of its own' and yet remain 'random,' Jameson borrows the theoretical vocabulary of Gilles Deleuze. '[T]he modern work of art,' Deleuze writes, 'is a machine and functions as such . . . To the *logos*, organ and organon whose meaning must be discovered in the whole to which it belongs, is opposed the antilogos, machine and machinery whose meaning . . . depends solely on its functioning, which, in turn, depends on its separate parts' (*Proust* 28–9). Narrative(s) may 'remain partitioned, fragmented, *without anything lacking*: eternally partial parts, open boxes and sealed vessels, swept on by time without forming a whole or presupposing one . . .' (142–3, Deleuze's emphasis).

21 Looking conversely from 'within' the enclosure of narrative, Gail Fincham closely echoes Karl in her reading of *Heart of Darkness*: 'Marlow's narrative, communicated . . . to nameless, voiceless, disembodied auditors, draws the reader's attention to qualities of self-enclosure and narcissism. Elaborately framed as dialogue, it is in effect monologue' ('Living' 66). The monologic relation between teller and reader in a third-person novel would presumably not draw attention to any 'qualities of self-enclosure'; nor, apparently, would it raise questions in the reader about her inability to respond to the monologue, to have a 'voice' in the exchange.

22 Even the careful mind of Ian Watt somehow discerns the metaphysics of subjectivity in the four-word dictum Conrad made famous in affirming his role as an artist ('to make you *see*'). Watt writes that Marlow was likely born of Conrad's desire '"to make us see" the individual's subjective life' (*Conrad* 202). Elsewhere in the book Watt addresses the phrase from the opposite pole, reading in the author's work the concerns of a literary objectivist: '[Conrad] maintains his own correspondence theory of literature: after all, what we are to be "made to see" is the real world of man and nature' (88). For a broad sampling of criticism that automatically ties Conrad or the modern novel in general to a philosophical project that would enclose the human subject in an inescapable, always 'filtering,' and always distorting subjectivity, see Najder 90–1; Friedman 64–78; Winner 186–7; Krajka 37 and 96–102; Anderson 162–6; Batchelor chapter 2; and Roussel vii.

23 *Narrative Discourse Revisited* 87. Genette's earlier *Narrative Discourse* and its
sequel will be abbreviated henceforth *ND* and *NDR*.

24 For a further survey of the effect of this logic within literary criticism,
which silently establishes as a simple axiom that we can never fully trust
narrated narrators, see Auerbach 534–6; Batchelor 37; Hunter 311–13; Lothe
166; Melnick 118–19; and Roussel 46.

25 Rick Altman's recent *A Theory of Narrative* represents an interesting and
fruitful attempt to replace focalization as a means of conceptually organiz-
ing narrative with what he calls a 'following pattern' (29). The 'following
units' that constitute this pattern, however, remain utterly dependent on
character – problematically so, perhaps, as major portions of a 'novel of
ideas' by the likes of Robert Musil or Milan Kundera would remain out of
the theory's reach.

26 For a glimpse at how the logic, if not the terminology, of 'external focalization' has governed even the most perceptive non-narratological readings
of the modernist novel, we need look no further than Leon Edel's conception of the '"compositional key" to the structure of The Wings of the Dove'
(5:118). In order to avoid sensational scenes of emotional confrontation that
'the sentimental novelists' would have expected (5:118), James 'resorted
to omission and indirection, thereby further disposing of the omniscient
author, as he had done in The Ambassadors . . .' (5:120). In the absence of a
posture of omniscience, Edel posits an omniscient presentation that really
would be comprehensive – as if the fabulist does not invent each scene,
inscribing it on otherwise blank paper, but rather selects or 'omits' it from
a diegetic totality that already exists. The critic must silently posit a fabula
with a determined existence over and beyond whatever has been written
whenever he asserts that the novelist has not fully reproduced its totality.

27 Wollaeger's study is a perceptive restaging of Conrad's 'sustained interrogation of the very categories that permit rational discussion to begin'
(xvii). In order to retain the author's commensurability with a Cartesian
scepticism, however, Wollaeger must systematically bracket the countless
ways Conrad's discourse erases the subject-object categories structuring
any such systematic epistemology. Conrad's scepticism is palpable, to be
sure, but of a wholly different order from Descartes's, whose *Pensées* questions everything except the discretion of the thinking subject, its identity
with the grammatical 'I,' and the certainty of an authentic existence from
which that subject may or may not be alienated. When Wollaeger finds
Conrad explicitly evoking – then erasing – Cartesian dichotomies ('It
is impossible to know anything, tho' it is possible to believe a thing or
two'; '[A]ll is deception only to those who have never been sincere with

themselves') he is forced to set these aside as part of 'an exasperated effort to end the conflict' of Cartesian scepticism (6; Wollaeger quotes Conrad in *Letters to R.B. Cunninghame Graham* 45, and *Tales of Hearsay* 48). On the very rare occasions when Conrad writes in an explicitly metaphysical register, he shows scant respect for 'identity' or 'the subject' as reliable concepts. In a letter to Edward Garnett he writes:

> When once the truth is grasped that one's personality is only a ridiculous and aimless masquerade of something hopelessly unknown, the attainment of serenity is not very far off. Then there remains nothing but the surrender to one's impulses, the fidelity to passing emotions which is perhaps a nearer approach to truth than any other philosophy of life. And why not? If we are 'ever becoming – never being' then I would be a fool if I tried to become this thing rather than that; for I know well that I never will be anything. (Garnett 46)

In a telling but familiar reading of these lines, Linda Anderson replaces their positive critique of a metaphysics of identity with a despairing cry that '[t]he individual can have only the precariousness of his perceptions for security' (166). Finding in it a 'futility,' 'a pessimistic discounting of the possibility of anything more than fleeting truths and momentary insights,' Anderson attributes to Conrad's work the very orientation it persistently critiques: the valuation of eternal certainty as the highest good. As is so often the case with the institutional articulation of modernism, the crisis of epistemology diagnosed here belongs not to the text, but to the critic. Conrad's 'pessimism' nevertheless remains a truism in a critical tradition that rarely includes in its analysis the author's surprising use of the term:

> We are inclined to forget that the way of excellence is in the intellectual, as distinguished from the emotional, humility. What one feels so hopelessly barren in declared pessimism is just its arrogance . . . That frame of mind is not the proper one in which to approach seriously the art of fiction. It gives the author – goodness only knows why – an elated sense of his own superiority. (*Notes* 8–9)

Only the pessimist could claim the 'superior' vantage required to see Anderson's non-fleeting truth on the horizon, and to confirm our distance from that truth. Anderson ultimately sees hope in Conrad, however – a potential escape from his pessimism – in something that turns out to be identical to the promise of a narratological structuralism: the assurance that 'continuity could be found in another sense of time, not time now as flux, but as an underlying pattern of recurrence' (173).

28 Chatman here follows Dorrit Cohn, who writes that an external narrator can 'effectively articulate a psychic life that remains unverbalized,

penumbral, or obscure,' and can do so – always, in every possible case – 'better than the character himself' (*Transparent Minds* 46).

29  See again Derrida, 'La Facteur de la Vérité' in *The Post Card*. It may seem that my more general critique could fall entirely within the compass of another of Derrida's works, his *Demeure: Fiction and Testimony*, which looks at the spectres of 'fiction, perjury, and lie' that haunt all testimony. The axiomatics that Derrida studies, however, are very different from those we have seen so far. Whereas the theoretical premise I have been isolating is that testimony is necessarily tainted by subjectivity – the distorted, 'filtered' product of consciousness – Derrida rather keeps in view the necessity by which perjury or fiction is an ever-present possibility of testimony, as are their opposites. If testimony is 'irreducible to the fictional,' he writes, 'there is no testimony that does not structurally imply in itself the possibility of fiction, simulacra, dissimulation, lie and perjury.' If this possibility 'were effectively excluded, if testimony thereby became proof, information, certainty, or archive, it would lose its function as testimony' (29–30).

30  Seshagiri 488, quotes György Lukács, 'Realism in the Balance' 39.

31  Letter from John Quinn, 23 May 1912, John Quinn Memorial Collection, New York Public Library; quoted in Stape 62.

32  Narratology will argue there is no such ouster in the novel because the third person does not absolutely disappear. The later chapters are in fact punctuated by a handful of scattered sentences that reestablish the scene of Marlow's narration and its setting, and the quotation marks surrounding the entirety of Marlow's discourse will be said to be further confirmation of the third person's continuous reign. It is an argument based on the Genettian rule we encountered earlier whereby the addition of even a single pair of quotation marks to either end of a first-person narration will transform it from the 'emancipated' utterance of immediate speech into a mere report of immediacy that could never emerge from the shadow of 'narrative patronage.' The simpler, competing conception of narrative *succession* does not require us to commit to this somewhat absurd absolutism, and in the case of *Lord Jim* it is much more responsive to what is, despite the sprinkled reminders of his storytelling setting, the total domination of Marlow's reign after his dramatic succession as the primary narrator. To the formalist the novel does not even throw the bone of an 'end bracket,' a summation or final reflection by the anonymous narrator; Marlow's discourse is the novel's last word. In the end, of course, a compelling reading of this or any such work, whether or not in relation to testimony and anonymous authority, could never emerge from a privileged attention to its regulation of 'narrating instances.' The merely automatic elevation of

such signals in a novel above the relevant features of its mise en scène, its discourse, its thematics, or its dramatic action will always be an arbitrary choice.

33  Again, it is Kafka who will write modernity's most explicit investigation into this condition. In *The Trial*, Joseph K. awakes into a proceeding in which his testimony is necessarily inadequate in relation to the narrative of his 'case.' This case is continually articulated, but always elsewhere, invisibly and inaudibly, by the anonymous authority of 'the court.'

34  In *The Novel and the Police*, D.A. Miller draws our attention to the first page of Wilkie Collins's *The Woman in White*, in which the narrator writes of the 'case' about to unfold: 'As the Judge might once have heard it, so the Reader shall hear it now' (Collins 33). For an annotated sourcebook of such fiction, see Breen.

## 2. Theatre of Incursion and Unveiling I: Home

1  See Conrad, 'Henry James' in *Notes* 17. Conrad was probably referring to James's 'The Art of Fiction' 378–9.

2  As will be obvious by now, it would be ideal, philosophically – but painful, stylistically – to write all of the 'depth' tropes inherent in the vocabulary of representation *sous rature* when ventriloquizing Conrad's position. In this case, the ambassadorial function of testimony should be understood to instate a diplomatic ~~front~~.

3  James's concern with Flack's sense of entitlement to panoptic power would have been aggravated by an incident of the previous year. James writes in a letter that he was invited to dine by one Mrs Sherwood, who 'then wrote a fearful letter about it (I having gone, all unconscious) to the American journals, which she afterwards sent me as if I should be delighted to see it' (*Henry James Letters*, vol. 3. Ed. Leon Edel. Cambridge, MA: Harvard UP, 1980, p. 189).

4  In his study of a self-critique that had always circulated among Enlightenment thinkers and their nineteenth-century progeny, however, David Bates shows that such scepticism was often directed at the trope of enlightenment itself and the rhetorical privileges it automatically arrogates.

5  For the 1908 'New York Edition' of his collected fiction, which I have been citing, James dropped this reference (as I see it) to *The Reverberator*. The quotation can be found in *Henry James: Complete Stories*, vol. 3. New York: Library of America, 1999, p. 229.

6  'The political,' for Seltzer, is a strangely undifferentiated blend of material and conceptual apparatus: within it is 'the law,' for instance, but it is

unclear upon any given deployment of that term whether it refers to the ideal, registered decrees of public policy, or to the actual engagement between state apparatus (including the police) and the individual – the historical reality of power that always exceeds the law. We will see below that this conflation is embedded in the very structure of certain influential and reportedly materialist reevaluations of the novel in general, and would itself be a prime target of Foucaultian revision.

7  Seltzer 22; he quotes de Man's 'The Purloined Ribbon' 39.

8  Rousseau, *Confessions* 252. The translations are mine.

9  In the narrative George Flack extracts from Francie in *The Reverberator*, the decadent activities it depicts are irrelevant to the newspaper except insofar as they can be linked to a name. When Flack coaxes Francie to expand on the marital 'complications' she mentions in connection with one of her future in-laws, James makes it clear that what will allow Flack to 'take hold' of his subject, to use Foucault's phrase – or 'close over it,' to use James's – is not the disclosed moral transgression, but rather the proper name appended to it. Of this woman, whose name otherwise means nothing to Flack, Francie says:

> 'She's very unhappy.'
> 'Do you mean through her husband?'
> 'Yes, he likes other ladies better. He flirts with Mme. de Brives.'
> Mr. Flack's hand closed over it. 'Mme. de Brives?' (137)

10  See, for instance, Brian Reynolds and Joseph Fitzpatrick, who join Michel de Certeau in critiquing *Discipline and Punish* for suggesting that the scope of discipline is ultimately circumscribed by the optic and architectural limits of the panopticon. These authors ascribe a foundational role to panopticism that Foucault's analysis explicitly denies. For Foucault, Bentham's panopticon is merely an attempt to schematize physically, in ink and in mortar, the 'political dream' of a fully disciplined society (198): 'The Panopticon . . . must be understood as a generalizable model of functioning; a way of defining power relations in terms of the everyday life of men' (205). It is an 'architectural figure,' a 'schema . . . destined to spread throughout the social body; its vocation was to become a generalized function' (200, 207). To propose that disciplinary apparatus is something confined to architecture or to particular institutional configurations is to keep hidden its 'more profound' reality, ultimately archival in nature. Discipline is ultimately limited only by the storage requirements of data and means by which individuals can be detailed, registered, and held accountable to power by and for those details (210).

11  Invoking Foucault in a discussion of H.G. Wells's *The Future of America*, Seltzer writes: 'Wells's account of the future in America is backed by the

comprehensive social redistribution of power that has been characterized as the formation of the "age of organization" and, more recently, as the institution of the panoptic or "disciplinary society"' (105).

12 Arguing against the 'simple polarization' between the aesthetic and the political, Seltzer writes that there is

a criminal continuity between the techniques of the novel and the social technologies of power that inhere in these techniques. It is in this rigorous continuity established in James's novel between seeing, knowing, and exercising power that the politics of the Jamesian text appears. (57)

Here and throughout his study, Seltzer states explicitly that James's fictional 'manipulation' and surveillance, his imaginary exercise of power, is identical to the historical acts of registration and subjection that Foucault traces.

13 Any discussion of James's narrative technique and his own conception of worldly power should acknowledge Leon Edel's observations on the matter in 1962. James experiences a certain 'uneasiness,' Edel writes, when considering the relation between ancient Roman art and the imperial power behind it:

Power was acceptable to him only in some attenuated or disguised form . . . Perhaps this was because he had always known it in disguise . . . and by the disguises he himself had assumed when he gave himself a motionless observer's role . . . while his eyes and mind took possession of them . . . [I]t was the observing of one who could play omniscient author in the lives of his characters while finding many ingenious technical devices to conceal his omniscience. He was to become, as a consequence of this, one of the masters of the *devious* in the modes of narration, and was to invent many new ways of concealing the storyteller from his readers. (1:101)

14 Donzelot 92, qtd in Armstrong 18.

15 As if it had been important to James to infuse into the novel the vocabulary he had since refined in *The American Scene*, these lines were new additions to the New York edition of 1908. Reprinted by Penguin, the eyes that had 'put up no shutters' appears on p. 535, and the 'comprehensive as a new issue' on p. 138.

16 See Schiller, chapter 3.

## 3. Overhearing Testimony: James in the Shadow of Sentimentalism

1 Letter to William James, 8 Feb. 1876.

2 See O'Connor 1. No source for the Ford quotation is given, and I cannot find it elsewhere.

3 Even if the donee refuses a status of indebtedness, this refusal, as Derrida points out, 'is already the mark of a duty, a debt owed, of the duty-not-to. The donee owes it *to himself* even not to give back, he *ought* not *owe* and the donor ought not count on restitution' (*Given Time* 13, Derrida's emphases).

4 Throughout the novel's history, 'disinterestedness' would suggest a renunciation of words and self-expression almost as readily as it would refer to a rejection of worldly gain. This conception of the term survives in Henry James's 1903 portrait of John Marcher in 'The Beast in the Jungle':

> He had thought himself, so long as nobody knew, the most disinterested person in the world, carrying his concentrated burden, his perpetual suspense, ever so quietly, holding his tongue about it, giving others no glimpse of it nor of its effect upon his life . . . [T]his was why, above all, he could regard himself, in a greedy world, as decently – as in fact perhaps even sublimely – unselfish. (77–8)

'Greed' becomes the name of a desire not to grasp and hoard, but to expel and to speak. Marcher is nonetheless tempted 'to take his stand on the intimacy of his loss, in order that it *might* be questioned and his retort, to the relief of his spirit, so recorded' ('Beast' 115). James frequently calls attention to the testimonial reality of the personal statement, as that which has created a 'record.'

5 As is common in the genre, the novel's primary conflict is between Julia's competing suitors: Savillon, sentimentally endowed but without worldly inheritance, and the wealthy Montauban, who asks Julia to be moved not by sentiment but by 'reasonable motives' for marriage, i.e., that an alliance with him will return her family to fiscal solvency. I will revisit in the next chapter how Savillon goes on to perform a miraculous alchemy by which he transforms his sentimental holdings into worldly currency, thus saving Julia from having to marry Montauban.

6 Such sentimental 'still-lifes' in the novel are likely Mackenzie's attempt to duplicate in prose the engraved tableaux interspersed in the pages of Rousseau's *La Nouvelle Heloise*. Compare these, for instance, with the picture Mackenzie paints of the Roubignés in the throes of their misfortune:

> When I saw the old man, with indignant pride, stifling the anguish of his heart, and pointing to the chaise that was to carry them from Belville, his wife, with one hand clasping her husband's, the other laid on her bosom, turning up to Heaven a look of resignation; his daughter, striving to check her tears, kneeling before him, and vowing her duty to his misfortunes . . . (2:6–7)

7 The terms of this particular 'marking' of testimony are governed by yet another strategic unconsciousness famously diagnosed by Jacques Derrida –

the selective recognition that even the most personal, non-circulating iteration is always for the other. An iteration is read 'from the outside,' even at
the moment of its assertion. See especially *Writing and Difference*.

8  With this aspect of its mimetic project, of course, the epistolary novel often
took great and sometimes comic liberties. A famous passage in Rousseau's
*Julie*, for instance, finds the epistler narrating, at the very moment of its oc-
currence, her lover's unexpected arrival into her room, and into her bed.

9  Over the course of the narrative, Mr Slope and Mrs Proudie unexpectedly
turn against one another in a battle over yet another official appointment.
Even as she automatically arrogates her husband's official power, in a
climactic final scene, to drive the chaplain from his service, Mrs Proudie's
power is shown to derive solely from the moral authority granted by the
conduct-book / domestic-novel matrix mapped out by Nancy Armstrong.
Yet this authority in Trollope, as Armstrong might have predicted, continually fails to limit itself to the domestic sphere. As Mrs Proudie fumes
under the pretext of moral outrage over Slope's flirtation with a 'doubtful'
continental socialite, the preacher's last rhetorical card is precisely the dangerous question of domain: 'I have yet to learn, Mrs Proudie, that you have
the power to insist either on my going from hence or on my staying here.'

> 'What!' said the lady; 'I am not to have the privilege of saying who shall
> and who shall not frequent my own drawing-room! I am not to save
> my servants and dependants from having their morals corrupted by
> improper conduct! I am not to save my own daughters from impurity! I
> will let you see, Mr Slope, whether I have the power or whether I have
> not. You will have the goodness to understand that you no longer fill
> any situation about the bishop.' (484–5)

10  The scene of intrusion is itself an intrusion within the narrative. As Eleanor
subsequently 'hurrie[s] out of the room' to recompose herself, the narration uncharacteristically doubles back on itself: 'And while she is gone,
we will briefly go back and state what had been hitherto the results of Mr
Slope's meditations on his scheme of matrimony' (130).

11  In the United States, Herman Melville will eventually portray sentimentalism as one of the most important tools of the grifters in *The Confidence-Man*.
As that novel mocks figures like Lord Shaftesbury and Mark Akenside,
its con man achieves familiarity and friendship with everyone he meets,
insisting that they open their hearts to one another and bring forth in conversation everything within. The con man sometimes creates scenarios of
'overhearing' to achieve this trust and familiarity. As he speaks in apparent
soliloquy at the railing of the steamship *Fidèle*, for instance, he only pretends to be unaware of his mark's overhearing. '[T]hrowing off in private

the cold garb of decorum, and so giving warmly loose to his genuine heart,' the con man's apparent innocence of this overhearing 'attested his earnestness' (31). Testifying to the con man's earnestness is not, purportedly, the man himself – the one uttering the words – but rather his false ignorance of being overheard.

12 Anonymous review, 'Mr. Trollope's Novels.' *National Review* 7 (October 1858): 416–35.

13 In The *Warden*, Trollope parodies Dickens in the figure of the widely read 'Mr Popular Sentiment,' whose novel *The Almshouse* is shown to depict the controversy in Barchester in easy moral terms.

14 Campos 135, cited by Christopher Butler in the 1985 Oxford UP edition of *The Ambassadors* 446–7. Butler mistakenly cites p. 137.

15 The relationship between consciousness and sacrifice in James is explored at length in Krook.

#### 4. 'Abominable Confidence' from *The Nigger of the 'Narcissus' to Lord Jim*: Toward a New Sympathetic Novel

1 Although I would advocate the 1923 Dent Uniform edition as the control text for any future editions of Conrad's works, as opposed to the oft-used but corrupt Heinemann edition of 1921, I do not consistently cite Dent-based editions in this study. I have chosen, for instance, Penguin's single-volume edition of *A Personal Record* and *The Mirror of the Sea*, since it alone among readily available editions of *The Mirror* includes the passages deleted from the periodical publications. I have relied on Norton critical editions of *The Nigger of the 'Narcissus'* and *Heart of Darkness* for similar reasons.

2 The charge was deleted from the *Pall Mall Magazine* article, 'Gales of Wind,' when it was reprinted in *The Mirror*.

3 Published in its final form in the 30 August 1923 *Times Literary Supplement*, the argument of Curle's 'The History of Mr. Conrad's Books' was apparently reversed after Conrad's chastisement, although its subject remains unchanged. It begins with the rather self-negating assertion that '[t]he material facts on which great novels are founded and the places in which their scenes are enacted are of no vital importance . . .'

4 In Norman Sherry's readily accessible *Conrad: The Critical Heritage*, examples of such criticism can be found in reviews by John Masefield 141–2, Charles John Cutcliffe 152–5, and I. Zangwill 94–6. The effects these critics cite that would thwart 'immediate communion' with the reader are usually

either the 'overly precious' and 'highly poetic diction' of the narrative, which is 'not suitable' to believable first-person presentation (Zangwill 96), or its zealous lack of sentimentality.

5  That Rousseau's fiction is under consideration in these sentences at least as much as his *Confessions* is suggested by the fact that the only work Conrad actually mentions in his short discussion of the author is *Émile*.

6  Some will counter that there really does exist a particular 'weakness' belonging to the ship, even if it is nowhere instantiated by or within the text. It is an argument committed to an artificial contract of diegetic comprehension that I critique in the opening chapter: the false notion that any imaginable nook or cranny of the fictional world, left unarticulated in the text, could exist in a determined (even if fictional) state. Such 'secret' features would have to have been determined 'somewhere else,' beyond the text – and they would have to have been determined *by* something other than the novel – since the text itself makes no such determination. See my critique of Mieke Bal's reading of *What Maisie Knew* in chapter 1, pp. 44–6.

7  See also Najder's conclusion that Conrad's letters to Curle promoted 'a shallow understanding of his own works' (*Joseph Conrad* 468).

8  The biographer's strategic blindness to his subject's critique of biography reaches a certain logical perfection, in the twentieth century, in James Miller's study of Michel Foucault. Demonstrating that the author's life, politics, and scholarship are expressions of his sexual desire and behaviour, Miller must remain completely innocent of *The History of Sexuality*'s major topics: the historical steps by which 'sexuality' became so conceptually elevated it began to determine the makeup of a subject's essential 'identity'; and the institutional apparatus – including biography – that has deployed an ever more detailed taxonomy of sexual behaviour to map out that identity and render it knowable.

9  Conrad, who frequently mixes languages in his correspondence, writes the last sentence of this excerpt, and much of the letter as a whole, in French.

10  To consider why this political sceptic so consistently embraces the nation as an indispensable atomic unit, and realpolitik as national policy, one might well take up this invitation to think about his 'life' and to recall the Polish nationalism for which his parents had died, which he takes to be the only possible bulwark against the Russian aggression that had ousted him from his childhood home. As Avrom Fleishman points out, however, the nation 'is not an end in itself for Conrad, but is justified as a stage in the development of international peace' (69). Conrad elaborates this doctrine

in his most extensive geopolitical analysis, 'Autocracy and War,' collected in *Notes on Life and Letters*.

11  *Narcissus* 107. The phrase refers to a well-known shipping reformer, Samuel Plimsoll.

12  *The Princess Casamassima*, Henry James's attempt to tackle questions of political reform and social revolution, similarly embodies the ignorant, wealthy, dabbling, would-be revolutionary in a woman. In keeping with his political vocabulary, the name of this sentimentalist is Christina Light.

13  Conrad addresses this theme quite explicitly in 'An Outpost of Progress,' a story he wrote the same year *Narcissus* was published:

> They were two perfectly insignificant and incapable individuals, whose existence is only rendered possible through the high organization of civilized crowds. Few men realize that their life, the very essence of their character, their capabilities and their audacities, are only the expression of their belief in the safety of their surroundings. The courage, the composure, the confidence; the emotions and principles; every great and every insignificant thought belongs not to the individual but to the crowd: to the crowd that believes blindly in the irresistible force of its institutions and of its morals, in the power of its police and of its opinion. Society . . . had taken care of those two men, forbidding them all independent thought, all initiative, all departure from routine; and forbidding it under pain of death. They could only live on condition of being machines. And now, released from the fostering care of men with pens behind their ears . . . they were like those lifelong prisoners who, liberated after many years, do not know what use to make of their freedom. ('Outpost' 89–91)

> Note, too, that, just as we had seen in James Wait's dream, Conrad anticipates Foucault in his vision of modern civic society as all but coextensive with its prisons.

14  See Michael North's *Dialect of Modernism* and Gail Fincham's 'Living under the Sign of Contradiction' for relevant readings.

15  In a conversation with Conrad recorded by Gerard Jean-Aubrey, the author discusses his own stint aboard the *Narcissus* in 1884. Conrad reports that 'the voyage of the *Narcissus* was performed from Bombay to London in the manner I have described,' and that there was a 'real Nigger of the *Narcissus*,' although he has forgotten his name (1:77). The crewman who died on that voyage is now known to be one Joseph Barron, whose place of birth was recorded as 'Charlton.' In *The Sea Years of Joseph Conrad*, Jerry Allen notes that 'the only place of that name with a Negro population [was] Charlton County, Georgia' (165).

16 Modelled on William Lingard, a famous captain and trader in the East during Conrad's sea years, Tom Lingard appears in *An Outcast of the Islands* and *The Rescue*, in addition to *Almayer's Folly*. Norman Sherry's research suggests, significantly, that Conrad probably never met Lingard, but had come to know the lore about the man that had already spread over the Malay Archipelago. See Sherry 116–18.

17 The significance of this intervention is underscored by an inverse movement soon after, when Donkin rouses the crew into a boiling resentment of Allistoun's pronounced judgment of Wait. As officers and regular sailors stand in tense confrontation on either end of the ship, Donkin hurls an iron belaying pin into the air, across the fore-aft divide, and it crashes violently on the poop deck among the captain and his mates.

18 Michael Greaney argues that written documents within Conrad's fiction tend to 'attest to a strain of cultural imperialism that enshrines authority in the written word' (14).

19 See Maus for a transcription and analysis of such testimony.

20 Yehiel Dinoor, or De-Nur, wrote under the name Ka-Tzetnik 135633 in reference to the 'K.Z.' (or Concentration Camp) number branded on his arm. The passage is from page 32 of *Shivitti: A Vision*.

21 As John Mullan points out, the operation of sensibility to eighteenth-century observers could be described in terms of a stimulation of 'nerves' (420).

## 5. Theatre of Incursion and Unveiling II: Empire

1 Citing only the title of the book, the letter-writer is probably referring to the American Swedenborg Printing & Publishing Society's translation of *A Continuation Concerning the Last Judgment and Concerning the Spiritual World*, published the previous year.

2 *New York Herald*, 21 July 1872; the writer cites one of the dispatches published on 15 July. Citations of the *Herald* will be abbreviated henceforth as NYH.

Although they seem to have emerged from the 'Prester John' myths sometimes taken seriously in the fifteenth and sixteenth centuries, in which the patriarch was said to have disappeared into a heathen land and built a Christian kingdom there, Swedenborg's white Africans are said to have always existed there, and to have always enjoyed an essentially direct contact with the divine.

3 It is likely that James Gordon Bennett, Jr, the magniloquent editor of the *Herald*, was personally intrigued by this hypothesis, as he had made it a

habit of late to devote long columns – written by anonymous contributors – to the Swedish philosopher. The most recent prior article appeared a week earlier on 14 July.

4  See appendices C–I in Bennett for Noe's, Stanley's, and Cook's testimonies on the matter. The totality of these narratives creates a surprisingly clear and striking impression of an abusive master-slave relationship between Stanley and Noe, to which they both appear to have been attracted.

5  As historian Adam Hochschild reports, Leopold would eventually staff his own 'Press Bureau' to this end. His agents 'surreptitiously passed cash to editors and reporters all over Europe; by 1907, the Brussels correspondents of both the *Times of London* and Germany's *Kölnische Zeitung* were on the take' (239).

6  My specific consideration in this chapter of the role Conrad and the *Herald* play in forging colonial discourse might fruitfully be read within the larger purview of Mark Wollaeger's *Modernism, Media and Propaganda*.

7  *London Telegraph* 4 July 1872. Henceforth the *Telegraph* will be cited LT.

8  This fragment belongs to Heraclitus, but Hartog notes that Lucian attributes it ultimately to Herodotus (Hartog 262).

9  Edel 5:221, quoting *The Golden Bowl* 489.

10  Because they were under the care of British authorities in Africa, the letters arrived in London before being forwarded to New York.

11  Stanley apparently made a brief attempt to take the reins of his famous greeting and lead it in another direction: in December of 1872, a brochure advertising a series of badly attended lectures he was to give in New York reprinted the hailing as 'Dr. Livingstone, I Believe' – which may have been Stanley's attempt to Americanize the phrase. The purpose of the brochure was to disseminate a biography that depicts the Welshman as wholly American.

12  See especially Said, *Culture* 70.

13  Stanley writes:

> The weapons of defence which the expedition possesses consist of one double-barrelled smooth bore No. 12, two American Winchester rifles or 'sixteen shooters,' two Starr's breech-loading carbines, one Jocelyn breech-loader, one elephant rifle, carrying balls eight to the pound; two breech-loading revolvers, twenty-four flint-lock muskets, six single-barrelled pistols, one battle axe, two swords, two daggers, one boar spear, two American axes, twenty-four hatchets and twenty-four long knives. (NYH 22 Dec. 1871)

14 *Globe*, 19 Jan. 1887 qtd in McLynn 146. In Bennett's recap of how the successful Arab onslaught against Mirambo rested entirely on Stanley's shoulders, he points to the 'great importance' of the 'superior armament of the Herald expedition' (2 July 1872).

15 The phrase 'die nobly' appears only in manuscript.

# Bibliography

Allen, Jerry. *The Sea Years of Joseph Conrad*. Garden City, NY: Doubleday, 1965.

Althusser, Louis. *Lenin and Philosophy and Other Essays*. Trans. Ben Brewster. New York and London: Monthly Review P, 2001.

Altman, Rick. *A Theory of Narrative*. New York: Columbia UP, 2008.

Anderson, Linda R. *Bennett, Wells and Conrad: Narrative in Transition*. London: Macmillan P, 1988.

Arendt, Hannah. *Eichmann in Jerusalem*. New York: Penguin, 2006.

Armstrong, Nancy. *Desire and Domestic Fiction: A Political History of the Novel*. New York: Oxford UP, 1987.

Atkinson, William. '"Try to Be Civil, Marlow": Authority at the Site of Narrative in Conrad's Early Fiction.' *Epoque Conradienne* 23 (1997): 51–67.

Auerbach, Erich. *Mimesis: The Representation of Reality in Western Literature*. Princeton: Princeton UP, 1953.

Bacon, Alan, ed. *The Nineteenth-Century History of English Studies*. Aldershot, UK: Ashgate, 1998.

Baines, Jocelyn. *Joseph Conrad: A Critical Biography*. London: Weidenfeld and Nicholson, 1960.

Bakhtin, Mikhail. *The Dialogic Imagination*. Trans. Caryl Emerson and Michael Holquist. Ed. Michael Holquist. Austin: U of Texas P, 1981.

Bal, Mieke. *Narratology: Introduction to the Theory of Narrative*. Trans. Christine van Boheemen. Toronto: U of Toronto P, 1997.

Barthes, Roland. *The Realist Novel*. Ed. Dennis Walder. *Approaching Literature 1*. New York: Routledge, 1995.

Batchelor, John. *The Edwardian Novelists*. London: Duckworth, 1982.

Bates, David. 'Idols and Insight: An Enlightenment Topography of Knowledge.' *Representations* 73:1 (2001): 1–23.

Benjamin, Walter. *Illuminations*. New York: Shocken, 1969.

Bennett, Norman R. *Stanley's Despatches to the* New York Herald: *1871–1872, 1874–1877*. Boston: Boston UP, 1970.

Billy, Ted, ed. *Critical Essays on Joseph Conrad*. Boston: G.K. Hall & Co., 1987.

Blackwood, William, ed. *Joseph Conrad: Letters to William Blackwood and David S. Meldrum*. London: Cambridge UP, 1958.

Bloom, Harold, ed. *Marlow*. New York: Chelsea House, 1992.

Bohlmann, Otto. *Conrad's Existentialism*. New York: St Martin's P, 1991.

Booth, Wayne C. *The Rhetoric of Fiction*. Chicago: U of Chicago P, 1961.

Borges, Jorge Luis. 'Pierre Mendard, Author of the *Quixote*.' *Collected Fictions*. Trans. Andrew Hurley. New York: Penguin, 1998. 88–95.

Bradbury, Malcolm, and James McFarlane, eds. *Modernism: A Guide to European Literature 1890–1930*. New York: Penguin, 1976.

Brake, Laurel. 'The Old Journalism and the New: Forms of Cultural Production in London in the 1880's.' *Papers for the Millions*. Ed. Joel H. Wiener. New York: Greenwood P, 1988. 1–24.

Brake, Laurel et al., eds. *Investigating Victorian Journalism*. New York: St Martin's P, 1990.

Breen, Jon L. *Novel Verdicts: A Guide to Courtroom Fiction*. Metuchen, NJ: Scarecrow P, 1984.

Brooks, Peter. *Reading for the Plot: Design and Intention in Narrative*. Oxford: Oxford UP, 1984.

– *Troubling Confessions: Speaking Guilt in Law and Literature*. Chicago: U of Chicago P, 2000.

Buelens, Gert. 'Henry James's Oblique Possession: Plottings of Desire and Mastery in *The American Scene*.' *PMLA* 116 (2001): 300–13.

Burns, Allan. 'Henry James's Journalists as Synechdoche for the American Scene.' *The Henry James Review* 16.1 (1995): 1–17.

Butler, Judith. *Giving an Account of Oneself*. New York: Fordham UP, 2005.

Butte, George. 'What Silenus Knew: Conrad's Uneasy Debt to Nietzsche.' *Comparative Literature* 41.2 (1989): 155–69.

Certeau, Michel de. *Heterologies: Discourse on the Other*. Trans. Brian Massumi. Minneapolis: U of Minnesota P, 1986.

Chatman, Seymour. 'Characters and Narrators: Filter, Center, Slant, and Interest – Focus.' *Poetics Today* 7.2 (1986): 189–204.

– 'Ironic Perspective.' *New Perspectives on Narrative Perspective*. Ed. Willie van Peer and Seymour Chatman. Albany: SUNY P, 2001. 117–132.

Cohen, Margaret. *The Sentimental Education of the Novel*. New Jersey: Princeton UP, 1999.

Cohn, Dorrit. *The Distinction of Fiction*. Baltimore: Johns Hopkins UP, 1999.

– *Transparent Minds: Narrative Modes for Presenting Consciousness in Fiction.*
   Princeton: Princeton UP, 1978.
Collier, Patrick. *Modernism on Fleet Street.* Farnham: Ashgate, 2006.
Collins, Wilkie. *The Woman in White.* Harmondsworth: Penguin, 1974.
Conrad, Jessie. *Joseph Conrad and His Circle.* London: Jarrold's, 1935.
Conrad, Joseph. 'Certain Aspects of the Admirable Inquiry into the Loss of the
   *Titanic.' The English Review* 11 (July 1912): 581–95.
– *Chance.* New York: Signet, 1992.
– *The Collected Letters of Joseph Conrad.* 7 vols. Ed. Frederick Karl and Laurence
   Davies. Cambridge: Cambridge UP, 1988.
– *Heart of Darkness.* Ed. Robert Kimbrough. New York: W.W. Norton, 1971.
– *Last Essays.* Ed. Richard Curle. London: Dent, 1947.
– *Letters to R.B. Cunninghame Graham.* Ed. C.T. Watts. Cambridge: Cambridge
   UP, 1969.
– *Lord Jim.* Oxford: Oxford UP, 1996.
– *The Mirror of the Sea* in *A Personal Record and The Mirror of the Sea.* New York:
   Penguin, 1998.
– *The Nigger of the 'Narcissus.'* New York: W.W. Norton, 1979.
– *Nostromo.* Oxford: Oxford UP, 1992.
– *Notes on Life and Letters.* New York: Doubleday, 1923.
– 'An Outpost of Progress.' *Tales of Unrest.* Garden City, NY: Doubleday, 1924.
   86–117.
– *A Personal Record* in *A Personal Record and The Mirror of the Sea.* New York:
   Penguin, 1998. 3–135.
– *The Secret Agent.* Oxford: Oxford UP, 1998.
– 'Some Reflexions, Seamanlike and Otherwise, on the Loss of the *Titanic.' The
   English Review* 11 (May 1912): 304–15.
– *Tales of Hearsay.* Garden City, NY: Doubleday, 1928.
– 'To My Readers in America.' (1914) Manuscript holograph in *Conrad's Mani-
   festo: Preface to a Career,* by David R. Smith. Philadelphia: Gehenna P, 1966.
   41–2.
– *Twixt Land and Sea: Tales.* New York: Doubleday, 1925.
– *Under Western Eyes.* Ed. Paul Kirschner. New York: Penguin, 1996.
– *Youth.* London: Dent, 1902.
Conroy, Mark. *Modernism and Authority: Strategies of Legitimation in Flaubert
   and Conrad.* Baltimore: Johns Hopkins UP, 1985.
Culler, Jonathan. *The Pursuit of Signs: Semiotics, Literature, Deconstruction.* Lon-
   don: Routledge, 2001.
Curle, Richard. *Conrad to a Friend.* New York: Doubleday, 1928.
– 'The History of Mr. Conrad's Books.' *Times Literary Supplement.* 30 Aug. 1923.

Cutler, Francis Wentworth. 'Why Marlow?' *The Sewanee Review Quarterly* 26 (1918): 28–38.

DaRosa, Marc. 'Henry James, Anonymity, and the Press: Journalistic Modernity and the Decline of the Author.' *Modern Fiction Studies*. 43.4 (1997): 826–59.

Davidoff, Leonore, and Catherine Hall. *Family Fortunes: Men and Women of the English Middle Class, 1780–1850*. Chicago: U of Chicago P, 1987.

Davis, Lennard J. *Factual Fictions: The Origins of the English Novel*. New York: Columbia UP, 1983.

Day, Geoffrey. *From Fiction to the Novel*. London & New York: Routledge & Kegan Paul, 1987.

Defoe, Daniel. *Serious Reflections during the Life and Surprising Adventures of Robinson Crusoe: With His Vision of the Angelick World*. London: W. Taylor, 1720.

Deleuze, Gilles. *Difference and Repetition*. Trans. Paul Patton. New York: Columbia UP, 1994.

– *Proust and Signs*. Trans. Richard Howard. New York: George Braziller, 1972.

Deleuze, Gilles, and Felix Guattari. *A Thousand Plateaus*. Trans. Brian Massumi. Minneapolis: U of Minnesota P, 1987.

De Man, Paul. *Allegories of Reading*. New Haven: Yale UP, 1979.

– 'The Concept of Irony.' *Aesthetic Ideology*. Ed. Andrzej Warminski. Minneapolis: U of Minnesota P, 1996. 163–84.

– 'The Purloined Ribbon.' *Glyph I: Johns Hopkins Textual Studies*. Baltimore: Johns Hopkins UP, 1977. 28–49.

– *The Resistance to Theory*. Minneapolis: U of Minnesota P, 1986.

DeMille, Barbara. 'Cruel Illusions: Nietzsche, Conrad, Hardy, and the "Shadowy Ideal."' *Studies in English Literature, 1500–1900*. 30.4 (1990): 697–714.

Derrida, Jacques. *Demeure: Fiction and Testimony* in Maurice Blanchot and Jacques Derrida, *The Instant of My Death / Demeure: Fiction and Testimony*. Trans. Elizabeth Rottenberg. Stanford: Stanford UP, 2000.

– *Given Time*. Trans. Peggy Kamuf. Chicago & London: U of Chicago P, 1992.

– *Margins of Philosophy*. Trans. Alan Bass. Chicago: U of Chicago P, 1982.

– *Of Grammatology*. Trans. Gayatri Spivak. Baltimore: Johns Hopkins UP, 1976.

– *On the Name*. Trans. David Wood et al. Stanford: Stanford UP, 1995.

– *The Post Card*. Trans. Alan Bass. Chicago: U of Chicago P, 1987.

Donzelot, Jacques. *The Policing of Families*. Trans. Robert Hurley. New York: Pantheon, 1979.

Edel, Leon. *The Life of Henry James*. 5 vols. Philadelphia: Lippincott, 1953–72.

Ensor, R.C.K. *England 1870–1914*. Oxford: Clarendon P, 1936.

Ermarth, Elizabeth Deeds. 'Realism and the English Novel.' *Encyclopedia of Literature and Criticism*. Ed. Martin Coyle et al. London: Routledge, 1991. 565–75.

– *Realism and Consensus in the English Novel*. Princeton: Princeton UP, 1983.

Eysteinsson, Astradur. *The Concept of Modernism*. Ithaca: Cornell UP, 1990.

Felman, Shoshana. 'A Ghost in the House of Justice: Death and the Language of the Law.' *Cultural Analysis, Cultural Studies, and the Law*. Ed. Austin Sarat and Jonathan Simon. Durham, NC: Duke UP, 2003. 259–303.

Felman, Shoshana, and Dori Laub. *Testimony: Crises of Witnessing in Literature, Psychoanalysis, and History*. London and New York: Routledge, 1992.

Fincham, Gail. 'The Dialogism of *Lord Jim*.' *Conrad and Theory*. Ed. Andrew Gibson and Robert Hampsons. Amsterdam & Atlanta: Rodopi, 1998. 58–74.

– 'Living under the Sign of Contradiction: Self and Other in Conrad's "Heart of Darkness."' *The English Academy Review* 7 (1990): 1–12.

Fleishman, Avrom. *Conrad's Politics*. Baltimore: Johns Hopkins UP, 1967.

Fogel, Aaron. *Coercion to Speak: Conrad's Poetics of Dialogue*. Cambridge, MA: Harvard UP, 1985.

Ford, Ford Madox. *Return to Yesterday*. New York: Horace Liveright, 1932.

Foucault, Michel. *The Archaeology of Knowledge*. Trans. A.M. Sheridan Smith. New York: Pantheon, 1972.

– *Discipline and Punish*. Trans. Alan Sheridan. New York: Random House, 1979.

– *Language, Counter-Memory, Practice*. Ed. and Trans. Donald F. Bouchard. Ithaca: Cornell UP, 1977.

Freedman, Jonathan. *Professions of Taste*. Stanford: Stanford UP, 1990.

Friedman, Alan Warren. 'Conrad's Picaresque Narrator.' *Marlow*. Ed. Harold Bloom. New York: Chelsea House, 1992. 61–79.

Gard, Roger, ed. *Henry James: The Critical Heritage*. New York: Barnes & Noble, 1968.

Garnett, Edward, ed. *Letters from Joseph Conrad 1895–1924*. London: Bobbs-Merrill, 1928.

Genette, Gérard. *Narrative Discourse*. Trans. Jane E. Lewin. Ithaca: Cornell UP, 1980.

– *Narrative Discourse Revisited*. Trans. Jane E. Lewin. Ithaca: Cornell UP, 1988.

Gikandi, Simon. 'Preface: Modernism in the World.' *Modernism/modernity* 13.3 (2006): 419–24.

Glassman, Peter J. *Joseph Conrad and the Literature of Personality*. New York: Columbia UP, 1976.

GoGwilt, Christopher. *The Invention of the West: Joseph Conrad and the Double-Mapping of Europe and Empire*. Stanford: Stanford UP, 1995.

Golanka, Mary. 'Mr. Kurtz, I Presume? Livingstone and Stanley as Prototypes of Kurtz and Marlow.' *Studies in the Novel*. 17.2 (1985): 194–202.

Graham, Kenneth. 'Conrad and Modernism.' *The Cambridge Companion to Joseph Conrad*. Ed. J.H. Stape. Cambridge: Cambridge UP, 1996. 1–24.

Greaney, Michael. *Conrad, Language, and Narrative*. Cambridge: Cambridge UP, 2002.

Harris, Michael, and Alan Lee, eds. *The Press in English Society from the Seventeenth to Nineteenth Centuries*. Rutherford: Fairleigh Dickinson UP, 1986.

Harris, Whitney R. *Tyranny on Trial: The Evidence at Nuremberg*. Dallas, TX: Southern Methodist UP, 1958.

Harrison, Thomas. *Essayism: Conrad, Musil and Pirandello*. Baltimore: Johns Hopkins UP, 1992.

Hartog, François. *The Mirror of Herodotus: The Representation of the Other in the Writing of History*. Trans. Janet Lloyd. Berkeley: U of California P, 1988.

Haywood, Eliza. *The Female Spectator*. Ed. Gabrielle M. Firmager. London: Bristol Classical P, 1993.

Henricksen, Bruce. *Nomadic Voices: Conrad and the Subject of Narrative*. Urbana & Chicago: U of Illinois P, 1992.

Herd, Harold. *The March of Journalism: The Story of the British Press from 1622 to the Present Day*. Westport, CT: Greenwood P, 1973.

Herman, David. *Universal Grammar and Narrative Form*. Durham: Duke UP, 1995.

Hochschild, Adam. *King Leopold's Ghost: A Story of Greed, Terror, and Heroism in Colonial Africa*. Boston: Houghton Mifflin, 1998.

Hopkins, Tighe. 'Anonymity? I.' *New Review* 1.6 (1889): 513–31.

– 'Anonymity? II.' *New Review* 2.10 (1890): 265–76.

Horkheimer, Max, and Theodore Adorno. *Dialectic of Enlightenment*. Trans. John Cumming. New York: Herder & Herder, 1972.

Howells, Richard. *The Myth of the Titanic*. New York: St Martin's, 1999.

Hunter, Paul. *Before Novels: The Cultural Contexts of Eighteenth-Century English Fiction*. New York: W.W. Norton, 1990.

Huyssen, Andreas. *After the Great Divide: Modernism, Mass Culture, Postmodernism*. Bloomington, IN: Indiana UP, 1986.

Hynes, Samuel. *Edwardian Occasions: Essays on English Writing in the Early Twentieth Century*. New York: Oxford UP, 1972.

Jackson, Tony E. *The Subject of Modernism: Narrative Alterations in the Fiction of Eliot, Conrad, Woolf, and Joyce*. Ann Arbor: U of Michigan P, 1995.

Jaffe, Aaron. *Modernism and the Culture of Celebrity*. Cambridge: Cambridge UP, 2005.

James, Henry. *The Ambassadors*. New York: Penguin, 1986.

– *The American Scene*. London: Hart-Davis, 1968.
– *The Art of Criticism: Henry James on the Theory and Practice of Fiction*. Ed. William Veeder and Susan M. Griffin. Chicago: U of Chicago P, 1986.
– 'The Art of Fiction.' *Partial Portraits*. London: MacMillan, 1888.
– *The Art of the Novel*. New York: Scribner's, 1934.
– *The Aspern Papers*. *The Novels and Tales of Henry James*. Vol. 12. New York: Scribner's, 1908.
– 'The Beast in the Jungle.' *The Novels and Tales of Henry James*. Vol. 7. New York: Scribner's, 1922.
– *The Bostonians*. *Novels 1881–1886*. New York: Library of America, 1985. 801–1219.
– *The Complete Notebooks of Henry James*. Ed. Leon Edel and Lyall H. Powers. Oxford: Oxford UP, 1987.
– *The Figure in the Carpet and Other Stories*. Ed. Frank Kermode. New York: Penguin, 1986.
– *The Golden Bowl*. New York: Penguin, 1987.
– *Henry James: A Life in Letters*. Ed. Philip Horne. New York: Viking, 1999.
– *The Portrait of a Lady*. *Novels 1881–1886*. New York: Library of America, 1985. 191–800.
– *The Portrait of a Lady*. New York: Penguin, 1986. [Based on the heavily revised New York edition (Scribner's, 1908)].
– *The Princess Casamassima*. *The Novels and Tales of Henry James*. Vol. 5. New York: Scribner's, 1908.
– *The Reverberator*. *The Novels and Tales of Henry James*. Vol. 13. New York: Scribner's, 1908.
– *The Sacred Fount*. New York: New Directions, 1995.
– *The Turn of the Screw*. *The Novels and Tales of Henry James*. Vol. 12. New York: Scribner's, 1908.
– 'The Younger Generation.' *Times Literary Supplement* 2 Apr. 1914. 157–8.
Jameson, Fredric. *The Political Unconscious*. Ithaca: Cornell UP, 1981.
Jean-Aubry, Gerard. *Joseph Conrad: Life and Letters*. 2 vols. Garden City, NY: Doubleday, 1927.
Jones, Doris Arthur. *Taking the Curtain Call: The Life and Letters of Henry Arthur Jones*. New York: Macmillan, 1930.
Kaplan, Amy. *The Social Construction of American Realism*. Chicago: U of Chicago P, 1988.
Karl, Frederick R. *Joseph Conrad: The Three Lives*. New York: Farrar, Straus, and Giroux, 1979.
Ka-Tzetnik 135633. *Shivitti: A Vision*. Trans. Eliyah Nike De-Nur and Lisa Herman. New York: Harper & Row, 1989.

Knight, Diana. 'Joseph Conrad, *Heart of Darkness.*' *Literary Theory at Work: Three Texts.* Totowa, NJ: Barnes & Noble, 1987. 9–28.

Knowles, Owen. 'Conrad's Life.' *The Cambridge Companion to Joseph Conrad.* Ed. J.H. Stape. Cambridge: Cambridge UP, 1996. 1–24.

Krajka, Wieslaw. *Isolation and Ethos: A Study of Joseph Conrad.* Boulder: East European Monographs, 1992.

Krook, Dorothea. *The Ordeal of Consciousness in Henry James.* Cambridge: Cambridge UP, 1962.

Levine, Lawrence W. *Highbrow / Lowbrow: The Emergence of Cultural Hierarchy in America.* Cambridge, MA: Harvard UP, 1988.

Livingstone, David. *The Last Journals of David Livingstone, in Central Africa, from 1865 to His Death.* Vol 2. London: John Murray, 1875.

Lord, Ursula. *Solitude versus Solidarity in the Novels of Joseph Conrad: Political and Epistemological Implications of Narrative Innovation.* Montreal & Kingston: McGill-Queen's UP, 1998.

Lothe, Jakob. 'Conradian Narrative.' *The Cambridge Companion to Joseph Conrad.* Ed. J.H. Stape. Cambridge: Cambridge UP, 1996. 160–78.

Lukács, György. *The Meaning of Contemporary Realism.* Trans. John and Necke Mander. London: Merlin P, 1963.

– 'Realism in the Balance.' Trans. Ronald Livingstone. *Aesthetics and Politics.* Ed. Ernst Bloch et al. London: New Left Books, 1977. 28–59.

Lyotard, Jean-François. *The Différend: Phrases in Dispute.* Trans. Georges Van Den Abbeele. Minneapolis: U of Minnesota P, 1988.

Mackenzie, Henry. *Julia de Roubigné.* London: Strahan, Cadell, & Creech, 1777.

Mao, Douglas, and Rebecca L. Walkowitz. 'The New Modernist Studies.' *PMLA* 123.3 (2008): 737–48.

Martelli, George. *Leopold to Lumumba: A History of the Belgian Congo 1877–1960.* London: Chapman & Hall, 1962.

Maus, Katharine Eisaman. 'Proof and Consequences: Inwardness and Its Exposure in the English Renaissance.' *Representations* 34 (1991): 29–52.

McKeon, Michael. *The Origins of the English Novel: 1600–1740.* Baltimore: Johns Hopkins UP, 1987.

– 'Prose Fiction: Great Britain.' *The Cambridge History of Literary Criticism.* Vol. 4. Cambridge: Cambridge UP, 1997. 238–63.

McLynn, Frank. *Stanley: Sorcerer's Apprentice.* London: Constable, 1991.

Melnick, Daniel. 'The Morality of Conrad's Imagination.' *Joseph Conrad.* Modern Critical Views Series. Ed. Harold Bloom. New York: Chelsea House, 1986.

Melville, Herman. *The Confidence-Man.* Oxford: Oxford UP, 1989.

Miller, D.A. *The Novel and the Police.* Berkeley: U of California P, 1988.

Miller, James. *The Passion of Michel Foucault*. Cambridge, MA: Harvard UP,
  2000.
Moore, Gene M. et al., eds. *Conrad: Intertexts and Appropriations*. Amsterdam &
  Atlanta: Rodopi, 1997.
Morley, Christopher. *Conrad and the Reporters*. New York: Doubleday, 1923.
Morrisson, Mark S. *The Public Face of Modernism: Little Magazines, Audiences,
  and Reception, 1905–1920*. Madison: U of Wisconsin P, 2001.
Mullan, John. 'Sensibility and Literary Criticism.' *The Cambridge History of Lit-
  erary Criticism*, Vol. 4. Cambridge: Cambridge UP, 1997. 419–33.
Murfin, Ross, C., ed. *Conrad Revisited: Essays for the Eighties*. U of Alabama P,
  1985.
Murray, David. 'Joseph Conrad, *Heart of Darkness*.' *Literary Theory at Work:
  Three Texts*. Totowa, NJ: Barnes & Noble, 1987. 115–34.
Musil, Robert. *The Man Without Qualitites*. Trans. Sophie Wilkins and Burton
  Pike. New York: Random House, 1995.
– *Posthumous Papers of a Living Author*. Trans. Peter Wortsman. Hygiene, CO:
  Eridanos P, 1987.
– *Precision and Soul: Essays and Addresses*. Trans. and ed. Burton Pike and
  David S. Luft. Chicago: U of Chicago P, 1990.
Najder, Zdzisław. *Conrad in Perspective: Essays on Art and Fidelity*. Cambridge:
  Cambridge UP, 1997.
– *Conrad's Polish Background: Letters to and from Polish Friends*. London: Oxford
  UP, 1964.
– *Joseph Conrad: A Chronicle*. New Brunswick, NJ: Rutgers UP, 1983
Nettels, Elsa. *James and Conrad*. Athens: U of Georgia P, 1977.
Nico, Israel. *Outlandish: Writing between Exile and Diaspora*. Stanford: Stanford
  UP, 2000.
Nietzsche, Friedrich. *Thus Spake Zarathustra* in *The Portable Nietzsche*. Trans.
  Walter Kaufmann. New York: Penguin, 1976.
North, Michael. *The Dialect of Modernism*. New York: Oxford UP, 1994.
O'Connor, William Van. 'The Novel in Our Time.' *Forms of Modern Fiction; Es-
  says Collected in Honor of Joseph Warren Beach*. Ed. William Van O'Connor.
  Minneapolis: U of Minnesota P, 1948. 1–8.
Page, Norman. *A Conrad Companion*. New York: St Martin's P, 1986.
Perosa, Sergio. *Henry James and the Experimental Novel*. New York: New York
  UP, 1983.
Politi, Jina. *The Novel and Its Presuppositions: Changes in the Conceptual
  Structure of Novels in the 18th and 19th Centuries*. Amsterdam: A.M. Hakkert,
  1976.
Porter, Carolyn. *Seeing and Being*. Middletown: Wesleyan UP, 1981.

Ramsay, Roger. 'The Available and the Unavailable "I": Conrad and James.' *English Literature in Transition* 14 (1971): 137–45.

Ransford, Oliver. *David Livingstone: The Dark Interior*. New York: St Martin's P, 1978.

Retinger, J.H. *Conrad and His Contemporaries*. New York: Roy, 1943.

Reynolds, Brian, and Joseph Fitzpatrick. 'The Transversality of Michel de Certeau: Foucault's Panoptic Discourse and the Cartographic Impulse.' *Diacritics* 29.3 (1999): 63–80.

Richardson, Samuel. *Pamela; or, Virtue Rewarded*. 4 vols. Oxford: Houghton Mifflin, 1938.

Rousseau, Jean-Jacques. *Les Confessions*. Vol. 1. Paris: Imprimerie nationale, 1995.

– *Julie, or the New Heloise*. Trans. Philip Stewart and Jean Vaché. Hanover: Dartmouth College P, 1997.

– *Les Rêveries du promeneur solitaire*. Paris: Librarie des Bibliophiles, 1882.

Roussel, Royal. *The Metaphysics of Darkness: A Study in the Unity and Development of Conrad's Fiction*. Baltimore and London: Johns Hopkins UP, 1971.

Said, Edward. *Beginnings: Intention and Method*. New York: Columbia UP, 1985.

– *Culture and Imperialism*. New York: Random House, 1993.

Schalck, Harry. 'Fleet Street in the 1880's: The New Journalism.' *Papers for the Millions*. Ed. Joel H. Wiener. New York: Greenwood P, 1988. 73–87.

Schiller, Dan. *Objectivity and the News: The Public and the Rise of Commercial Journalism*. Philadelphia: U of Pennsylvania P, 1981.

Schudson, Michael. *Discovering the News*. New York: Basic Books, 1978.

Scott, Walter. *Sir Walter Scott on Novelists and Fiction*. Ed. Ioan M. Williams. London: Routledge & Paul, 1968.

Scudder, Horace Elisha. *James, Crawford, and Howells* [unsigned]. *The Atlantic Monthly* 57 (1886): 851–3.

Seaver, George. *David Livingstone: His Life and Letters*. New York: Harper & Bros., 1957.

Seitz, Don C. *The James Gordon Bennetts: Father and Son; Proprietors of the New York Herald*. Indianapolis: Bobbs-Merrill, 1928.

Seltzer, Mark. *Henry James and the Art of Power*. Ithaca: Cornell UP, 1984.

Senn, Werner. *Conrad's Narrative Voice: Stylistic Aspects of His Fiction*. Bern: Francke Verlag, 1980.

Seshagiri, Urmila. 'Modernist Ashes, Postcolonial Phoenix: Jean Rhys and the Evolution of the English Novel in the Twentieth Century.' *Modernism/modernity* 13.3 (2006): 487–505.

Shakespeare, William. *Coriolanus*. Ed. Philip Brockbank. New York: Routledge, 1976.

Shattock, Joanne, and Michael Wolff, eds. *The Victorian Periodical Press: Samplings and Soundings*. Leicester: Leicester UP, 1982.

Sherry, Norman. *Conrad's Eastern World*. Cambridge: Cambridge UP, 1977.

– *Conrad's Western World*. Cambridge: Cambridge UP, 1980.

Sherry, Norman, ed. *Conrad: The Critical Heritage*. London: Routledge and Kegan Paul, 1973.

Showalter, English. 'The Prehistory of Omniscience: Representing Minds in Early French Fiction.' *Romance Quarterly* 38:3 (1991): 355–62.

– 'Prose Fiction: France.' *The Cambridge History of Literary Criticism*. Vol. 4. Cambridge: Cambridge UP, 1997. 210–37.

Small, Ian, and Josephine Guy. 'The "Literary," Aestheticism and the Founding of English as a Discipline.' *English Literature in Transition (1880–1920)* 33.4 (1990): 443–53.

Stape, J.H. '"Conrad Controversial": Ideology and Rhetoric in the Essays on the Titanic.' *Prose Studies* 11.1 (1988): 61–8.

Staten, Henry. 'Conrad's Mortal Word.' *Critical Inquiry* 12.4 (1986): 720–40.

– *Eros in Mourning: Homer to Lacan*. Baltimore: Johns Hopkins UP, 1995.

Trollope, Anthony. *Barchester Towers*. New York: Penguin, 1987.

Tuchman, Gaye. *Making News*. New York: The Free Press, 1978.

Watt, Ian. *Conrad in the Nineteenth Century*. Berkeley: U of California P, 1979.

– 'Conrad, James and *Chance*.' *Imagined Worlds: Essays in Honour of John Butt*. Ed. Maynard Mack and Ian Gregor. London: Methuen & Co., 1968.

– *The Rise of the Novel*. Berkeley: U of California P, 1957.

Watts, Cedric. *The Deceptive Text: An Introduction to Covert Plots*. New Jersey: Barnes & Noble, 1984.

White, Andrea. *Joseph Conrad and the Adventure Tradition*. Cambridge: Cambridge UP, 1993.

Wiesenfarth, Joseph. *Henry James and the Dramatic Analogy*. New York: Fordham UP, 1963.

Winner, Anthony. '*Lord Jim*: Irony and Dream.' *Marlow*. Ed. Harold Bloom. New York: Chelsea House, 1992. 182–201.

Wollaeger, Mark. *Conrad and the Fictions of Skepticism*. Stanford: Stanford UP, 1990.

– 'Killing Stevie: Modernity, Modernism, and Mastery in Conrad and Hitchcock.' *Modern Language Quarterly* 58:3 (1997): 323–50.

– *Modernism, Media, and Propaganda*. Princeton: Princeton UP, 2006.

Woodmansee, Martha, and Peter Jaszi, eds. *The Construction of Authorship: Textual Appropriation in Law and Literature*. Durham: Duke UP, 1994.

# Index